Tales of MAN SINGH

Kenneth Anderson (1910–74) was a hunter, nature enthusiast and an adventure-seeker. His love for the denizens of the jungle led to some of the best literature on wildlife and his books are acclaimed as classics. He wrote about eight books and sixty short stories which recount many of his real-life adventures and hunting exploits in the jungles of South India.

Anderson belonged to a Scottish family settled in India for six generations. He spent most of his life in Bengaluru, where he was employed with an aeronautics company. His invaluable contribution to the shikar literature in India continues to inspire scores of wildlife lovers.

Tales of MAN SINGH
King of Indian Dacoits

Kenneth Anderson

Published by
Rupa Publications India Pvt. Ltd 2018
7/16, Ansari Road, Daryaganj
New Delhi 110002

Sales centres:
Allahabad Bengaluru Chennai
Hyderabad Jaipur Kathmandu
Kolkata Mumbai

Edition copyright © Rupa Publications India Pvt. Ltd 2018

The views and opinions expressed in this book are the author's own and the facts are as reported by him which have been verified to the extent possible, and the publishers are not in any way liable for the same.

All rights reserved.
No part of this publication may be reproduced, transmitted, or stored in a retrieval system, in any form or by any means, electronic, mechanical, photocopying, recording or otherwise, without the prior permission of the publisher.

ISBN: 978-81-291-5117-9

First impression 2018
10 9 8 7 6 5 4 3 2 1

The moral right of the author has been asserted.

Typeset by Saanvi Graphics, Noida

Printed at Repro Knowledgecast Limited, Thane

This book is sold subject to the condition that it shall not, by way of trade or otherwise, be lent, resold, hired out, or otherwise circulated, without the publisher's prior consent, in any form of binding or cover other than that in which it is published.

This book
is
dedicated
to the
Spirit of Adventure,
and to all the red-blooded youths and men
of all countries
who pursue her

Contents

Introduction   ix

Acknowledgement   xi

Chapter 1
    Chota Singh of the C.I.D.   1

Chapter 2
    Jhani and Lotibai   50

Chapter 3
    The Policemen Who Sought a Reward   121

Chapter 4
    The Invasion of the Ravine Kingdom   137

Chapter 5
    The Rich Landlord and the Poor Maiden   163

Chapter 6
    The Three Travellers and the American Journalist   195

Chapter 7
    The History of Man Singh   229

Epilogue   260

Introduction

The young men and women of free India are indeed fortunate in many ways. They have a beautiful country as their homeland, second to none in the world. A country where they can find every type of geography and scenery that is to be found anywhere else. Some of the highest mountains in the world; wide, rolling plains; marsh land; desert land; magnificent rivers and beautiful sea beaches. They can have any climate; from the freezing cold of snowy Kashmir, to the burning, unrivalled heat of some of the central districts. They have a Venice in Kashmir, lagoons and waterways in Malabar, glorious forests where the King of the Jungle—the tiger—still roams at liberty; picturesque waterfalls; and ancient cities, rich in folklore and history.

The pages of Indian history are generously pageanted by unique personalities. They range from the very bad, like Timur the Lame, to the very good, like Akbar the Great. There are warriors who carved their names forever in the memories of the living, such as Shivaji, the Maratha, and Tipu Sultan, the Tiger of Mysore; there are apostles of peace who shook the world with their doctrines of love, such as Gautam Buddha and Mahatma Gandhi; and there are martyrs who shed their blood for India, in ancient times and modern, including that Joan of Arc of the East, the Rani of Jhansi.

These figures of Indian history, both good and bad, have one attribute in common. As personalities, they are unmatched, unparalleled, unique. No boy or girl in India who has the ability to read need seek for adventure stories abroad, for his and her own land abounds in them. The stage is set, teeming with heroes and heroines and in deeds that thrill and chill the blood; requiring but more writers to record them, and the youth of the country to read.

Such a unique personality was Man Singh, King of Dacoits. A man possessing diametrically opposing attributes, he was at once a murderer and thief, generous benefactor and upholder of the poor. Cruel, cunning and sly, he was brave with the heart of a lion. A fugitive from justice for years, he exhibited attributes of true equity to those who followed in his band.

In no way are these stories intended to glorify or even commend Man Singh and his ideals. They are merely yarns of adventure which I truly hope will afford a degree of pleasure to those who read them. That pleasure will be my reward.

Sit with me, then, in your imagination, around the flickering light of a campfire and hearken to the tales I have to tell you. The smoke curls upwards to the twinkling stars, floating in the unlimited space above. At times the fire erupts with a shower of sparks and then dies down again.

Throw on a fresh log of wood, friend. For outside the narrow circle of light is utter darkness, punctuated by the distant chirrup of crickets and the nearer croaking of a bullfrog.

It is dangerous to be left in the darkness, friend. For mysterious and unknown things lurk there, unseen in the Stygian gloom.

And Dacoits!

The Author

Acknowledgement

The author wishes to acknowledge, with grateful thanks, his indebtedness to Shri Vishwa Nath, Editor and Publisher of *The Caravan*, one of India's foremost publications, for giving him permission to use much of the data in recording the *History of Man Singh* that appeared in an article entitled 'Raja Man Singh' by Tapan Ghosh.

Chapter One
Chota Singh of the C.I.D.

His real name was not Chota Singh at all. (Chota, as those of you who have been in India know quite well, is merely an adjective in the Hindi language, signifying 'small'; or maybe, 'short' or 'diminutive'.) His real name was Katar Singh.

But he had been called 'chota' from childhood, because he was a puny-looking youth, far shorter than the average boy of his age. And the epithet stuck to him like glue and followed him into the Police Force which he joined when 19 years old as an ordinary constable.

Katar Singh, or to give him his nickname of 'Chota' by which we shall hereafter allude to him, made up for his poor physique and short stature—he was about 5 feet 3 inches—by a powerful personality and outstanding intelligence.

The story is told that when Chota applied to join the Force as a young man, he, with other applicants, was duly interviewed by the District Superintendent of Police. As those were the days of the British Raj, this officer was a European—an Englishman who had put in many years of service with the Police in India.

The recruits were called one by one in turn. At last Katar Singh stood before the D.S.P. The police officer looked at him somewhat disdainfully and then remarked, 'We want "burra admi", (well-built men) in the Force, and not "chota admi" (small men) and weaklings like you. Go home, little man, and apply for the post of a clerk somewhere else; not that of a policeman.'

A rebuff like that would have unnerved a normal applicant at any time.

But Chota was far from being such a normal applicant.

He answered without a moment's hesitation, 'But, sahib, do "burra admi" always possess "burra akul" (great intelligence)? That is something to be considered, is it not?'

The D.S.P. lost his temper. 'Meaning…' he began.

'Exactly what I say, sahib.'

'What makes you think you are so smart?' queried the police officer, turning red.

'That you will have no doubt about, but will come to know for yourself, sahib; and within two months—If you employ me.'

Impertinent little devil, thought the D.S.P. Thinks no end of himself. Conceited to the very core.

And then, aloud, to the little man. 'Suppose I take you at your word and enrol you right away and put you on probation on night duty. Will you still be able to make me agree within those two months?'

'Without the least shadow of doubt, huzoor', Katar Singh had returned immediately.

And throughout the whole conversation he had looked the D.S.P. in the eyes, without once turning his head away.

'Dammit, I will take you at your word. But remember, out you go after the two months are over, unless you do something very unusual to prove your mettle.'

'That is all I ask for, sahib,' Chota had concluded.

Within five weeks of that day, Katar Singh, alone on night duty, caught and brought in a notorious cat burglar. Single-handed.

The police had been searching unsuccessfully for that cat burglar for the past two years.

And that was how Katar Singh, or 'Chota' as he was better known from top to bottom in the Police Force, came to be confirmed after his probation, although his medical sheet recorded figures which were far below the standard required for a 'pass' with reference to his height, chest measurements and weight.

That was only the beginning.

Chota showed unusual abilities for turning in reports that were brief and to the point. He appeared to have the natural gift of being able to discern facts that were of evidential value, and to discard matters that were of little importance. Above all, he had the powers of reasoning and deduction that are not very commonly found in men of his class and grade.

Within six months he was transferred to the Traffic Branch; and within a year of that date had achieved the double distinction of not having lost a single case he had brought in, as well as of having the largest number of prosecutions to his credit from among the members of his branch.

At that time the Government had issued a circular to all chiefs of the Police Force to send some of their best men for special training in the Criminal Investigation Department (C.I.D.). Chota, with only one-and-a-half years service to his credit had more recommendations, and more grounds for them, than many of his colleagues with 10 and 15 years.

An important factor that had contributed very largely towards his success was his inherent honesty and interest in his work. On the one hand he never accepted a bribe, however large. On the other, he did not invent cases against people in the hopes of getting money from them to withdraw the charge later, or for reasons of vindictiveness or petty spite.

When Chota filed a charge sheet, he only did it against somebody who had really done something wrong; and he succeeded in his prosecution.

Hence he came to be strongly advocated as a very promising policeman, suitable for assignment to the C.I.D.

He underwent the year's training that was prescribed and took to the work as naturally as a duck takes to water, topping the list of successful candidates in the examination.

His career in the C.I.D. thereafter was meteoric. In a comparatively short time he was promoted to Head Constable; and then was made a Sub-Inspector at the first vacancy that offered itself.

Two years later he was Inspector Katar Singh of the C.I.D.; but still 'Chota' to his superiors and friends, and 'Chota Sahib' to those whom he had superseded and left far behind.

Chota was a Rajput by birth, although he did not seem like one in appearance. He did not look martial nor warlike by any means; being puny and slightly-built; affable and mild.

He was clean-shaven and wore his hair closely cropped to the skull. These features were the despair of his family and his closest friends and relations, who deplored his unsightly looks.

Chota himself knew well enough the reason why he deliberately did these things. But he did not tell that reason to anyone.

He was an adept at disguise and could dress and act any part he set himself to impersonate. And Chota knew a clean-shaven and closely-cropped man could wear a false beard, moustache and wig; whereas a man who already had long hair or a beard, or whiskers, could not disguise himself—unless he chose to shave them off.

So, he wisely determined not to grow them in the first instance. Then the necessity for removing them could not arise. It was easy enough to take them off at any time; but they took long to grow.

His round, pleasant face and mild, brown eyes enabled him to wear any sort of disguise with little risk of penetration. His features had no distinguishing factors.

Chota spoke five dialects fluently, and could read and write four of them.

When Rajah Man Singh and his band of followers commenced to grow in numbers and their depredations increased by leaps and bounds, the police authorities sought means to circumvent him. It was generally known that the bandits had their headquarters among the Chambal ravines, but exactly where, nobody could tell.

That was what the police wanted to find out very much, and quickly, too.

It was most dangerous work. Many informers and police spies had already paid dearly for their temerity in trying to discover the answers to these questions, with their lives.

Headless corpses, bloated, disfigured and decomposed, had been hauled out of the rolling waters of the Chambal and Kunwari rivers. They had been so long immersed that their flesh was soft and rotting. It came off in chunks as the grapnel hooks tried to draw the bodies ashore. Many could not be identified at all. Now and again, by the presence of some trinket or particular mark, the police knew they were gazing at the cadaver of one of their secret agents.

At other times plain heads, minus their bodies, were left behind by the dacoits, spiked to a bamboo or a cut stem in the dense, thorny scrub. Very frequently the head would carry a piece of paper clenched tightly between the teeth even where the rest of the flesh had rotted away. Scrawled on the paper would be a message reading, 'Let this be a warning to all police agents and informers as to what will befall them when we catch them'. Underneath the message would follow four words. 'Rajah Man Singh Rathore'.

It was not a popular assignment, therefore, to be ordered to try to get information regarding this redoubtable outlaw. Police agents came to regard it as a form of official punishment; possibly their death sentence.

Some would try to evade the issue by reporting sick. Quite a number escaped by resigning when commissioned on this duty. A few panicked—and deserted.

Chota went to his immediate superior one morning—an Assistant Superintendent of Police. 'Sir, please use your influence and recommend me for special duty; the duty of arresting Man Singh,' he asked, blandly.

'Say that again,' asked the A.S.P., scarcely believing his ears.

Chota said it again.

The A.S.P. wondered. Did this man know what he was asking for? Possibly his own death sentence. The A.S.P. told him so in confidence.

Chota merely replied, 'It is appointed to every man to die but once.'

To those words the A.S.P. could find neither an appropriate nor an effective answer.

So he made the recommendation.

And the Inspector General eagerly jumped at it.

Chota was paid three months' salary in advance. He was also given some extra money to defray incidental expenses. Thereafter he was on his own for the next ninety days.

Chota had heard all the current stories about how Man Singh defended the poor, particularly men who had been wronged by the moneylenders, by the zamindars, and by the rich in general.

He immediately set about becoming one such poor man who had been wronged in exactly that way.

He dressed himself in rags and tatters—as a beggar.

Then he walked the 63 miles to the village of Dhowd, situated on the nearer bank of the Chambal River and not far from the 'ravines'.

All day he sat himself in the marketplace and begged for alms. At night he slept in the dust of the roadside. And he ate only what he could buy with the few copper pice he was given by the way of charity.

He found out who was the 'baniya', (moneylender) of the place and appeared at his 'dukaan' (shop or business premises).

'Alms for a poor man,' he whined.

Nobody, looking at the bent and haggard figure dressed in rags, covered with filth, matted hair that had apparently never been washed, a straggling beard and tottering, dragging walk, would have recognised him as an Inspector of Police. The disguise was complete.

The baniya promptly ordered him out.

'I am starving, your honour. Spare me a pice,' he cringed, not making any effort to go away.

'Arre badmash!' (Oh rascal!), cried the moneylender, 'if you don't get out this instant I will teach you a lesson.'

'Charity, huzoor; for a poor, starving man,' he begged.

'Oh, Ram, Dehu,' called the baniya to his servants, 'kick this creature out at once; he is annoying me.'

Ram and Dehu promptly, and literally, kicked him out.

But the beggar was back again the next day. Once more he cried out, 'A copper for this poor man,' while standing in front of the baniya's place of business.

'So you are back again', cried the moneylender, testily. 'Yesterday I told my servants to kick you out. Today I will tell them to soundly beat you.'

'Give me an anna, please huzoor,' was the imperturbable reply.

The baniya became enraged. He clapped his hands and his two henchmen presented themselves before him.

'Useless dogs,' he said to them, 'can you not do a simple thing for me? Rid me of this persistent beggar who pesters me each day. Teach him a lesson and beat him hard. Do anything; but make certain he does not show himself here, ever again.'

Ram and Dehu hastened to obey their patron. They administered many whacks with bamboo sticks on the person of the unfortunate beggar in the open street. So much so that even the passers-by felt sorry for him, and murmured beneath their breaths at the harsh treatment of this poor man by the 'sowcar' (usurer) and his servants.

Chota smarted with pain from the blows he had received. But he was also satisfied that he had given a good public performance in keeping with his disguise as a poor beggar being harassed and beaten by the rich. He wept loudly and lamented that Fate could think of being so unkind to the downtrodden as to permit this ill-treatment of a beggar at the hands of a member of the moneyed class.

That evening he sat in the marketplace and showed the stripes on his bare back—real ones—to all who passed by; and he cried very bitterly as he told them the story. 'See for yourselves, Sirs, how the wealthy oppress the poor in this land.'

But the result he had been hoping for did not come about at once. Chota cursed his ill-luck and determined to try again.

Two days later he appeared once more, this time as if by accident at the residence of the same baniya whose name was Kunjilal. On this occasion, not only was he beaten but also dragged to the police station. Chota did not reveal his identity there, so he received a second thrashing at the hands of the police.

In the marketplace that evening his lament was couched in slightly different terms. 'Is there none to help the down-and-out in this cruel land? If there was but a leader, I would gladly join him and teach these wealthy dogs a lesson.'

Towards sunset a stalwart villager threw an anna on to the open kerchief spread by Chota on the road before him.

'God bless you, huzoor,' he said fervently. 'Oh, if only the land was left to the peasants how happy we would be. It is these rich people; these wealthy landlords and baniyas, who oppress us. If only someone would lead us against them, they could be overthrown for ever.'

Instead of passing on his way immediately, the tall man regarded him speculatively. Chota felt that he was being closely scrutinised. The dark eyes of the unknown man appeared to bore through and through him.

The beggar pretended not to notice. He stooped down, picked up the anna, and put it into a small, dirty cloth bag which he produced from the waistband of his dhoty.

The stranger had time to notice that the bag contained a few small copper coins only.

Then the beggar restored the bag to its former place, tucked next to the bare skin of his stomach where it was encircled by the dhoty.

The newcomer said, 'Suppose there was such a man, oh beggar. What would you do then?'

Chota looked up, the light of fanaticism in his eyes. 'Just tell me where to find him, huzoor,' he replied, 'and I will offer myself to him this instant. I will serve him faithfully, if only it is to teach these rich bastards a lesson. See for yourself where I was beaten by the baniya's servants. Not content with that, they dragged me to the police, who beat me too.' And pulling up the ends of his ragged shirt, he turned his back so that the stranger could see for himself the scars he carried from the various beatings he had received.

But the tall fellow said nothing. Just coughed.

He turned and began to walk away.

Chota felt disappointed. Would he never succeed in establishing the contact he had been trying so hard to do?

Then the stranger halted a few feet away, hesitated for an appreciable time, and retraced his steps.

He said to Chota, 'There are rumours that a certain dacoit hangs around these parts. It is said that he is not really a thief. He merely robs the rich to feed the poor. Is that the type of leader you would wish to join?'

'Oh yes,' returned Chota eagerly. 'If your honour will but tell me where to find him, I will go to him right away.'

The tall man laughed. 'It is not so simple as all that, brother,' he said. 'If it was so easy to find Man Singh; well, I guess there would have been no Man Singh by now.' And he smiled cryptically. 'However, we shall see.'

He rummaged in his pocket and produced a silver rupee which he passed unostentatiously to Chota. The beggar allowed his countenance to beam with gratitude.

But there was more than gratitude that shone from Chota's eyes. There was the glint of exultation. The sheer joy experienced by the trained sleuth who knows that, at long last, he is hot upon the trail.

Chota did not see the tall man all of next day. But he came again the following evening at sunset and handed the beggar another rupee.

The mendicant began to thank him, humbly and happily; but the tall man cut him short.

'Before a disciple can join a master,' he spoke enigmatically, 'it is necessary for that disciple to prove himself to be in earnest, and above all, trustworthy.'

'I am ready to be tried at any time,' Chota answered unhesitatingly. 'Let the master put me to any test he wants.'

The tall man said, 'I cannot be seen holding a prolonged conversation with a beggar in such a public place as this. People would wonder what it is all about. Meet me at midnight beneath the large banyan tree that grows by the road besides the second milestone on the way to Bhind. I may have something to tell you then.'

He moved away. Chota salaamed profusely in the manner of a beggar who had just been handed some alms.

～

It was inky black beneath the spreading boughs of the gnarled banyan tree near the second milestone as Chota arrived that night, about fifteen minutes to midnight. He had deliberately come before time, because he wanted to know in what manner the tall man was going to approach him, and from where. After all, he felt no suspicion would be attached to his early arrival, even if it was noticed. A beggar would not be expected to own a watch. Apart from that, what more natural than a poor man coming early to an appointment, particularly with the hope of getting some money through it?

But Chota was disappointed in expecting he would be the first to arrive.

Three figures emerged from the blackness cast by the shadows of the banyan's branches. They surrounded him. By his height, Chota made out one of them to be his benefactor who had arranged the rendezvous. His companions were strangers.

'You come before time, beggar?'

The voice came from one of the other men. It was a hard voice and seemed to hold a tinge of suspicion in it.

'Sirs, I am a stranger to these parts and have never been to this spot before. Besides, I own no watch. When the village 'ghadi', (a bell or gong sounded in some public place to record each hour) struck the hour of eleven, I set out to give myself enough time to come here in order not to keep the tall gentleman waiting.'

'I see,' replied the man, apparently satisfied with the simple explanation.

'We are told that you have been beaten by the village baniya and the police,' he continued. 'Why did that happen?'

'I begged for alms before his shop,' Chota toned his voice down to a complaining whine, 'and he ordered his servants to thrash me. Very foolishly I went a second time, although I didn't know it then, to his residence. I was hammered again and dragged to the police station, where the police beat me some more.'

'Show me the marks of these beatings,' asked the speaker, flatly.

'You may certainly see them for yourself, huzoor. But the darkness.—'

Chota's further words came to a stop as the stranger pressed the button of a small electric torch, sending a ray of light directly into his eyes. He blinked.

Then he turned around and commenced to pull up his torn shirt as he had done so often before.

'Take it off completely,' ordered the same voice, brusquely.

Chota complied immediately.

He felt the three men examining his back closely, and at that minute congratulated himself upon undergoing the various trouncings in reality. Had the scars not been genuine, Chota knew that he would have died violently on the spot. Yes indeed, he owed his life to those real weals across his back. Because they testified that he had been beaten very cruelly in all truth.

A little later he felt a moist finger touching the bare skin of his back. The finger began to rub up and down, vigorously. The wound thus rubbed commenced to burn as the scab was broken off. Then he knew what the man was doing. He had spat on his own finger and was rubbing one of the scabs caused by the bamboo that had been used in belabouring him. Should the scab be unreal and put there by some colouring agent, the spittle would remove it and the deception would be revealed.

On the other hand, the friction now caused by the rubbing finger tore off the newly-forming scab over the healing wound and made it bleed. It also began to smart him sharply.

Chota felt more moisture beneath the rubbing finger. It commenced to tickle him unpleasantly. He could feel a faint trickling of something running down his back and realised it was his blood.

What the devil is the fellow going to do next, he wondered. The dacoits were being cautious, no doubt, and he smiled inwardly to himself.

The rubbing finger started working on one of the other scabs till it also began to bleed.

Then on a third scab. And that bled also.

God damn you, Chota thought; are you going to rub off every bloody scab and make my back as sore as hell—you bastard!

But when the third scab bled the man became satisfied.

There was a distinctly more friendly tone in his voice when he spoke to Chota again.

'Excuse me for hurting you afresh, brother. But we cannot afford to run any risk. There are so many police spies about.'

Chota noticed the use of the word 'brother'. Apparently he had passed the test satisfactorily and the brigands were about to accept him into their fold.

'Let us sit here under this tree and talk softly,' the voice continued. 'We won't be seen.'

All this while Chota had been trying hard to pierce the darkness with his eyes to see what manner of men he was conversing with. His companion of the evening, of course, he knew to be the tall man. But he could not see the other two clearly. The man who had been doing all the talking and was no doubt the leader, was the shortest of the three. He appeared to have some kind of moustache, but was otherwise clean-shaven. The third man who had not uttered a word so far, was slightly taller and fairly heavily built. Chota could make out he was bearded. Every one of them wore turbans.

That was about all that he could distinguish in the darkness.

They sat on the ground and the leader began to talk to him in a whisper.

'What is your name and where do you come from? Have you been a mendicant all your life?'

Chota had carefully prepared the answers to questions of this sort long before he had set out on the assignment of trying to catch Man Singh. He had those answers ready on his lips now.

'My name is Bapat Rao,' he said, 'and I come of Maratha stock from the far away town of Sholapur. My father and my father's father before him were farmers. Our family possessed many acres of land then.

'But the monsoons failed successively and a long drought set in. The crops withered and there was no grain. Then the cattle began to die in scores. The little money we had saved up, we spent in buying gram for the animals and grain for ourselves, imported into the town from other districts. In our area, there was not a single green blade of grass to be seen anywhere.

'My father, in his desperation, mortgaged our land to the local baniya, Mohan Lal, intending with the next monsoons, when the crops grew again, to redeem it.

'But there was no next monsoon, Sirs; nor did the crops grow again. At least, not that next year nor the year after. For three years in succession God scourged Sholapur and the district around it, for hundreds of miles. All the money we had borrowed from Mohan Lal was spent. My father went to him again and the wily moneylender advanced still more money on our farm. And then there was a third mortgage.

'The rains came on the fourth year. But God was still angry with us. After withholding the monsoon for three years, He sent the rain on the fourth year. But He sent it in overabundance.

'The rivers rose and the floods came. Our fields, that had been parched for so long, were now inundated. And our house, which was built mostly of mud and unbaked bricks, collapsed entirely.

'That was the last blow, Sirs, from which my poor father could not recover. The cruel Mohan Lal prosecuted and our lands were auctioned to discharge the mortgage that had been raised on them. After paying Mohan Lal his capital and accrued interest on the three loans, and the cost of the case at court, there was just a few rupees left for food for a few days.

'We were landless, homeless and put on the streets.'

'The blow killed my poor mother within two months. She had always been a frail and sickly woman, of small stature—and that is why I am short and frail, too, as I have taken after her. The exposure of sleeping under trees by the wayside at night, unprotected from the cold and dew gave her pneumonia, to which she succumbed within six days.

'My father became practically mad after that. Our mother had been his sole consolation through all his troubles. With her death he felt he could face the world no longer.

'The very night of the day on which mother died, my father hung himself from a branch of the mahua tree under which we were all sleeping.

'You can imagine our plight next morning when we awoke, Sirs. Dangling before our eyes was the corpse of our father. The rope which he had tied around his neck, and the other end of which he had attached to a branch that spread above us, before he had jumped off, was stretched taut with the weight of our poor father which hung from it. His eyes bulged in a ghastly manner; his tongue lolled out and had become quite black. Slowly his body swayed and revolved on the tightly-stretched rope, blown by the fresh breeze of that early, but dreadful dawn.

'On the ground lay the yet-uncremated remains of our beloved mother. She had died the previous morning. By that evening she would be stinking in that hot climate. We had no money to conduct the two cremation ceremonies.

'My young brother and I and my sister who was still younger—a comely girl not yet 14 years old—had been left behind to face the cruel hard world, without an anna for the three of us.

'I well remember that awful morning, Sirs,' continued Chota reminiscently, a sob creeping into his voice. 'For some time we were silent, too shocked and bereft of words even to speak. Then my sister began to cry, and my brother and I joined her.

'Next my brother, who had always had the most brains amongst the three of us, did a very dreadful thing. In a paroxysm of pent-up and confused rage, he began to curse the corpse of our dead father as it dangled in the air.

'"You beast," he cried loudly, with tears streaming down his face and shaking his fists in the air, "you have brought us to this state. You mortgaged our lands and home. You starved our dear mother so that she became too weak to resist the sickness that overtook her. And now, damned coward that you are, you killed yourself because you were too much of a bandicoot (a very large rat the size of a guinea pig) to carry the burden you had thrust upon her. We are your children. You begot us. Now, how are we to live?"

'His voice rose to a frenzied scream. "Don't just hang there and stare at us with those dreadful bulging eyes and your tongue lolling out of your mouth, but answer us," he wailed. "You, who were our father; speak and answer us."

'And then, in a fearful outburst of hysterical tears, "Damn you! And I say it again and again. You, who were our father; damn you! damn you! damn you!"

'His behaviour had momentarily shocked my sister and myself into stemming our tears.

'I loved father dearly, and knew in all fairness he could not be entirely blamed for all the misfortunes that had befallen us. This outrageous behaviour by my brother, Scinji Rao, infuriated me beyond reason.

'Although shorter than him in stature, I sprang upon him, seized his throat in both my hands, and commenced to squeeze and squeeze and squeeze. As from a great distance I could hear my sister, Kamala, screaming to me to release him.

'People rushed to the rescue and tore me away from on top of my brother. I had knocked him down and was sitting astride his chest, strangling him with my bare hands. Had they not dragged me away, I would have killed him that very morning.

'Then the police came.

'That evening, after a post-mortem held by them, the bodies of our poor parents were cremated. A huge crowd attended out of curiosity, hushed by the awful tragedy of the drama.

'The inquiries went on and on for days after that. Nothing seemed to satisfy the police. They appeared bent upon unearthing some crime where there had been none, but only a dreadful tragedy.

'A few people gave us a little food and money. But that was soon finished and we had to work.

'I never spoke to my brother again after that tragic morning. He went away a few days later to Poona to try to get work. The last news I heard of him was that he had gone mad and was in an asylum.

'My sister, Kamala, was a beautiful girl; the charms of youthfulness were rapidly becoming replaced by budding womanhood in her rising figure, upright stance and pretty face.

'The scoundrelly Mohan Lal, not content with all the harm he had done to our family, somehow contrived through his agents to inveigle her to come and live with him. I heard later that, after keeping her for over a year, he had suddenly turned her out into the streets, and that she had gone to Bombay where she is living the life of a harlot.

'I went as far north as Delhi myself, seeking work but finding no permanent employment. The ill-luck of our family appears to dog my footsteps. And so I come to be here before you all today—a beggar! And for the second time, I have been the victim of the rich and of a moneylender into the bargain; Kunjilal, the village baniya.'

It had been a lengthy tale, and Chota had related it well. Indeed, it was not for nothing that he had spent such a long time in making it up. It just had to be a story that would call for immediate sympathy.

Chota felt he had succeeded and that the men before him had been moved.

He was right. The leader commenced speaking again, but his voice was quite changed. It no longer held the note of curtness and suspicion that had been there before. It was kindly. Moreover he now talked in a brotherly tone as used between long and trusted friends.

'Indeed brother,' he said, 'yours is a very sad story. It all but brought tears into my eyes. But be of good cheer now, we are your friends. In time to come you will meet another who will prove to be the greatest benefactor you could ever hope for. I am referring to our peerless leader, Rajah Man Singh Rathore, the noble.

'But for now, let us get down to business. This moneylender in the village, Kunjilal by name. Not only has he hurt you, but the Rajah has heard many tales of his oppression, harsh treatment, and his atrocities against the poor.

Are you aware for instance that he is in partnership with his brother in Bombay? They are running a brothel there with over a dozen girls in it. About half of them are from this very village; the daughters of poor peasants who have fallen into this villain's clutches through being in debt. These poor fathers and mothers have been compelled to surrender their growing girls to him for this nefarious purpose.

'In fact,' he continued, 'this Kunjilal is doing the very same thing that your moneylender, Mohan Lal, did in Sholapur. As their names indicate, they are from the same accursed stock—the Marwaris (a caste of usurers).

'Will you help us then to teach him a lesson?' and the speaker came to a stop.

Although the tale of Mohan Lal had been but a figment of Chota's imagination, Kunjilal was very real. The weals across his back that smarted so terribly reminded him of that fact every little while. And the story about the girls in the brothel at Bombay shocked Chota. If it was really true, this blackguard, Kunjilal, definitely needed to be taught a severe lesson.

He found himself wondering what sort of person Man Singh actually was. If it was a fact that he spent a good part of his time punishing scoundrels like Kunjilal, Chota felt that he would genuinely like to make his acquaintance.

Almost with a start he pulled himself out of the reverie into which he had fallen.

'Most assuredly,' he returned; 'in fact, I was just thinking what I would do to him were he left alone with me for only five minutes.'

Chota caught the faint outline of white teeth before him as the stranger smiled in the darkness.

'My name is Sundar,' he said, 'the tall man who spoke to you in the village marketplace is Datar Singh. This other man here who has not spoken so far is Hyder Khan.'

The last named individual, who was a Muslim as his name indicated, acknowledged the introduction with a low, 'Salaam-alaykum' (Greetings; God be with you).

Sundar continued, 'This Kunjilal eats his food in his own house, but on certain evenings, particularly a Saturday, after dinner at about nine o'clock, he goes to a cottage that he owns in another part of the town to spend the night with some unfortunate girl who has fallen into his meshes, or with one or two of the village prostitutes with whom he has regular dealings. His wife and family know about these affairs but are powerless to stop him.

'We are arranging that a certain very handsome girl of our acquaintance will act as a decoy. She will be introduced to this rascal. Of course he will lose no time, thereafter, in inviting her to his secret villa. On that night his servants, Dehu and Ram, will open the door of the villa, and the girl will be told to go there in advance and wait for him. It has always been worked thus,' he added.

'It will be your job to help Datar Singh and Hyder Khan to overpower these servants—but soundlessly. On no account should they be killed. You three must knock them out; then bind and gag them. When that has been done, send Hyder Khan to call me. He knows where I will be found.

'In the meantime, Kunjilal will hasten to the villa. Datar Singh and you must secure him also—and again noiselessly. That should not be difficult at all,' he added, 'for Datar Singh is a very powerful man.' Once again Chota caught the flash of his smile in the darkness.

'About one o'clock in the morning I will come along with Hyder Khan and we will spirit Kunjilal away. That part of the responsibility is mine. It should not be very difficult, as the village "chowkidars" (watchmen) are our friends to a man.

'You may accompany us after all this has happened as it will not do for you to remain in the village.

'Oh, by the way. When the three of you overpower the two servants, you must also truss and gag the girl, so that no one the next morning will suspect she was part of the plan. The police must be made to think it is just one of the many clever raids executed by Rajah Man Singh and that the woman played no part in it.

'Come now; let us revise each detail carefully so that there are no mistakes.'

Chota was surprised to find himself entering enthusiastically into this scheme of abducting the village moneylender. He felt he was killing two birds with one stone. Not only could he look forward to meeting the far-famed king of dacoits soon; but that slimy fellow, the baniya, was going to get what was coming to him. Chota could not help but enjoy thinking of the latter prospect.

The plan worked to perfection. Two evenings later the stalwart Datar Singh and the squat Muslim, Hyder Khan, sat talking in the marketplace till late. Not far away, Chota stood before his kerchief, spread upon the ground. He was begging.

Just after 7.30 p.m., when it was quite dark, the girl who was the pièce de résistance of the whole scheme, and who had the previous day been secretly pointed out to Chota by Datar Singh, passed close by the three of them on her way to the villa.

Chota could not help admitting that she was a comely wench.

Datar Singh and Hyder Khan casually followed some distance behind her. Back of them again, hobbled Chota. Ostensibly, his begging, at least for that night, was over.

By the time they reached the villa, the girl had already been admitted by the two servants, Ram and Dehu, who were there in advance to let her in and prepare the place for their master's night of debauchery.

In the darkness, Chota and his two companions stood outside. Then the three of them approached the entrance door, with Datar Singh in the lead.

Gripping the handle, Datar Singh tried to open it.

As was to be expected, the door was fast closed.

He knocked loudly upon the panels. There was no reply for a time. He knocked again.

The door flew open, to reveal Ram on the threshold.

'What do you dogs want—', he began.

Datar jammed his foot against the open door to prevent it being closed again, and the three of them rushed inside.

Chota found himself taking the precaution of closing the door behind them.

Datar struck Ram over the head with some small object he had produced from his pocket, and Ram fell as if pole-axed.

Dehu, the remaining servant, who had been in the next room, heard the thud of the fall and entered to find out what had caused the sound. Hyder Khan tackled him from the rear and pinioned his arms behind him. Chota clapped his hand over the man's mouth. And Datar Singh struck him with the same object he had used on Ram, and with exactly the same result. Dehu sank to the ground in a heap. Chota saw, for the first time, that the object was a wooden ball fastened upon a bamboo stick, six inches long.

So far, so good. It had all been very easy.

The girl had been a silent spectator to the whole scene.

As both the servants were unconscious, Datar Singh now addressed her.

'Come girl; we will tie you up now, so that when these beauties recover and see you bound and gagged—and disarrayed, too—they will think you were as much a victim of the attack as themselves.'

He produced several rolls of cord from his capacious pocket. Not ungently, they bound her hand and foot; and then gagged her with a 'rumal' (shawl), which he had also brought with him. Finally they tore her sari and jacket in places to make it appear she had been molested by them.

Just as they finished, Ram emitted a low groan.

Within the next ten minutes the two servants lay on the floor, efficiently bound and gagged. And it was Inspector Chota Singh of the C.I.D. who took particular pains to ensure that the gags and cords were so thoroughly well tied that the victims could not possibly escape unaided or make any noise.

With this part of the proceedings successfully accomplished, Datar Singh told Hyder Khan to go and inform their leader, Sundar, that everything had, so far, gone according to plan. It was a few minutes after eight o'clock and the two men estimated that the well fed Kunjilal would hardly arrive before half-past nine, after he had dined sumptuously, to enjoy himself with the girl awaiting him.

They were nearly right. At about a quarter after nine o'clock there came a soft knock at the door, and Kunjilal's voice could be heard calling, 'Open up; it is me.'

The two men had thought it wise to keep the oil light burning in the front room in case the baniya should become suspicious if the place was to be in total darkness. But, as it happened, this was not what he had evidently wanted to be done.

Chota and Datar Singh stood to a side as the latter swung open the front door. The door itself kept them from being seen immediately as Kunjilal stepped inside the room.

He was annoyed, and he was saying, 'Damned fools that you both are. Did I not distinctly tell you to keep the house in darkness?'

Just then Chota closed the front door softly, while Datar Singh hit the baniya over the head with his improvised weapon. Kunjilal collapsed.

The Inspector could not help thinking to himself, and smiling slightly as he thought, that the wooden ball had indeed played its part most efficiently that evening in silencing three men in quick succession.

They were both sickened by the scent of perfume that arose from the prone man. The baniya had evidently saturated himself with it before coming to the villa.

In a few minutes they had him trussed and gagged as efficiently as the two servants.

Ram and Dehu had, in the meanwhile, recovered consciousness. Helplessly, and with eyes wide open in fear, they stared at their master and at Datar and Chota. In the latter they recognised the beggar they had twice beaten. No doubt he would now avenge the injuries they had caused him and would cut their throats. Perspiration poured down their faces at the thought, and they trembled in their bonds.

But they found themselves still alive as the hours dragged by. Kunjilal took a long time to regain consciousness. When he did so he could not speak because of the gag. But tears rolled down the ash-grey skin of his flabby cheeks.

The girl lay bound and gagged in her corner. Kunjilal and his two servants noted her torn jacket and sari, and all three of them concluded that their captors had had her while they had been unconscious.

Meanwhile Datar Singh and Chota carried on a whispered conversation at the far end of the room. His tall companion offered Chota an endless succession of beedies (small cigarettes wrapped in tobacco leaf), as he smoked them himself.

Datar was speaking. He seemed to be in a talkative mood and the Inspector let him prattle on in order that he might learn as much as possible about him.

'Like you, brother,' Datar was saying, 'I was once upon a time a happy man. I ran a small-scale business. I owned a flour mill in the town of Bhind. It did not earn large profits, but it kept my family and me alive; I should say, comfortably alive.

'Then one day one of the rich men in the town who was, incidentally the President of the town Panchayat (local municipality), bought another mill. I was his sole competitor.

'Actually, the town was big enough for us both to do the same business and profit by it. He was a "lakh-eer", and had hundreds of thousands of rupees to his name, besides lands and houses. The few rupees, more or less, earned by my mill would have mattered nothing whatever to him.

'On the other hand I was a poor man. My wife and two children and myself were entirely dependent on what our mill brought in for our day-to-day food. To us it was our vital bread and butter.

'But this rich man, this president, whose name was Arjun Singh, could not bear the thought of competition. He determined to eliminate us and our little mill, entirely.

'As a first measure, he used his influence with the village Panchayat members to decree that the building in which the mill was housed belonged to the Village Council and that it was now required for other purposes.

'We were thrown out, and could not operate the mill until such time as some other building became available for our use.

'So I rented a small godown and stored the machinery in it, while I tried to find some other room large enough for setting up the mill. You must understand that at the moment there was no other empty place in the village big enough to accommodate the machinery.

'One night some persons broke into the godown by removing the zinc sheeting that formed the roof. They smashed the motor of the machine and removed the cutter.

'It was quite plain to me that no ordinary man, however evil he might be, would have done such a thing without rhyme or reason. Our machine had obviously been damaged at the instigation of Arjun Singh.

'I was hot-headed in those days and I publicly accused him. The President retaliated by making the Panchayat order me to refrain from ever operating my mill in that town again, even if I was able to repair it, and rent a building to house it. Thus this evil and greedy man succeeded in his purpose of removing me altogether from ever competing against him.

'Realising the hopelessness of fighting against Fate as far as running my mill in that town was concerned, I sold the broken machine as junk and set myself up in business in a petty shop, vending cigarettes, sweets and a few odds and ends.

'But Arjun Singh was not content with just wiping me out as his competitor as far as the flour mill came into consideration. He now set himself the task of eliminating me altogether. I really could not tell you why, as I had done him no harm. Possibly he bore me a grudge for publicly accusing him of being the instigator behind the persons who had damaged my machine.

'Be that as it may, he started harassing me directly and indirectly in a hundred different ways. It culminated one night with the premises of my petty shop being completely gutted by fire and all my stock destroyed. Inside the shambles, next morning we found a two-gallon petrol tin, twisted and blackened by the flames, but still recognisable as a petrol tin. Somebody must have entered through the roof and set fire to the place after pouring petrol over it. It had burnt to cinders.

'I was ruined entirely and for life.

'Then the landlord who owned the room which had been burned along with my stock, instigated by Arjun Singh, took legal proceedings against me for damages, saying that I was responsible for the fire through carelessness.

'In the face of all these troubles there was nothing we could do. At the dead of night I fled with my family from that accursed town.

'But disaster dogged our footsteps continuously. Exactly six months after the day of the fire—to the very date—the ferry boat in which my family and I, along with several others, were crossing the river Jamuna, foundered in midstream. The river was in spate. Many were drowned, including my wife and both our sons. I was picked up for dead on one of its banks a mile downstream.

'From that day, brother, I wandered in this land with hatred in my heart against Arjun Singh. It was he who was the beginning of all our misfortunes.

'All this while stories had reached me about the wonderful accomplishments of Rajah Man Singh, the gentleman dacoit who helped the poor. One day I determined to seek him out.

'How I found this great man will be of no interest to you. But I found him. Into his sympathetic ear I poured out my sad tale. Never, to my dying day, will I forget his reply.

'He said, "Be of good courage, Datar Singh. Maybe God has chosen you to help me to help the poor. Would you like to join my band?"

'I was so happy that I could hardly believe my own ears. That very moment I joined the great leader, Bapat Rao, as I hope you too will join him soon. And never to this day have I regretted it.

'Some months later, Arjun Singh undertook a business journey across the Chambal River. I happened to be with a batch of Man Singh's outlaws when we raided and captured a caravan. I am sure our chief knew about it and deliberately assigned me to that band, because among the members of that caravan was my old enemy, Arjun Singh.

'I took him to the Rajah and said, "Maharaj, remember I once told you about an evil man who had destroyed me and my family? Here, before you stands that very man in the flesh. Let me be avenged and kill him."

'"No, Datar Singh, you must not do that now," he had answered me, "every man should be given a fair trial and a chance to defend himself. It is my custom, always, to do this. Then, if the members of the band who sit in judgement on him pass the death sentence, he may be executed. But not till then."

'So the next day a number of the troupe assembled, to whom I told my story just as I have related it to you. Arjun Singh was asked to defend himself. He did so by flatly denying he had ever seen me before.

'Man Singh kept him a prisoner after the trial and sent some of his agents to the town of Bhind to inquire which of us was telling the truth. Those agents came back with ample proof that what I had said had been true, while Arjun Singh was lying.

'The outlaw band passed sentence against him. He was to die. And I was to kill him in whatever manner I deemed fit.

'Bapat Rao, the old rage and hatred that had burned within me for years against that accursed man, Arjun Singh, who had blasted my home and was indirectly the cause of the deaths of my wife and two sons, surged back into me in an irresistible wave of hatred. I drew the blade of the knife I was carrying, and before them all I cut the throat of Arjun Singh from one ear to the other.

'As his warm life-blood spurted between my fingers, my revenge was achieved.

'Among Arjun Singh's effects we found much money and some concealed jewellery. All this booty Man Singh handed to me with the words, "They are rightly yours, Datar Singh, for all the wrong that you have suffered at his hands. Keep the lot, or give some to the poor, just as you please."

'I returned everything to him with the reply, "Maharaj, I don't want one anna of the accursed swine's belongings. You may give everything to the poor. I ask only to follow you wherever you may go."

'That was nearly two years ago, Bapat Rao. Since then I have faithfully served this wonderful leader, nor have I ever regretted my decision to do so. More and more have I seen his chivalry and kindness. More and more do I love him. This very night I would sacrifice my life to save his.'

Datar Singh was silent. He had brought his poignant narrative to a close.

Chota pondered long and deeply about everything that had been said. Truly, he thought, the lot of a policeman is sometimes very hard. He has to make the most difficult decisions as to what is right and what is wrong.

Exactly at one o'clock in the morning they heard a soft knocking at the door. Lowering the oil-light, Datar Singh drew the bolts and opened the door a few inches. Outside stood two muffled figures whom they recognised as Sundar and Hyder Khan.

Datar opened the door still wider; and they both entered.

Sundar now spoke, 'Brothers, you have done your part of the work exceedingly well indeed. A closed car is standing outside. We will put this lout'—indicating Kunjilal, who was staring at them with renewed fright—'inside, and take him along with us. Come on, let us get going.'

The four of them lifted the weighty figure of the baniya to their shoulders and carried him outside, Sundar stopping just long enough on the threshold to close the front door behind them. Then they bore him down the few steps that led to the level of the street.

Before them stood a Buick sedan of ancient vintage.

Into the rear seat of the sedan they bundled the trussed Kunjilal. Then they got in themselves.

Chota noticed a silent figure standing at the street corner. The man gave no indication whatever of having seen them. He realised that it must be one of the village chowkidars whom Sundar had told him were favourably disposed towards the outlaws.

The driver, who had remained seated in the car, pressed the self-starter and the engine came to life with a splutter. They moved off and soon had left the village behind.

It was too dark outside to see much, but the headlamps of the vehicle cut a swath of light before them. Soon Chota noticed that they were traversing scrub jungle. It was also becoming chill, as the night air blew in through the open windows of the sedan.

Some hour-and-a-half later the road emerged from the scrub jungle and turned to the left. A few minutes more and they came upon the river running parallel to the roadway. They must be at least 30 miles down the course of the Chambal River from the point where it touched the village of Dhowd, he reckoned.

Ten more minutes passed. Then the headlights showed men standing on the road before them. The car drew to a halt.

'Some owls are wise,' mumbled the muffled figure of one of the men on the roadside.

'So are a few men,' returned Sundar, without hesitation.

The driver switched off the ignition.

'Is all well, brother?' queried the same voice.

'All is well,' intoned Sundar. 'The guest sits here amongst us.'

The other man chuckled softly.

'All right, then. Fetch him out and dump him into the boat. It is right here, at the waterside.'

They hauled the recumbent Kunjilal out of the car and carried him a few paces to the water's edge. Floating there was a boat with a man seated inside.

The four men who had stood on the roadside now joined them. Between them they lowered the baniya into the bottom of the boat.

As they all clambered in, the driver restarted the engine of the car and moved off.

In the boat two men, one on either side, commenced rowing. It slid silently into the night. They were in total darkness except for the reflection of the stars, mirrored on the oily surface of the water that lapped in gentle thuds against the wooden sides of the craft. For all Chota could feel, they might have been floating on a placid pond rather than crossing a river.

After a while, a deeper darkness loomed ahead, and Chota knew they were approaching the opposite bank of the river. With a faint rustling, the prow of the boat broke through the tall rushes that grew there, and grounded smoothly on the sand.

Evidently they had been expected, for another group of men suddenly appeared, their figures but dimly visible in the darkness.

Leaving the boat, the party waded ashore, carrying the trussed Kunjilal.

Then they untied his legs but not his arms. Nor did they remove his gag.

'Get up and walk, you fat hound,' said Sundar, prodding the baniya roughly with the toe of his sandal.

But Kunjilal had been bound for so long that his legs were benumbed. He groaned with pain and discomfort as the blood coursed through them, setting up the stinging sensation known as 'pins and needles' in his feet and calves. There was nothing for it but to let him lie there for five minutes or so.

When that time had passed and his captors judged the circulation had been restored, Kunjilal was hauled unceremoniously to his feet. With a man on either side, supporting him beneath the armpits, he was marched ahead, while the rest of the party which now numbered over a dozen men, followed in single file.

Dawn was breaking in the eastern sky. They had walked for almost two hours, up and down over extremely rough country, crossing what appeared in the darkness to be deep gorges whose sides rose to towering heights above them. The baniya tottered with exhaustion, and for the last half hour or so had been practically dragged along by the two men who supported him. Chota himself felt dead beat from loss of sleep and his physical exertions.

Then halfway down the face of the gorge they were traversing, they turned a corner caused by a spur of the hillock they had just descended. Suddenly before them loomed the entrance to a cave.

It was quite dark inside as they entered the tunnel, but the party shuffled along, one behind the other.

Chota knew they were following a secret passage of some kind, leading into the bowels of the earth, for he could feel the gentle but steady decline.

The passage negotiated a double-bend and must have continued for a couple of hundred yards at least, when they found themselves in a large amphitheatre, open to the sky which was tinged with the pink flush of dawn. All around in a circle, stony crags reared above them, the walls rising almost perpendicularly from the floor of this natural coliseum.

They stood, as it were, on the inside and bottom of a huge cylinder, open at the top, whose surrounding sides were of towering rock, rising to the height of perhaps two hundred feet. The area of the arena was considerable, and at a rough estimate in the greying light of dawn, Chota judged it to cover about ten acres of ground, forming an almost regular circle.

A few trees grew here and there. Spread beneath them, Chota caught sight of a number of nomad tents. For the rest, the ground was overgrown with coarse grass interspersed with boulders, large and small, that had probably rolled down from the top at various times.

The Police Inspector became lost in retrospection. No wonder it had proved so difficult to find the hideout of this notorious bandit when there was such a natural, secret camping ground available to him. From outside, the terrain would appear to be just an unbroken range of hills. Even from an aeroplane, the significance of the valley would be lost unless the pilot was flying very low. It would appear as normal country in keeping with the surrounding contour of rolling hills and broken ground that extended along these ravines, for miles upon miles on end.

At the same time, he thought that if he could only learn the way to this place and then escape, he would come back with an armed party who could be hidden among the rocks above and around, while another party could cover the entrance to the secret passage. Then the whole outlaw band would be trapped, like rats inside their own hole, in this natural amphitheatre.

It seemed a wonderful opportunity for him, Inspector Katar Singh of the C.I.D., to bring about the liquidation of the notorious Man Singh and his entire gang of dacoits, at one stroke.

They crossed a tiny stream that twined its way through the glade and approached the group of trees with the tents pitched below them.

Looking up to the ridges above, Chota could now make out in the orange rays of the rising sun that bathed them in a golden glory, the figures of armed men squatting behind boulders.

Sentries no doubt, he mused. Although they were clearly visible to the people on the inside of that hidden coliseum, from without they would be unseen.

The glade they were traversing was still cast in shadow as yet unreached by the rays of the rising sun.

Man Singh had a really marvellous hideout here, Chota conceded in his own mind. He did not even want for water with that little stream they had just crossed.

The grove of trees became alive with men who had issued from the several tents, or had perhaps been sleeping in the open. They turned out to inspect the new arrivals as they reached the fringe of the trees.

With a brief word of command, Sundar bid them to halt and sit down on the grass. Kunjilal tumbled to earth in exhaustion. Chota sat down gratefully. Sundar continued alone towards the centre of the group of tents.

They waited expectantly after that.

Ten minutes or so later, Chota saw three men approaching. He rivetted his attention on the first one of them.

He was an old man, stately and tall. His abnormally lofty forehead was streaked with horizontal white chalk marks, from temple to temple. On his head was a high turban of bright blue muslin. Glittering, steely-grey eyes, as hard as the metal they resembled in hue, were topped by shaggy eyebrows. The whole face was hidden by thick whiskers, a fierce out-jutting moustache, and a heavy beard, all the hair being snowy-white. The whiteness set off to advantage the determined profile of his countenance or such as could be seen of it through the beard, moustache and whiskers.

That was his first sight of Rajah Man Singh Rathore, king of the many outlaw bands that roamed the area.

Behind the Rajah was a burly figure armed with a tommy gun carried in the crook of his right arm, and the curved blade of a dagger strapped around his waist.

That would be the bodyguard who, he had heard, always accompanied the leader night and day.

Bringing up the rear of the approaching group, was Sundar.

Chota rose to his feet respectfully.

Man Singh came close, stopped, and gazed at the bound Kunjilal. Sundar stepped forward and spoke.

'Maharajah, that is the baniya' he said, rather unnecessarily.

Man Singh smiled vacuously. 'I can see that,' he replied; 'and is this the other man, the beggar you told me about?' indicating Chota.

'It is the Maratha beggar, Bapat Rao, your highness,' confirmed Sundar, by way of a formal introduction.

Chota salaamed, bowing low before the dacoit leader.

'Welcome to our camp and to our band,' Man Singh greeted him, heartily. 'I hope you will find here the justice that the world has denied you.'

With a musing half-smile on his face, he continued, 'So, we have the accuser and the accused, face to face, eh? That will make for a fair trial, indeed.'

They were all silent for a moment.

Man Singh turned then, and spoke to Sundar. 'Unbind the prisoner and remove his gag,' he commanded, 'the poor devil must be feeling terrible. Let them both rest and give them food. Tonight, after supper, the trial of the baniya will be held.'

Chota salaamed again, and the dacoit leader acknowledged it with a pleasant smile. He walked away after that, but Sundar remained to untie Kunjilal and remove the kerchief which had gagged him all this while.

Just as soon as he could speak, Kunjilal came to Chota and fell on his knees before him, 'Oh, spare me Sir,' he implored, almost grovelling on the ground with terror. 'After all, I did not beat you. It was my servants who did it. They are to blame. Please don't tell the old man anything against me. Only persuade him to let me go free. If you will do this, as soon as we get back, I will give you fifty thousand rupees. I swear it, on my honour.' The words came tumbling from his lips in a torrent.

Chota did not answer him. He just stared at the baniya stonily, and in that implacable look Kunjilal saw no mercy—no hope, whatever.

They ate and rested that afternoon.

Just after sunset, they ate again.

Then the bandits gathered around in a circle, a few lanterns were lit here and there among them, and the trial commenced under the open sky, with the line of serrated hills around, as witnesses.

Man Singh sat on his haunches within the circle. His armed bodyguard with the tommy gun ready for instant use, stood immediately behind him. To his right side and ten paces in front, squatted Chota the accuser. To the left, and an equal ten paces in front, sat the man on trial, the accused, Kunjilal.

Chota could see the sweat break out on the baniya's forehead and heavy cheeks and roll down to the tip of his chin in a successive stream. Kunjilal was so frightened that he never even thought of wiping his face, but permitted the perspiration to drip from his chin on to his lap, creating a spreading circle of wetness there.

Man Singh was speaking and addressing the accused. 'Your name is Kunjilal and you are a moneylender, is it not?' he queried.

'Oh yes,' gasped the baniya, 'but I take only a very small rate of interest…'

The old dacoit did not wait for him to finish, but put his next question, 'Do you know this man here, the beggar?'

'His face is familiar, your honour.'

'Did he come to you for alms?'

'Yes, I remember now. He came once, I think.'

'Did you cause him to be beaten on more than one occasion by your servants, and also by the police?'

'My servants may have beaten him, Sir; but how can you blame me for that?'

'And why did the police beat him?'

No answer.

'Did your servants not drag him to the police station?'

'If they did, I know nothing about it, Sir.'

'And how come you to be here tonight?'

This question was so unexpected that Kunjilal did not know what to reply. His jaw hung open and he was speechless for a while. After that he blurted rapidly, 'Why, your honour, all these men came inside my house and kidnapped me.'

'Where were your servants at the time?'

'They had already been assaulted and tied up,' he complained.

'And was anyone else there, besides you and the two servants?'

No reply.

'Was there not also a young woman present?'

Still no answer.

'Come,' said Man Singh, 'we have ways of making you speak the truth, but we would much prefer it if you did so voluntarily, when questioned.

'How came the young woman to be there?'

'She was sent to me as a prostitute and I had arranged for her to come to that house and meet me,' stammered the moneylender in admission.

'That is quite in order and we find no fault in it whatever,' cut in Man Singh. 'If a woman comes willingly to a man, it is entirely their business, not ours.'

'But tell me,' he continued, 'were you not in the habit of forcing women, obligated to you or bound by debt, to visit you in the same house where you would have them all night long?'

Kunjilal remained silent.

'There are other grave charges against you,' continued the old man, 'which have reached my ears from time to time.'

'Is it not a fact that, 14 months ago, when a certain bullock cart driver, Rajendra by name, paid you back the sum of two hundred rupees for which he had mortgaged his cart and two bulls to you, having already paid you an enormous interest, you took the money from his hand, while at the same time you declined to return the mortgage bond, thereby robbing him of the cart and bulls and of the two hundred rupees as well, while continuing the debt?'

'Is it not a fact that, when this cartman protested and pleaded with you on bended knees for what was his own property, you ordered your two servants to beat him soundly although he had fully repaid you all the money due to you, both as regards principal and interest?

'Is it not a fact that, in the course of the beating, one of your servants struck that poor man on the skull with a heavy bamboo?

'Is it not a fact that he fell unconscious at your feet?

'Is it not a fact that you bribed the police to say that he had been knocked down by a motor car which had caused severe injuries to his skull?

'Is it not a fact that he never regained consciousness, but died in the village Local Fund Dispensary two days later, from concussion?

'Are these charges true, or not, baniya Kunjilal?'

'Are you not guilty of the robbery and murder of an innocent, inoffensive, poor cartman for no reason, whatever?

'Do you not possess money in abundance—some hundreds of thousands of rupees of your own, together with many houses and much land that you should have coveted that poor man's bullock cart and his oxen?

'And when he repaid you in full for the loan he had taken, both as regards interest and capital, was it right of you to have refused to give him back his bond as well as his property, and then have him beaten up because he begged for it, thereby causing his death?

'For the last time, I say to you, answer me,' thundered the old man's voice inexorably, 'what have you to say? Why did you do these things, oh most wretched among men?'

But Kunjilal could make no answer. He fell on his face and grovelled on the ground and said, weakly, the one word, —'Mercy'.

'You beg for mercy yourself,' said Man Singh coldly, 'but did you extend it to that poor cartman; or to Bapat Rao the beggar, here, when he asked for alms; or to those unfortunate girl-children whom you raped when they begged for mercy from you, and whom you later sent to a brothel in Bombay when you had done with them?'

Kunjilal began to wail aloud in a high-pitched, hysterical voice, just like a woman.

'For the very last time, I give you the opportunity to answer and defend yourself,' continued the dacoit leader relentlessly. 'It is our custom at these trials of wicked men like yourself, to afford them a fair chance of speaking in their own defence. So, speak up. If you remain silent, it will mean you have no defence to offer.'

But how could Kunjilal put up any defence to those awful charges; especially as all of them were true?

Therefore he continued to say nothing.

'Oh children,' Man Singh addressed his band, 'you have heard the charges. We have given the accused an opportunity of defending himself. He has not done so, which appears to indicate he has no defence to offer. What say you, my sons? Be quite fair now. Is he guilty, or not? In your opinion should he be punished or not? And how?'

There was an unanimous roar of the one word, 'Guilty!' followed by desultory shouts of 'burn him', 'bury him alive', 'cut him to ribbons', and so on.

Kunjilal rolled on the ground, howling ever louder for mercy.

'Let the beggar-man beat him first and then cut his throat,' counselled a voice.

Man Singh turned to Chota and said, 'Do you agree to carry out the verdict of this gathering?'

Chota felt that he was in a predicament now, and in right earnest. If he refused, the outlaws would think him a weakling. They might even grow suspicious of him. Whereas, if he accepted, he would be compelled to murder the baniya in cold blood. As much as he detested Kunjilal, he could not possibly do that.

He thought fast, and inspiration came to him in a flash.

He said, 'Great Maharaj, you are a just man yourself. For me to beat him, as he had me beaten, would be nothing but right and I will gladly do it. But for me to cut this baniya's throat, when he has not killed any of my kith and kin would, I fear, respected sir, make me commit an unjust and unwarrantable action myself which I will have had no excuse whatever for performing.'

'Spoken like an oracle, Bapat Rao; shabash! (well done)' agreed Man Singh readily, 'I perceive you are a man after my own heart. Therefore I will not ask you to do what your conscience forbids. I will not ask any man to do that. Pick a stick then, of as near as possible the same kind of wood and thickness as that with which you yourself were beaten; if you can remember the number of stripes you received, so much the better; and lay on. For the moment we will suspend the latter portion of the sentence.'

And he laughed heartily over that. Chota could understand that the old dacoit appreciated his viewpoint and sense of justice.

He remembered, and most vividly too, that he had been beaten with bamboos. So he borrowed one from a dacoit and approached the cringing Kunjilal.

'Be a man for once and take your punishment like one,' he advised.

Then he commenced to strike the baniya soundly across his buttocks and his fat thighs with the bamboo. To make things more realistic, he administered a few, although not too hard blows, across his back.

Kunjilal screamed with pain and howled yet louder for mercy. Chota began to feel he rather enjoyed what he was doing.

The encircling crowd of bandits applauded vigorously.

After a dozen well-administered strokes, Chota stopped abruptly. Addressing the dacoit chief, he said, 'That was about the number, Maharaj Sahib, perhaps one or two less in fact than I received myself; certainly not more. But I find little pleasure in thrashing this cringing wretch.'

He returned the bamboo staff to its owner and walked away.

'Not only have you the quality of justice within you,' observed Man Singh, 'but the quality of mercy as well. I like them both,' he added.

Kunjilal nursed his wounds and whimpered.

But the encircling gangsters were not satisfied. A voice called out, 'Maharaj, he has been suitably punished for the lesser crime he committed. But what about the death of the cartman? This stranger, who has just come, talks much about justice. What has he to say to that?'

All eyes were upon Chota once more. Man Singh was watching him amusedly, no doubt curious to see how he would extricate himself from that challenge.

'Brothers,' returned the disguised policeman, 'I merely said that, as this moneylender had not murdered anyone of my family, I was hardly the proper one to be chosen to kill him. A relation of that cartman, if he is here, would be the right person.'

An impasse had arisen and they were silent awhile.

Just then another figure approached. It was that of a tall man with a slight growth of beard. He possessed the old man's features, and Chota knew he was looking upon one of the brigand leader's sons.

'Tehsildar, my son,' said Man Singh, 'here is a curious situation; what would you advise?'

Then in a few clipped sentences, he acquainted his son with the position. Chota noticed Tehsildar Singh glance in his direction once or twice; and it seemed to him those glances were not very friendly ones, nor were they understanding.

The young man waited till his father had stopped speaking. Then he said very simply, 'Father, to my mind the solution is easy. May I have your permission to end the problem?'

'You have, my son,' returned the leader.

Tehsildar stepped backwards two paces till he reached the bodyguard standing behind his father. Stretching out his hand, he got hold of the tommy gun and almost pulled it away from the man. An instant later, four or five shots broke the stillness in quick succession, and Kunjilal dropped dead.

Tehsildar pushed the tommy gun back into the hands of the guard, saying to him, 'Don't forget to clean it.'

To his father and the other members of the band, he said shortly, 'That is the solution; vermin and parasites like this are not fit to live.'

Chota had stiffened as he witnessed the cold-blooded murder of the baniya. Undoubted parasite that he had been, he had still been a human being.

And he had been murdered before his very eyes.

Nothing of importance happened for the next few days, and Chota fell in with the routine of camp life with the brigands. The day after his arrival he was given intensive training in the use and maintenance of ordinary firearms, such as the gun and rifle, of which he pretended to be quite ignorant. He discovered, then, that the dacoit band had their own miniature rifle range, where four .22 target rifles were in almost daily use in teaching such new members as himself the fine art of shooting men—and shooting them accurately.

On the fourteenth day after the murder of Kunjilal, Chota was given his first assignment to front-line activities with the dacoit band. It was a tough one, and incidentally it proved to be his last.

A raid on the house of a rich zamindar, living in a village about 30 miles away, was to be staged. This raid was to be carried out under the personal supervision and leadership of the dacoit chief, Man Singh himself. Chota learned that it was the old man's policy to share the responsibilities and dangers equally with his lieutenants and ordinary rank and file.

To allow the main body to get away with the booty in the event of pursuit, a smaller band of dacoits was arranged to fight a rearguard action, and to distract the police should they come out in force. It would also be one of the duties of this separate detachment to stage a counter-attack if necessary and then beat a retreat in quite another direction to draw the police off the trail of Man Singh and the actual raiders.

Chota was chosen to be one of the members of this rearguard. In fact, it was Sundar himself who selected him. He wanted to test the courage of this new recruit.

The main body of men who were to conduct the raid under the personal leadership of the Rajah numbered twenty, inclusive of their leader. The rearguard unit with Chota and Sundar, numbered six men and was put in charge of Devi Singh, one of Man Singh's higher lieutenants.

The plan was detailed to them after sundown two evenings before the night fixed for the attack. They ate their suppers at about eight o'clock at night, and at 9 p.m. the combined units went forth through the secret passage into the outer world.

They marched all that night, and by dawn had covered a distance of 23 miles. They were now only 7 miles from the village that was to be raided the following night.

Throughout the day they lay in hiding in the jungle, eating the baked chappatties they had brought with them; and once more at nine o'clock at night they issued forth to cover the remaining distance.

It was not yet eleven o'clock when they reached the outskirts of the village.

Devi Singh with his six men now deployed in a flanking direction to the east of the village. The main force, under Man Singh, was scheduled to attack at exactly midnight. If all went well, and they didn't hear much firing, Devi Singh and his party would understand there had not been much resistance. In that event, their orders were to wait till the shooting ceased and then make their own way back over the 30 miles to headquarters as best as they could.

But if there was heavy firing when the attack was launched, they would know that resistance was being offered in force, either by the zamindar's own people or by the police. They were then to advance to the outskirts of the village at its eastern limits and open fire with their weapons to make the defenders think the dacoits were operating in that direction also.

As soon as the police, or whoever it was that were defending the zamindar, commenced to attack Devi Singh's unit, they were to fall back towards the south in order to draw off pursuit from the main group, who would retreat northwards as they had come.

Eventually the rearguard was to circumvent the village itself and then withdraw towards the heavy jungle that grew to the north. From there on, Devi Singh and his men would use their own initiative to eventually get back to headquarters.

Devi Singh himself was a fierce-looking Rajput, wearing the usual martial moustache and whiskers. He was a thin man, very wiry, and gifted with abnormal powers of endurance and energy. Above all, he was a daring leader, possessing immense personality and great courage.

He hid himself and his little squad in a mango-grove, within two furlongs of the sleeping village, to await events.

Punctually on the stroke of midnight they heard the sound of rifle fire. It grew rapidly in intensity, and soon they heard the rat-tat-tat of automatic weapons in use, and the return fire of other automatic weapons.

That could only mean one thing. There were police or military patrols in the village; and they were resisting Man Singh's attack.

Devi Singh whispered, 'Come along, my brothers; here comes our chance,' and led them at the double over the two furlongs to the eastern edge of the village.

There he halted them, and under his instructions, they fired five or six rounds each into the air.

The sound of shooting at the scene of the main attack continued unabated. It became clear that the battle being waged there was so fierce as to permit of no distraction.

So Devi Singh advanced with his six men into the by-lanes of the village itself and worked forward to where the fight appeared to be raging. The noise of battle grew even louder.

'Keep together men,' he cautioned, 'follow me closely.'

At the first sound of gunfire the villagers had barricaded themselves inside their houses. There was nobody about and consequently no danger of counter-attack from the rear or resistance from the villagers themselves. They might even be counted upon to render assistance in emergencies. It was only the zamindar's own hirelings or the police force defending him, that had to be taken into consideration.

When the plan had been originally explained to him, Chota had at first thought of deserting should the opportunity occur while the attack was taking place. But later he had abandoned that idea. Of what use would he be to the police now, even if he did desert? He had not yet discovered the exact locale of the outlaws' hideout, or even its general direction amongst that maze of ravines. He would only be able to tell the police that Man Singh had his headquarters in a hidden grove somewhere between the hills. And that the police knew already.

So after much consideration, Chota had decided to remain with the dacoits and go back with them after the attack.

Such an action on his part would bring about three results. Firstly, the bandits would develop more confidence and trust in him. Secondly, they might bestow upon him a greater responsibility the next time which he might then be in a position to usefully take advantage of to help the police. Thirdly, and what was most important, the longer he stayed with the dacoits the more would he be able to find out, particularly facts regarding the different members of the band and the way that led to the entrance of the secret passage to the grove. That last was a most important factor.

These thoughts again raced through Chota's mind as he followed Devi Singh and the other five bandits along the village lanes.

They turned a corner and came upon the scene of the skirmish.

Nobody had noticed them thus far, all being intent upon the fight. Thus they were able to take stock of the actual position which soon became clear to them.

Evidently Man Singh and his main body of men had succeeded in gaining access into the zamindar's house before the alarm had been raised.

And, when that had happened, the police had surrounded it.

Now knots of policemen could be identified by their uniforms and seen hiding behind walls and corners of buildings, firing up at the windows of the house, from where the fire was being vigorously returned.

Man Singh and his party were trapped inside the zamindar's house!

Again the temptation grew strong within Chota to desert and join his comrades of the police and lead them into capturing or killing Man Singh.

But would they believe him at this juncture? His assignment to penetrate the dacoit stronghold had been kept a top secret. The police patrol here would not know about it. Would they have time to listen to his story? In all probability they would shoot him on sight, thinking he was a dacoit who had been sent to mislead or entrap them.

In the meantime Devi Singh ordered his party into action. 'Take cover men, and open fire on the police. Kill as many as possible. Then follow me and run back to the mango-grove. Be sure that we stick together. Ready now—Fire!'

Within the next few seconds the little band had carried out his orders. They opened fire with a ragged volley. Devi Singh and Sundar carried tommy guns. Chota could see policemen falling in all directions, as he himself began to shoot—but at nothing.

Taken in the rear, the police onslaught on the building came to a stop. At first the policemen were unable to know from where the counter-attack was coming, and they began to fire at random and in all directions.

This afforded the marksmen and the tommy-gunners from among the main group with Man Singh inside the zamindar's house, and those who had a bird's-eye view from the top storey of the building, of the counter-attack by their small band of comrades, the opportunity they wanted. They took heavy toll of such policemen as exposed themselves, caught between the enfilading fire.

A few minutes later, Chota saw the rear door of the house suddenly open and the dacoits that had been inside make a run for it.

A couple fell to the ground as some of the bullets from the police struck them. But in a trice the rest had disappeared.

That meant that the main body of dacoits with Man Singh had made good their escape. The rearguard unit had performed its job successfully.

Chota could only hope that Man Singh himself had been among the couple who had fallen.

But now a fresh eventuality developed. No longer supported by the crossfire of their comrades from the zamindar's house, the rearguard party of six dacoits and Devi Singh now had to face the full brunt of engagement by the policemen. The latter had also partially recovered from the surprise of the counter-attack to which they had been subjected and were rapidly becoming organised.

The police fire increased in intensity as more policemen located their position. Their tommy-gunners also came into action.

It was soon clear to Devi Singh that his small band was hopelessly outnumbered and out-gunned, and would be wiped out to a man in a little while if they did not retreat.

Even as he thought this, one of the dacoits threw up his arms and crashed to earth with a bullet through his brain.

'Follow me and run for it—to the mango-grove,' he shouted above the rattle of musketry.

And suiting the action to his words, he ran down the village lane, zigzagging as he went to avoid the hail of bullets that screamed in his wake.

One by one the others followed.

Chota hesitated for a second. Should he desert now? It would be easy. Devi Singh would think he had been killed. But then he remembered he had no information worthwhile to report. And he would surely be shot by the police, anyhow.

So he turned and ran.

Towards the end of the lane he stumbled over the dead body of another dacoit. He recovered himself and continued running.

A little later he found that he had reached the mango-grove. There were only four of them there—and Devi Singh.

Stray shots followed, indicating the police were in hot pursuit.

'Come on, follow me,' said Devi Singh, 'to the south of the village.' They ran after him again, one behind the other, crashing blindly through the darkness, stumbling against thorny bushes and tripping over rocks and the ant-hills that abounded.

Torches began to flash behind them as their pursuers sought to find out which way they had gone.

That was when Sundar made the mistake which was to cost him his life; and some of them, theirs too.

He stopped running, swung around and fired a burst from his tommy gun at one of the shining torches.

The torch went out abruptly as the policeman holding it died violently.

But Sundar had unwisely given away their position and the direction of their retreat.

A burst of return fire came from the police. Sundar stopped in his tracks, turned around slowly, and crumpled to the ground.

There were now only three of them left—and Devi Singh.

They stumbled blindly after him as they heard the running footsteps of their pursuers and bullets whined thickly through the air. Two tommy guns spat viciously from somewhere behind them and the dacoit who was running alongside Chota screamed hideously and collapsed, rolling over and over as he clawed at his abdomen.

There were now only two of them and Devi Singh.

But he was a good leader, and he kept his head. When they were directly south of the village, he stopped for a few seconds till his two companions caught up with him. Then he whispered quickly, 'Silently now; we will work our way up towards the west of the village. They will think we have gone straight on. Try to make no sound.'

Bent double he started running in a northwesterly direction with his two companions behind him.

As he ran, Chota thought to himself that it was now too late for him to desert. If he did, and even if he was not shot by the police, he would have accomplished nothing. Man Singh had, in all probability, escaped with the main force.

There was nothing for it but to keep with the dacoits and go back to their headquarters with them, there to find out more.

It took them but a few minutes to realise that the chase had petered out since they had changed their course at the southern point of the village. Devi Singh's strategy had succeeded and their pursuers had evidently continued on southwards, assuming they had fled in that direction. No more shots followed, nor did they hear any sounds to indicate they were still being chased.

Eventually they arrived at the western limits of the village. Here Devi Singh halted them for a few minutes to regain their breath. Then he led them north-eastwards. By following that direction he knew they would eventually rejoin the path along which they had originally come when approaching the village earlier that unfortunate night.

They were walking now, silently, and still in single file.

It was just after three o'clock in the morning when they at last met the pathway. Just over three hours ago they had traversed it in good spirits. It seemed like three days. All of them had been alive and happy then. Many of their number lay behind dead now.

But the path led directly northwards and to safety.

They now quickened their footsteps. Still another six miles or more lay between them and the friendly shelter of the forest.

It was 4.30 a.m. and the jungle loomed darkly and directly ahead, when a sudden shot rang out from somewhere in front of them.

The dacoit walking second-in-line, immediately behind Devi Singh, fell dead.

Now only he, Chota, was left alive—and Devi Singh. More shots rang out and bullets whistled around their heads.

They had been ambushed.

Simultaneously, he and Devi Singh dropped to the ground on their bellies and waited for what might come.

Bullets continued to whine above. It was dark and they could see nothing.

Then a voice came out of the blackness, 'Surrender, or you will all be shot,' it ordered.

That voice had come from a little to the right of them.

Devi Singh held his tommy gun ready for action in his hand, while with his right he groped for the stone upon which he had fallen. It was hurting his belly.

Suddenly an idea came to him. Gripping the stone with his right hand, he threw it as hard as he could to his left. The stone landed on the earth some yards away with a dull thud.

Immediately flashes of flame stabbed through the night as the ambushing police patrol opened fire in the direction from which the sound had come.

Devi Singh pressed the trigger of his tommy gun and kept it pressed as he swept the muzzle of the weapon in a slow arc at the spot from which the flashes were coming. There were screams and cries of pain as his bullets took effect on the hidden members of the police party.

Once more, lead screamed over their heads and around them.

In the midst of that confusion a strange thing happened.

From quite close by and in the direction of the forest in front, a horned owl hooted dismally—once, and then again.

And from Devi Singh, immediately to the left of him, Chota was surprised to hear the answering hoot of another owl, again twice in succession.

Only then did he understand the significance of the signals.

Man Singh and the main body of outlaws had reached the forest and had been hiding there. The police patrol had been following them when Devi Singh and his depleted group had turned up from the direction of the village. The main party had heard the sound of gunfire and counter gunfire, and had guessed that their returning comrades from the rearguard party had run into trouble. No doubt they had also seen the flashes issuing from the muzzles of many guns. But in that darkness they had no means of knowing which party was which.

So they had signalled by means of imitating the call of the horned owl, to establish contact. Devi Singh had understood the message and had replied. Man Singh and the main party would now know the police were in the other group.

The very next second proved that he had surmised correctly. Concentrated gunfire from the jungle was opened upon the police in which Devi Singh joined wholeheartedly with his automatic weapon. Chota himself began to fire his rifle rapidly, but shot into the air above the hidden policemen.

Once more, caught by an enfilading fire and this time hopelessly outnumbered, the policemen in the small patrol began to die, one by one.

Their return fire had almost ceased when Chota suddenly felt a terrible searing pain in his chest. Vaguely, he wondered what was the matter with him. Then he realised the irony of fate. He had been shot—by a policeman!

Oblivion followed after that.

Once during the following day he regained consciousness to find himself lying in the jungle. Man Singh sat beside him and was trying to force some water between his lips. But he relapsed into a coma before that could be done.

At night he awoke again to a peculiar and not unpleasant swaying motion. It took him some time to realise that he was lying in an improvised stretcher which was being carried on the shoulders of four of the outlaws.

The pain in his chest was excruciating. It burned cruelly, as if a red-hot knife was being twisted inside. He had high fever and his throat was parched.

Chota tried to speak. But the only sound that issued from his lips was a faint croak.

A hand clasped his and went up to his forehead; while a kindly voice said, 'Bear up, son; we shall be home by morning.'

That kindly voice had been Man Singh speaking to him. Before he could try to answer, he fell into a stupor once more.

Chota awoke for the third and last time. The sun was shining brightly outside. He was lying on a rasai (mattress) just within the entrance to a tent.

The dacoits had succeeded in carrying him all the way back to headquarters. For twenty-three long miles they had borne him on their shoulders. It must have been a valiant and difficult undertaking, tired as they were and in momentary danger of pursuit themselves.

With all that they had not abandoned him.

Chota appreciated what they had done and marvelled.

Of what use was all this trouble, though? For Chota knew that he was dying.

The pain in his chest was unbearable. Yet he could think clearly.

'Call Rajah Man Singh—urgently,' he said in a feeble voice.

One of the outlaws heard, and bent over him with a beaming smile. 'So, you are awake at last, brother? Don't fret; you will soon be well again.'

'Call him, do you hear? Call the Rajah soon—very soon! For I am dying; but I have something to tell him first.'

The man disappeared, and in a few minutes, Man Singh stood in his place.

'I am glad to find you awake, brother Bapat Rao—,' he began.

Chota cut him short. 'Listen to me, Maharaj Sahib,' he whispered faintly, 'there is something—that I must tell you. There is hardly time—for I am going to die.'

Meanwhile Tehsildar Singh and Devi Singh had also appeared. They listened curiously.

'Maharaj Sahib,' continued Chota feebly, making a mighty effort to speak coherently, 'I—am not—Bapat Rao, the beggar. My real name is Inspector Katar Singh. I am a detective—a police spy who came—to trap you. Fate has ordained—otherwise. Forgive me—if you can, O grand old man! But—but I was only doing my duty—honestly—my duty—my duty…' Here his voice trailed off into silence, and his eyes closed tiredly.

Man Singh thought that he had died.

But Chota opened his eyes after a moment and continued to speak. But his voice was yet fainter now, so that Man Singh had to bend low over him to hear what was being said.

'I succeeded in finding your hiding place—but, thank God, I told nobody about it'. Here he smiled faintly. Then continued.

'Thank you—for trying to help me—for car—for carrying me all the way back here. I am—much honoured and glad—to have met you. You are—a great man. God—bless you—Rajah Man Singh—Ra—Ra—Rathore.'

A convulsive shudder shook the diminutive Inspector's frame; then he was dead.

Man Singh regarded the little body silently, with its chest soaked in clotting gore. His eyes were strangely bright.

Then he said, very very softly.

'Assuredly I forgive you, Inspector Katar Singh of the Police. And I salute you, for you are a brave man. You did your duty and you did it marvellously well. May God rest your departed soul.'

But Tehsildar Singh, his son; and Devi Singh, his lieutenant; had overheard him. They wondered how the fierce old man could yet have such tender feelings.

And they cremated the little Inspector with all religious ceremony.

While of the plucky little rearguard unit that had fought so gallantly, none were left alive now—

Except Devi Singh!

Chapter Two
Jhani and Lotibai

'Don't pull my hair, you rude boy,' said a little girl one day. Her name was Lotibai, and she was the only daughter of Kumar, a rich merchant in the town of Bhind. She was hardly 10 years old when she uttered those words, and the place was the quadrangle in front of the local primary school building, which afforded the highest education to the children of Bhind that the large majority of parents could themselves afford to pay for in the way of school fees.

'Why not?' asked the youth, 'I like pulling girls' hair so as to make them cry,' and he pulled again.

He was a bright looking boy of about 12 years, with merry, sparkling black eyes. He seemed inordinately thin of body, but that was because he was growing rapidly, and all boys who grow suddenly appear thin. His wavy black hair was tousled and hung over his right temple. There was a glistening display of white teeth and a mischievous dimple on each cheek.

And his name was Jhani.

'Don't think, because you are a boy and I am a girl, that you can annoy me,' retorted Lotibai, 'for I will smack your face for you just now.'

'Go on, really,' laughed Jhani, as his right arm darted out once more, suddenly, to give her hair another tweak, 'maybe I like being smacked by girls.'

But Lotibai had begun to cry.

The smile died suddenly from Jhani's face and he looked wonderingly at the girl beside him.

'Now that is what I don't like about women,' he spoke the words with all the weight of sagely wisdom behind him. 'You try to joke with one and she begins to cry. Thank heaven, I was born a boy.'

'Get away from here, you nasty beast,' answered Lotibai vehemently, stamping her tiny bare feet on the ground with rage. 'I shall tell the teacher all about you as soon as class starts.'

'You sneak', blurted Jhani, contemptuously.

Just then the school bell rang, breaking in with a discordant clang upon the jabbering falsetto of the other children's voices that came from all around them.

There was a rush to enter the classroom.

For the teacher, old Mulki Ram, a Brahmin, was a strict man, and moreover very cruel. He would beat children who came late upon the palms of their hands with a thin cane. Rumour had it that that cane had been pickled in vinegar.

It certainly hurt terribly.

The children sat down in their accustomed places at the long desks that traversed the room. Out of the corner of his eye Jhani noticed that Lotibai had stopped crying, although she snivelled every now and again.

He also noticed that the tip of her nose, which tilted upwards a little, was moist and deliciously red, where she dabbed at it and her eyes with a small coloured handerchief.

Jhani felt that he would like to tweak that nose too.

He hoped she would not sneak on him to the Brahmin, Mulki Ram. If she did, he would surely be given a caning, and a severe one too.

All the other boys and girls would laugh at him.

The door opened and Mulki Ram entered the room, walking briskly.

The children stood up in unison and intoned in a sing-song chorus, 'Goodmorning, Sir.'

Mulki Ram had, meanwhile, stepped upon the foot-high platform at which stood his large desk and chair. Facing the assembled children, he replied crisply, 'Morning; boys and girls.'

He was above middle age and had flabby cheeks that sank down to his jaws and pouches beneath his eyes. He wore horn-rimmed spectacles with exceptionally thick lenses. From the angle of vision of the children before him, these greatly magnified the size of his eyes, which assumed ogre-like dimensions as they glared balefully around, accentuated by his rather predatory nose and thin-lipped mouth. He looked very much like an owl, and 'the owl' was the nickname the children called him behind his back.

Mulki Ram was clean-shaven, including the whole of his head, except far a tuft of long, greying hair which hung from a point high up at the back. This tuft and the three parallel vertical caste marks in vermillion powder that had been drawn down the centre of his forehead between his eyes and up to the bridge of his nose, proclaimed to all and sundry that here was a Brahmin indeed, of pure untouchable lineage.

'I will take roll call,' he announced, 'and then we will begin our history period. I hope you have all brought your textbooks?'

Again those ogre-like eyes looked around, and Jhani fancied they wore an expression of eager expectation. Woe betide the boy or girl who had forgotten.

Once again Jhani looked sideways across two rows of desks at Lotibai. Now was the time. If she was going to tell on him, she would have to do it now.

Lotibai appeared to become conscious of his gaze. She looked up slowly, then turned her head slightly and glanced backwards in his direction. Their eyes met.

There appeared the faintest trace of a smile at the corners of her mouth, and Lotibai did not sneak upon Jhani.

Thereafter, their eyes were rivetted upon their history books.

～

Seven years rolled by, but they seemed like seven days.

Lotibai was seventeen now, and she was the apple of her father's eye.

Indeed, she was a beautiful girl.

Of medium height and with raven-black hair which she invariably wore in two long tresses falling down her back, her face was symmetrically oval, her skin as smooth as velvet and of a creamy, chocolate tint. Her eyes were large and lustrous, and appeared to look out upon the world with the innocence and much of the surprised wonder of a startled doe. They were a very dark brown, had beautifully long, curving eyelashes, and naturally arched eyebrows. Her tiny nose, slightly up tilted as a little girl, had become provocatively pugged. Her warm, luscious pale pink lips set off the pointed chin, dainty yet determined, below it. A pretty red 'bottoo' (dot), glistened on her forehead between her eyes—the religious adornment of Hindu ladies.

Her figure had assumed the full proportions of budding womanhood. The sky-blue silk sari she was wearing bulged gracefully to reveal a black chiffon jacket that clasped the twin mounds of her breasts in a tight embrace.

Lotibai was in love; very much in love.

The object of this affection was the same Jhani; yes, the very same boy who had pulled her hair before school had commenced that far-off morning.

Somehow, they seemed to have just naturally grown into lovers.

They had been playmates throughout their schooldays and had passed out together.

Thereafter, Lotibai did not see much of Jhani in the mornings for he was kept busy, working in the fields with his father, old Balaji.

Jhani was Balaji's only son, just as Lotibai was Kumar's only daughter. But there the resemblance ended. For Balaji was a poor man, a farmer, who toiled with his son to plough the fields and scatter the seeds on the 12 acres of dry land they owned and from which they were just able to eke out a poor living provided the monsoons did not fail, or did not descend upon the land out of season, or in superabundance.

When any of these calamities happened, old Balaji and his son, Jhani, had to live on borrowed money and hope for a good crop the next year.

Kumar, however, had prospered. Everything he touched had turned to gold. Not only did his business as a merchant flourish and increase, but he had taken up a new line—that of a contractor to the Government—who supplied all the military garrisons and the local police detachments in the area with their everyday wants, from food to safety pins. This had brought him in enormous profits, and he was now the owner of many hundreds of thousands of rupees.

Every evening—or nearly every evening—Lotibai and Jhani would meet at the marketplace, or sit on one of the small benches in the public park, talking.

(The boys and girls of India, unlike those of western countries, are not encouraged into developing pre-marital friendships between the opposite sexes. Normally and invariably, marriages are pre-arranged by the respective parents and only during the ceremony do the boy and girl see each other for the first time.

So, Lotibai and Jhani were doing something quite unusual in meeting each other, even if it was but to chat for a few minutes in the open marketplace, or on a bench at the park, in broad daylight.

Any such thing as going to the movies together, or for a picnic or even a stroll outside the village precincts was not to be thought of. In fact, they themselves never dreamt of it.)

Somehow, their friendship with each other became to be looked upon by their respective fathers as an accepted, harmless thing. For had they not known each other for more than seven years? Were they not in school together; even in the same class?

Indeed, the townsfolk of Bhind thought the same thing and did not gossip about it; at least not overmuch. Such few of the old hags as did whisper with heads together and sidelong glances, as the young couple passed by, were known to be frustrated old scandal mongers anyhow; and nobody paid much attention to them. Frustrated people do not attract sympathy all the world around.

Even Jhani and Lotibai themselves did not recognise they had fallen in love with each other. If they had, they would probably have been very frightened about it. They were just good pals—buddies since their schooldays—who still got along well together and enjoyed each other's company. It was all very innocent. Neither of them had ever thought about themselves or each other in terms of sex.

That is, until the day the storm came.

'Jhani, it is going to pour with rain in a minute,' said Lotibai, seated next to him on their usual bench in the park one evening. 'Come, let us go. If we walk quickly, there may just be time for me to reach home.'

'But it is only five o'clock and we've just met,' answered Jhani, glancing up at the darkening sky, resentfully. 'Hang the odds; let it rain. We can always take shelter in the old 'moosafarkhana' (travellers' bungalow) across the road.

'And suppose it doesn't stop?' Lotibai put in, apprehensively.

'How silly. It must stop sometime. Probably by six o'clock or so. It will still be daylight.'

Lotibai was not so sure of the wisdom of remaining, but her liking for the wavy-haired young man seated next to her overcame her sense of caution.

For Jhani, now 19 years old, was no longer the lanky youngster he had been as a schoolboy. Tall, well-proportioned and muscular, the last two the result of his daily toil in his father's fields, he had grown into a strikingly handsome youth. The unruly hair was now naturally wavy, although one end of it yet persisted in falling over his right temple in the same way it had done so many years ago. The mischievous smile was yet there, to reveal the same gleaming white teeth. His dark eyes still sparkled with the joy of living.

But he no longer pulled her hair or tweaked her nose.

'Well, if I get drenched, you will be responsible for it, and I shan't meet you tomorrow evening,' Lotibai pouted, a softness in her tone quite belying the threat her words had been intended to convey.

Jhani knew they would meet the next evening; and every evening after that.

A growl of thunder issued from the black cloud above them, increasing in crescendo as if a giant drummer above beat a bass drum of titanic proportions.

'Here it comes,' said Lotibai, looking heavenward with her frightened, doe-like eyes, 'do you think there is enough time for me to get home before the rain starts?'

'What a scared little puss you are,' was Jhani's only reply.

Then the thunder came again; but now it was as if the heavens themselves were rent asunder. And the thunderclap was followed by the first few drops of rain;—not the small raindrops one sees in temperate climes, but large blobs that fell to the earth ponderously, to leave a splash of moisture on the sun-baked surface of the dry, hard land.

'Come on, let's run for it,' said Jhani lightly, springing to his feet and seizing her small hand in his large and powerful fist, 'let's see how fast you can move.'

And with the words he set forth at a trot in the direction of the old moosafarkhana standing across the road at the other end of the little park.

Lotibai tried to keep up with him, but the tightness of her sari around her thighs and calves prevented her from taking long strides. Each of her paces was forcibly short and Jhani felt that if he pulled her any harder she might trip and fall.

Halfway to the old bungalow there came a vivid flash of lightning which made itself seen in the gloom around them, cast by the clouds that had piled themselves together overhead and now covered the whole sky under an ashy-grey pall. The lightning was followed by another resounding thunderclap, and then the reservoir of the heavens, pent-up for the past six hot, thirsty and waterless months, opened itself fully upon them. The rain descended in a solid sheet of water, enveloping everything in its opaque shroud.

The bungalow, was but 50 yards ahead, directly across the road. But they were both soaking wet by the time they reached its sheltering porch.

For a moment they halted underneath to watch the wall of rain, and the trees in the park bend under the force of the sudden gale of wind that had come with it.

The smell of the moist earth seemed indescribably refreshing to Jhani's nostrils. A farmer himself, and descended from a long line of agriculturist ancestors, he knew that the rain meant life, growth, sustenance and the means of existence to the millions of square miles of land and the teeming millions of people, that were India. Without uttering the words aloud, he breathed them, 'God be praised.'

Then, in an exuberance of childish glee and gratitude, he suddenly ran out into the rain, pirouetted around twice, and rushed back beneath the porch.

'Jhani, you ass, what are you doing?' asked Lotibai, now all attention, once again stamping her feet upon the ground in anger just as she had done seven years ago. That was a little habit of hers in registering displeasure.

Before he could say anything, she continued, 'Sometimes I think you will never grow up. You will always remain the little schoolboy I knew.'

But once more the expression of her eyes belied the severity of her tone. There was an infinite tenderness in them. A softness that almost cried aloud in its very silence the words, 'Oh Jhani; you will always remain the schoolboy that I know, and love so well.'

Jhani, however, was in no mood for sentiment just then. He shook himself, as does a wet spaniel, spraying water from his soaked clothing all around him, and over Lotibai.

She was all concern. 'Get inside the verandah this instant,' she commanded, the mother instinct, pent up inside every woman, showing itself spontaneously, 'you will catch your death of cold and probably die of pneumonia. Here, wipe your face and hair with my hankie.'

Jhani grinned hugely at the diminutive handkerchief she offered him, a mere six-inch square of prettily coloured material. He solemnly took it from her hand and commenced to wipe his face with it and run it through his hair.

In no time the tiny handkerchief was saturated. With pretended seriousness Jhani rung out the sodden wisp of cloth between both his hands and then started wiping his head once again.

Together they walked up the four stone steps from the porch—or portico (as it is commonly known in India)—to the verandah of the building.

The moosafarkhana had been a popular construction in its time.

Built by the British over seventy years ago, it had been the one Travellers' Bungalow in the area for many, many miles around. Hence it had been a haven and an oasis for weary officials on their rounds of tour and inspection. These officials had hailed from all departments of Government Service; Military, Police, Excise, Land Revenue, Forest, the Survey Department, and such like; who had taken advantage of its existence to break journey for a few hours and camp in relative comfort before, once again, becoming exposed to the many discomforts and vicissitudes of tent life.

Rumour had it that a Viceroy had once stayed there. Certainly many Governors had, as the old bungalow registers would have proved had they been in evidence.

But those registers had long ceased to exist. Some of them had crumbled to dust; some been eaten by termites and mice. Perhaps a few had gone to light the kitchen fires of the chowkidars, who had still been kept in service to guard the bungalow long after it had stopped being used.

Now even the chowkidars had been withdrawn and the old moosafarkhana was crumbling into ruin.

Somebody had discovered that the building was unsafe due to an architectural or constructional fault—or so that somebody had said. In a great hurry Government had selected a fresh site and built a brand new bungalow. No one could tell how much pains had been expended, if at all, in considering whether the old building had been thought worth repairing.

The fact remains that the new building had mushroomed into existence while the old one was fading, slowly, into oblivion—like a weary old man, abandoned by the roadside and left to die peacefully of old age.

The wooden doors and windows, with their frames, had long been removed; then had followed the sky-lights, and then the wooden beams and rafters in many rooms, causing the roof to cave in. But the main walls of the old building still held firm, and the roof yet covered two or three of the silent, deserted rooms, striving against the hopeless task of defying the inroads of time and the elements.

Part of the verandah roof had collapsed, part remained.

Jhani and Lotibai took shelter under the roofed portion and stood there to watch the play of the elements without.

Forked lightning streaked the ever-darkening clouds with veins of phosphorescent silver, momentarily depicting in the sky above the giant tracings of a river, mapped in the heavens, that flowed towards the earth. Then the picture vanished, to be followed in a few seconds by the ear-splitting explosion of a thunderclap. They felt the walls of the old bungalow shiver as if from an ague. The rain that had been descending in torrents, poured even harder entering through the fallen portion of the verandah roof and flooding the stone flooring on which they stood, inches deep in water.

It beat in directly through the open front; it saturated them in the form of spray. Rain, and yet more rain. Even Jhani felt the awe of the elements.

Then the wind began. They heard the banshee howl of it in the distance, coming ever closer. And it was upon them. The row of 'neem' trees that lined the road in front of the old bungalow suddenly bent double with the impact of it; branches and leaves were wrenched off and sailed completely out of sight. It tore through every gaping door and window opening, and through the holes and crevices in the walls and roof. It cut through their saturated clothing, numbing them with the cold so that their teeth chattered.

'Let's go further in,' shouted Jhani to make himself heard above the howl of the wind and the hiss of falling rain outside, suiting the action to the word by seizing Lotibai above the elbow and piloting her before him.

They passed through the open doorway into what had once been one of the main rooms of the old moosafarkhana.

The roof here was in place, but the water flowed in through many cracks and ran down the walls in streams of moisture.

'Across there,' indicated Jhani, still propelling the girl by her elbow, 'through that doorway. Perhaps that room leaks less.'

They entered and found themselves in some sort of anteroom. It was almost dark inside, because there were no windows, and the only way in was through the doorway they had just come. For the same reason the room was less draughty and not leaking much. They huddled against the wall together for mutual warmth, Jhani's arm protectively around Lotibai, and held tightly.

Again and again thunder exploded overhead as the storm spent its fury. The old building quivered with each impact.

Suddenly there was a rending crash as the roots of one of the neem trees, strained to the utmost by the force of the cyclone that bent the trunk and branches above, were torn out of the earth, allowing the tree to heel over and topple to the ground.

The noise startled Lotibai, who thought the roof had fallen in. She threw both arms around Jhani's neck and hid her face in his breast.

'Jhani, oh Jhani,' she whimpered.

And at that moment time seemed to stand still for Jhani. In a flash, as rapid as the flash of the lightning outside, there was born within him a new conception of the girl who clung to him so tightly.

Gone was Lotibai, his schoolgirl friend and companion, and pal of so many years.

In her place stood Lotibai, the woman. The woman whom he now desired beyond anything and anyone else in the world.

Her wet blouse and his soaked shirt were inadequate to prevent the feeling of warmth and pressure upon his chest as the firm hardness of her breasts bore against him. Her face was upturned to him, the hair plastered to her wet skull. Her eyes were closed, and her full, moist lips were temptingly close.

A wave of passion, as fierce as the tempest outside, shook Jhani.

Impetuously he threw both arms around her and crushed her yet harder to him. His lips met hers hungrily in a long and passionate kiss.

'Loti darling, I love you,' he whispered tenderly, 'I don't know for how long it has been thus. But now I know it. I—I want you dearest. Now.'

'Jhani,' she replied tenderly, 'I love you too. I have always loved you, but I hesitated to show it. I was waiting for so long, just for you to tell me.'

They kissed again and again.

Instinctively the man in Jhani knew that the resistance of the woman he held in his arms was rapidly weakening, and relentlessly, almost cruelly, he pursued his advantage.

Loti's lips opened partially, and her breath came in little gasps of passion and increasing desire.

Jhani kissed her, long and lingeringly, forcing the tip of his tongue into her mouth, where it met hers trembling with eager desire.

Still holding her tightly against him with his left forearm, Jhani removed his right hand from behind her, gently sliding his fingers down her bare side and across her abdomen. Then he ran it over her blouse and forced it down from above and under the wet cloth, to finally cup her breast within his palm.

Exultantly he felt the tautening of her nipple as her body quivered with mounting lust.

'Oh Jani, we musn't,' she breathed feebly, 'it's wrong; we musn't.'

But there was no conviction whatever in her tone.

He knew he had almost conquered, and pressed home to complete the subjugation.

His hand tightened around her bare breast, and his tongue forced itself upon hers. A moan of surrender issued feebly from between Lotibai's parted lips.

Then active lust played its part, unrestrained.

Petulantly, shamelessly, she pressed her lips more tightly upon his—lips wet with exultant submission. Her tongue slid itself past his, and into his mouth.

As if glued together, they sank silently to the ground.

Time passed, and the ecstasies of passion, as they spent each other over and over again, gradually wore away. Lotibai was the first to become aware of it. 'Good gracious, darling,' she breathed, 'what must be the time?'

It was pitch dark inside the room now.

Jhani looked at the luminous dial of his wristwatch. 'Good gracious,' he exclaimed, 'it's five minutes to eight.'

They scrambled to their feet together. All sounds of the storm had abated outside. They had been entirely oblivious to everything but themselves.

Arm in arm they splashed through the pools of water that had formed in the driveway of the compound, and came out on to the road.

'Father will be worried,' said Lotibai, 'he will wonder what has happened to me. I have never been so late.' Then, and only then, did the full weight and significance of what they had just done forced itself into her memory.

She looked up into his face with a frightened expression in her eyes. Almost pleadingly, she asked, 'Oh Jhani. Jhani, what have we done? Why did we do it?'

At that moment Jhani was asking himself exactly the same question.

But he made a brave show at trying to calm her.

Taking the palm of her right hand in both of his, he squeezed it reassuringly, comfortingly.

Then he replied, 'I am very very sorry, Loti darling. Please forgive me. I don't know what happened, but I just could not control myself.'

'Don't blame yourself entirely, Jhani dearest,' she answered forthrightly, 'I was as much at fault myself'; adding lamely, 'it takes two hands to clap, you know.'

They walked on a few paces, each lost in thoughts of their own.

Then Lotibai asked, somewhat apologetically, 'What do we do now?'

But Jhani had regained his usual high spirits. He laughed lightly at her question.

'How silly! What do you think? We will get married of course.'

Loti thrilled to his words, and hugged his arm tightly against her breast.

'Tonight won't be advisable,' continued Jhani, 'but first thing tomorrow morning I'll come across to your place with my dad and tell your old man I'm going to marry you.'

Loti was delighted.

A few minutes later they had reached her home.

Lotibai was a bit anxious as to how her father, Kumar, would look upon her late return. The clock on the wall in the drawing room showed it was exactly 8.20 p.m.

But Fate had decided to be kind to the lovers, at least for that night. The servant who opened the door informed her that her father had gone out in a car with a friend who had called for him just before the storm started, and had not yet returned home.

Breathing a sigh of thankfulness that they had crossed the first hurdle, the lovers kissed each other quickly as soon as the servant had gone inside, and Jhani turned to go home and convey the good news to his father.

Balaji was happy; he was gloatingly happy.

He was delighted because the rain had not only watered his twelve acres of land plentifully, but had filled the small pond he had dug at the further end of it.

That water would be a boon to the hundred or so domestic ducks he kept. They would swim in it all day, and lay eggs in the grass on the banks at night.

And he would sell those eggs.

Sitting on the floor in the verandah of his little home, with his feet folded crosswise and tucked beneath him, he closed his eyes and gave himself up to reverie.

At the age of fifty-nine, Balaji could by no means be considered an old man. Tall and well-boned, the strenuous and healthy life he had led since a lad, when his own father had died suddenly from cholera while the epidemic had raged and left this farm in his sole charge, had kept him fit and busy and happy.

Thrown so unexpectedly upon his own resources, he had manfully shouldered the burden and worked hard upon the land since that very day.

Often indeed had the wheel of fortune doled out hardships and calamity to his lot. The water in his well sometimes dried up. The rains had failed; or had come out of season. Occasionally there had been too much of it. Twice a crop-pest had visited his land, killing the harvest before it was ripe in front of his very eyes.

But not for nothing had his father endowed him with a square, determined jaw; hazel-brown frank eyes; a jovial pleasant, face; an overflowing, optimistic nature; and an indomitable determination to win through. Not only did he look to have these qualities; he possessed all of them abundantly.

Early in life he married the rather thin girl his father had chosen for him, but had not lived to see him marry. She had been the daughter of another farmer, and so she had fitted perfectly into the hard life led by those who till the soil in India. She had proved herself to be the very best life-mate, companion and wife a man could ever have wished for.

In times of trouble and misfortune she comforted, consoled and encouraged him. At other times when things were going well, she praised him for the hard work he had done on the land, while she put something by for a rainy day.

Jhani had been their only child, and they had stinted themselves to educate him at the best school in the village.

One night, almost exactly four years ago, Fate had struck old Balaji the cruellest of blows, and incidentally the first and only one to which he had nearly succumbed.

His wife, Meerabai, had gone outside the house to answer the call of Nature and had trod upon a cobra with her bare feet. The cobra had promptly bitten her.

There was no doctor nearby in those days who knew the value of antiserum treatment. Neither was there any anti-venine serum available.

It had happened in the dead of night.

He had summoned the village magician, or 'mantram-man' as he was called, who claimed the powers of a witch doctor and assured Balaji that he could, and would, shortly cure the patient.

The magician had seized one of Balaji's fowls, plucked off the feathers from around its anus, and applied the vent itself to the two fang-marks made by the cobra near her ankle, in turn.

He claimed this treatment would draw out the venom.

Then he said he noticed the fowl was turning black about its head owing to the snake poison it had absorbed. He cut the fowl's throat. He said that by sacrificing its life the gods would spare the woman's.

He muttered mantras.

He set fire to a white powder that had flared up in a glaringly bright flame. That was to frighten away the evil spirits.

But nevertheless Meerabai, his wife, had died.

That was the time Balaji had lost interest in the farm, in his son and himself, and with life altogether for some months. He had contemplated throwing himself down his own well.

But his dominant nature reasserted itself. He won through, overcame his despondency, struggled on.

Now things were a bit easier. His son, Jhani, had grown up and helped him on the farm every day. Balaji was pleased that the boy had taken to farm life voluntarily. So many of the lads of his age these days were averse to it. They clamoured to migrate to the big cities and work in some industrial concern there.

They had said it brought in more money. Balaji knew for a fact it brought in more leisure—and more trouble and evil habits with that leisure. But his Jhani had not done these things. On the contrary, he had shaped himself admirably to life on the land.

Balaji was very proud of Jhani. He thought the world of him.

The old man continued his reflections, eyes closed tightly to concentrate his thoughts and keep them from going astray.

Jhani was nineteen years old now. High time he got married. He, Balaji himself, would have to look for a suitable wife for the boy.

And, by God, she would have to be really worthy of his Jhani.

For one thing, she would have to bring a big dowry of money and jewels with her. The former would be used for remodelling the farm and digging another well.

For another, she would have to be the daughter of a farmer herself, just as his beloved Meerabai had been. Then only could he ensure that the girl would be able to adapt herself to this life of toil and sweat. No woman from a city; no daughter of some worthless, white collared town man would he permit Jhani to marry.

For only too well did Balaji know the uselessness of a town-girl when she was brought face to face with hard manual labour on the soil of the land.

Footsteps splashed suddenly through the mire and water outside, and a cheery voice called through the darkness, 'Hello dad; are you asleep?'

Balaji opened his eyes. There was the ghost of a smile of pride upon his face.

For that voice was Jhani's.

A moment later his son took the three steps leading up to his verandah in a single stride and came to a halt, smiling happily, before him.

Balaji thought his son was happy because of the rain.

He said, 'A lovely downpour, eh, Jhani?'

To which Jhani replied spontaneously, 'Hang the rain; I have wonderful news for you.'

Balaji frowned noticeably.

'Hang the rain!' he exclaimed incredibly. 'Why, this downpour is the best thing that could have happened today.'

'Not on your life,' returned Jhani promptly, 'I have much better news for you—and far more important, too. I am going to be married.'

'Married did you say?' asked Balaji, not believing his own ears. And then again, openly dubious, 'Married?'

'Yes,' burst from Jhani exultantly, 'to the sweetest and best girl in all the world; Lotibai.'

Then Jhani continued excitedly, and before his father could put in a word. 'Do you know, dad, a wonderful thing happened today? I have always loved this girl, yet I didn't know it myself until tonight.

'It came down to rain, and we took shelter in the old moosafarkhana. Then suddenly, I—I—; well, I discovered I loved her, and am going to marry her soon.'

'That's rather unusual,' said his father; unfolding his legs from underneath himself and slowly rising to his feet, 'what led up to causing you to make such a sudden discovery?'

Jhani blushed beneath his brown skin. How could he possibly tell his own father what had happened.

'I—I really don't know myself, dad. You see, as I said, we had been talking in the park when it suddenly came down to rain. We rushed into the old moosafarkhana, as it was the closest building. There we remained till the storm had passed. In the meantime, we were just —well, talking. From the things Lotibai and I said to each other, we discovered we are deeply in love and wish to get married.

'Tomorrow I want you to come with me, dad, to ask old Kumar for his consent to marry Loti. It will be just a formal request of course as he is bound to agree. But we would like both our fathers to meet and to give us their blessings.'

'I see,' said Balaji, thoughtfully, 'in my time a boy and girl did not suddenly decide to get married while they were sheltering from a storm in a deserted building.'

He glanced up. Jhani thought he detected a knowing smile at the corners of his father's mouth. Could the old man have guessed what had really happened?

'Their respective parents arranged the match before ever they met,' continued Balaji.

'Nevertheless, I for one realise the times are changing. Nor am I bigotted or narrow-minded. I do not object to you choosing your own mate.

'But the vital question, Jhani, is just this. I know Lotibai is a pretty girl and a nice girl, and a decent respectable girl.

'I also know your marriage to her will bring in a considerable dowry. Her father, that merchant-contractor, Kumar, is a very wealthy man. I for one will bargain most rigidly for a large dowry, you may be very certain of it.

'But the all-important question, my son, is just this.

'Will Lotibai prove to be a good wife to a farmer-boy, like you? Is she not just a town-bred girl; rich, lazy, indifferent and probably unfaithful, too, along with it? Will she be able to stick the hard life by the side of her husband?

'Like your dear mother of ever-blessed memory endured it, along with me.' Then he added in an undertone, 'May God rest her soul in eternal peace.'

Jhani had listened to his father's words with growing impatience. To him it appeared ridiculous, if not sacrilegious, for old Balaji to even entertain such thoughts.

'Oh don't be so silly and old-fashioned, dad,' he cried petulantly, 'I have known Lotibai for years. For one thing, she is a plain, simple girl with no pretensions whatever. Surely we are not going to imagine faults in her just because her father happens to be a very rich man?

'Besides, we love each other too deeply for either of us to ever think of being unfaithful.' He uttered the words with an air of finality and as if the last word on the subject had been spoken.

After that they ate their evening meal of vegetable curry and the chappatties which Balaji had prepared, almost in silence, each engrossed in his own thoughts.

The old man was thinking to himself: is this going to be for the better or the worse?

After mother died we both managed the farm more like pals than like father and son. There was perfect understanding and never discord.

Jhani would work on the land while I attended to the household chores. Occasionally we would change over; and he would do the cooking while I pottered about on the land. Either way, there was always time between us for both duties and a chat when they were done.

Now this woman is coming along. She will claim his time and his attention both day and night. I will have to attend to the farm all by myself—and I am growing old. It may be too much of a burden for me at this age. The work may prove too hard.

If I call my son away from her, this woman will not like it. She will whisper sweet nothings in his ear and he will hurry back to her arms.

Worse still, this Lotibai is the offspring of one of the 'higher-set' of human beings—the hated rich—who never seem to work by the sweat of their brow like we have to work, but to whom money appears to come nevertheless—just like that, as if attracted by a magnet.

Would she make a good wife for his Jhani? Would she be able to accustom herself to sitting on the floor of their little home, and not on chairs, as she was wont to do in her father's mansion? Would she sleep on the ground, or would she want her spring-cot, probably equipped with a mattress of silk-cotton, gathered from the pods of the silk-cotton trees that grow in the jungle not so far away? Above all, would she soil her beautiful sarees and her prettily-manicured fingernails, toiling in their kitchen, or sitting on the floor grinding the 'curry-stuff' between the flat stone and the elongated oval stone roller which went with it, and with which the kitchens of the poor in India are equipped?

Would she do all these things?

Balaji doubted it; and in his heart he found himself resenting the advent of this Lotibai, or for the matter of that the intrusion of any woman into the home for his son as a wife.

But then, another thought came to him. In his memory, not clouded by the mists of forgetfulness but wondrous clear as if she stood before him at that very moment, appeared the face of a woman; rather lean of countenance but with lustrous, frank, honest brown eyes; a tiny, rosebud mouth, topped by an equally tiny nose and a delightfully rounded chin with a dimple in it.

The face was that of his beloved Meerabai as she was on the day he had married her.

His old eyes misted with tears as he allowed himself to float on the tide of memories. The sweet memories of what had been; those days of long ago that were so dear, so tender to him; days that had gone forever; that could never come back; but that brought with them recollections as if of yesterday; precious moments he relived and treasured and would keep sacred with him deeply hidden till his span of life ran out and he would once again be with his darling; this time reunited, never to part.

Old Balaji thought of those days.

He remembered that, far from hindering him with his work on the land, Meerabai had actually helped him with her own hands to plough to sow, and to reap the harvest. She had inspired him in everything he did.

And he also remembered the nests of the birds that were built in almost every tree and bush, on and around his boundaries, at the coming of summertime. The females would hatch the eggs while the males fed their mates. When the 'bacchas' (young) were out of their shells, both father-bird and mother-bird would feed the little family.

How sad had been the two bulbuls one day, years ago, when a sparrow-hawk had raided their nest and gobbled up their young. They had shrieked shrilly for help—when none had come. Their screechings had mingled with the wails of the last of their fledglings as it had been carried away in the cruel talons of the hawk. That incident had been a reminder of life—and sudden death.

He remembered that Meerabai had heard those sounds. She had seen the little tragedy enacted. Too late, she had rushed out of the house in an effort to drive away the predatory hawk. Then she had wept bitterly.

Even the hated crows showed love for their young and for each other at nesting time.

Then Balaji realised that it was the way of life—the rule of creation. The male and the female would meet; court each other; procreate their species; and die themselves. It had been happening since the world began. It would continue to happen, till the world ended.

Who was he, Balaji, stupid selfish old fool, to resent his son finding his own mate? Had he not fallen deeply in love himself with Meerabai?

Balaji snivelled, slyly wiped the corners of his eyes with the back of his gnarled right hand when Jhani was not looking, and munched his curry and chappatty, almost happily.

He had made up his mind now. Most certainly he would do his best to help Jhani to marry this girl of his choice. As for the rest, it lay in God's hands.

Father and son lay awake that night till a very late hour, their beds spread on the floor of their little living room.

The frogs sent up a cacophonious croaking from the many pools of water that had filled every depression and hollow in the land after the storm that had come earlier that evening.

It was a chorus hideous to listen to. The ululations of individual bullfrogs attained a pitch of noise that made them heard above the vibrations of the refrain, voiced by hundreds of the slimy creatures as they sat on their little haunches, half-buried in the mud by the waterside. The sound rose to a crescendo; fell in pitch and then rose again.

The humble creatures were thanking their Creator for the rain and the water that fell with it and in which they were enjoying themselves so happily.

Balaji, as he fell asleep, was thankful too.

But Jhani could not sleep. He had no ears for the chorus of the frogs, nor any thought for the rain.

All he could think of was Loti's beautiful face, almost unseen in the darkness of the old room in the moosafarkhana; her water-soaked hair; the passion of her kisses as her lips had clung to his; the plump mounds of luscious flesh that were her breasts under the pressure of his eager, questing, demanding hands; the upright tightness of her erect nipples; and the little bites she had given his lips and ears and cheek as she had attained each orgasm in her lustful passion.

It was nine o'clock the following morning when Jhani and his father reached the gate before the mansion-like building that was Kumar's residence. The sun was shining brightly from a cloudless sky. The leaves of the trees looked green and fresh after their recent washing in the rain. Even the earth smelled fragrant, and seemed alive with the promise of growth to come.

The farmer instinct, inborn in Balaji, told him that such a cloudless sky and the bright sunshine would probably bring with them another downpour of rain the following night. He was delighted at the thought.

The 'mali' (gardener), who was busy digging among the flower-beds saw them, opened the gate and asked whom they wanted.

Loti saw them too; through the iron bars and glass panes of the front windows that were always closed in her father's house—closed, for fear of thieves coming through them.

Like Jhani, she had lain awake long into the previous night, exulting in the love she had so suddenly discovered but now knew she had always entertained for him since that day years ago, when Jhani had pulled her hair before schooltime and she had not sneaked on him.

Over and over again during the night she had relived those hectic moments of passion they had experienced together the evening before, oblivious to the violence of the storm and the threat offered by the tumbling roof of the old moosafarkhana.

Her eyes gleamed with welcome, love, and lust too, as she opened the front door for Jhani and his father and waved them into the living room.

'Dad, this is Loti, whom I have been telling you about. The most wonderful girl in the world that I am going to marry.' Jhani spoke simply to his father, but his gaze was only for his sweetheart.

(It is considered very immodest and is against Indian custom for a boy and girl, or husband and wife for that matter, to embrace and kiss each other in public or before their elders; even their own parents.)

The old man acknowledged the introduction with an inclination of his head and an expansive smile. Loti returned it, demurely, with both hands folded, palms together, before her face.

Then she said, 'Be seated, please; I will call my father.'

With a flitting smile for Jhani and a bewitching glance at him, she drew aside the brocaded silken curtain hanging at the entrance to the door leading to the next room, and disappeared from sight.

Jhani waved his father to a chair and sat in another himself.

Balaji sat down very slowly and cautiously on the edge of the chair which Jhani had indicated to him, as if he feared that the act of sitting on it was sacrilegious, or that it might collapse with his weight.

Very obviously old Balaji was quite unaccustomed to sitting on chairs.

He was plainly nervous, too. He fidgeted and moved himself about and glanced alternatively at the large Japanese wall-clock hanging on the opposite side of the room and at the doorway through which the girl had just passed.

The room in which they were seated was a lofty one, with a ceiling of wooden panels, betraying the style of architecture in vogue in India about a century ago. From external appearances at least the remainder of the house had been renovated and modernised. But this room, for some reason, had been allowed to remain untouched except for the flooring which had been changed to one of polished white tiles.

There was a settee covered with green velvet at the further end of the room; a sofa and two padded chairs beside it, all in green, at the opposite end. Three comfortable armchairs made out of Singapore cane and painted green also, occupied intermediary positions. Jhani sat on one of these and Balaji on the other.

A heavily ornamented table, with top of brass and legs of mahogany, from Travancore, stood in the centre of the room. On the table was a brass vase crammed with multicoloured zenias from the garden. A radio, worked by an automobile battery, stood in the corner near the brocaded curtain.

Nearly ten minutes dragged by, and then they heard the sound of approaching footsteps. Abruptly the curtain was pushed aside and Kumar entered the room. Lotibai followed silently behind him.

Of medium height like his daughter, Kumar carried his age—which was forty-eight years—well. His step was firm and brisk, his frame thin but well-set, his shoulders squared under his tightly-fitting black silk coat with its neat row of buttons in front reaching from knee-length right up to the close-set, 'dog collar' at his neck.

His head was covered with carefully-brushed black hair, parted in the middle and mottled at the temples, where it was greying. Sharp eyebrows were raised, a trifle interrogatively above his keenly-piercing slate-grey eyes. An aquiline nose; thin-lipped, rather tight mouth; and a determined chin gave his clean-shaven face a terse, business-like expression.

His brightly-polished brown shoes creaked audibly below the tight-fitting, white-cotton jodhpurs that bulged above his knees.

Lotibai stepped forward and said in her musical voice, 'Daddy; this is Jhani's father, Shri Balaji; and of course, Jhani.' And then to Balaji and Jhani, she said formally, 'Please meet my father, Shri Kumar.'

Balaji and Jhani stood up from their seats with their palms together before their faces and bowed slightly in respect. Kumar acknowledged their greeting with a wave of his right hand in the direction of the chairs they had been occupying.

'Please be seated and be comfortable,' he said graciously. Then, addressing Jhani, 'You, of course, I know young man, as my daughter's schoolboy friend. She often speaks of you, and of how you both meet and chat every evening in the marketplace. Don't you ever grow tired?'

He smiled slightly and in almost the same breath, addressed Balaji.

'It is a pleasure to make your acquaintance, Shri Balaji. A real pleasure.

'Would you both care for a cup of tea?'

Father and son hesitated to accept the invitation. They were unaccustomed to society manners, being just farmers.

Kumar apprised himself of the situation at a glance. Turning to his daughter he asked, 'Lotibai, will you make us and yourself four cups of that delicious tea that only you can make?'

He was smiling fondly and proudly upon her as she left the room.

A rather strained silence fell upon the three of them after that. Kumar glanced expectantly at his visitors. It was apparent they had come to tell or ask him something. Otherwise they would never have called at his house. Perhaps they were going to ask for a loan.

Jhani looked at his father. It was clearly Balaji's duty, as his parent, to announce the purpose of their call.

Balaji had been preparing himself, since early that morning and all along the way to Kumar's house, as to what he would say. Now he was tongue-tied, however. He did not know quite how he should begin.

Noticing the glances between father and son, Kumar coughed discreetly. Then, to ease the tension and help them to start talking, he asked politely, 'To what do I owe the pleasure of this visit, gentlemen?'

Balaji looked flustered. Both Kumar and his own son were gazing expectantly at him. He would have to say something.

So he said, 'I—er, that is to say we, er—came to ask—rather to tell you—,' and then he broke off into silence. A few seconds later he asked, apologetically, 'I hope we are not disturbing you or keeping you from some engagement?'

Kumar smiled tolerantly. He knew the old man wanted to say something important but did not quite know how he should commence. Well, let him take his own time. Rather unusually, he found himself not very busy at the moment and could spare the few minutes it would take these two country yokels, seated so obviously ill at ease before him, to sort themselves out and gain sufficient courage to come out with whatever it was they had in their minds.

But when old Balaji eventually did blurt out the purpose of the visit Kumar received the rudest shock of his life.

With the true style of direct talk which is the stock-in-trade of all people who live in the country and on the land, Balaji said slowly and distinctly.

'My son, Jhani, wishes to marry your daughter and I have come here to negotiate the terms of the marriage with you.'

Kumar jerked himself bolt upright in his chair. There was an expression of profound astonishment on his countenance and in his voice, as he asked incredulously, 'What is that you said? Say it again?'

Balaji looked a little disconcerted. Perhaps he had not spoken loud enough for this man to hear.

So he repeated what he had just said, and this time sonorously, 'My son wishes to marry your daughter. I have come to negotiate terms and make arrangements.'

Kumar looked thoroughly startled. He glanced from father to son. In Jhani's forthright countenance he saw confirmed the statement that his father had just made.

As if speaking to himself, Kumar repeated flatly, ruminatingly. 'You have come to negotiate terms and make arrangements.'

And as if he had been asked this question, Balaji replied with alacrity, 'That's right. That is what we have come for.'

Kumar glanced at each of them in turn, his face becoming confused with rage. Were they really mad? Were they trying to have a joke at his expense?

Perhaps the fools were actually in earnest.

He hesitated another couple of seconds. Then made his decision.

Whether they were mad, joking or serious, the sooner he set these country bumpkins right and made himself clear to them, the better.

Kumar leaned forward in his chair and commenced to speak, plainly and deliberately. 'If you really mean what you are asking and this is not a silly joke, the answer is very emphatically, "NO".'

It was now the turn of father and son to register surprise. Before they could recover, Kumar went on, speaking with devastating frankness.

'In the first place, on the very face of things, the idea is absurd. My daughter comes of a respectable family—of genteel folk if you understand what I mean—she is a lady. Your son and yourself are just—well, just farmers.

Secondly, my daughter is accustomed to living in luxury. She does no work herself. The servants attend to all that. If she was to marry below her status—into a poor family of farmers—she would have to break her back working all her life. She was not born to enter into a future of that sort.

'Thirdly, I have high ideals and big plans for her. It is my intention to marry her to some rich zamindar, or big merchant or businessman, who will not only maintain her in the standard of luxury and comfort in which she has been brought up all her life, but who will be of direct assistance to me, through his influence and his money, to further expand and increase my own business in this town and elsewhere.'

Kumar stopped talking to take a deep breath. He was distinctly ruffled. Then, as deliberately as he had addressed them, he recommenced speaking as if to himself.

'I looked upon this friendship as a merely platonic acquaintance. A schoolboy and girl comradeship. Never did I suspect there was anything more behind it.'

Then, addressing Jhani, he asked, 'Since how long have you both come to be in love?'

'Why, since last night,' answered Jhani truthfully, 'the storm…'

'Tell me, what happened last night? What had the storm to do with it?' In his anxiety, Kumar leaned forward in his chair.

'The storm broke and we took shelter in the old moosafarkhana. We—well, we were just talking and—and we—we discovered we were in love with each other, had always been as a matter of fact, and wanted to get married.'

'So,' Kumar almost hissed the words, 'it took the storm and the old moosafarkhana to make you know you were in love, eh?'

He sprang to his feet and strode up to Jhani, standing defiant over him.

'Tell me, young man; and tell the truth. Else I will kill you. What else happened between the two of you in the old moosafarkhana last night.'

Balaji had been listening to the dialogue between his son and this man, without quite grasping what was happening. But when Kumar strode up to Jhani and said something about killing him, the old farmer, complacent till then, lost his temper.

He also leapt up and faced Kumar, their angry countenances but inches apart.

'Did you say something about killing, O feeble little man?' he asked with contempt. 'When it comes to killing, only men can do that. Men like farmers. Men like us. Not stinking little rats like you, who hide in rich houses and fight boldly—with the pen and tongue.'

Just then Lotibai re-entered the room, carrying a tray on which were set four inlaid silver cups brimming with steaming tea. Taking in the scene at a glance, she came to an abrupt halt.

Kumar swung on her.

'What did this young brat do to you in the old moosafarkhana last night?' he thundered.

How did her father come to discover what had happened, Loti wondered to herself in amazement? Had Jhani really been so shameless as to tell him what he and she had done last night?

She released her hold on the tray and it crashed to the polished floor, throwing the cups in all directions with the hot tea that was inside them.

'Tell me,' shouted Kumar inexorably.

Lotibai raised both her hands to cover her face that had crimsoned in shame. Then she turned and ran out of the room abruptly.

Kumar guessed what had happened to his daughter the previous evening, and guessed correctly.

He knew that she was no longer a virgin and that her marketable value as a bride with which to attract a rich and influential husband who could directly help him—Kumar—to expand his business still more, had dropped to zero.

Turning to Balaji and Jhani, Kumar gritted between his clenched teeth.

'Get out, the pair of you. You have ruined my daughter's whole future. You will never see her again.'

They turned and left the house without a backward glance.

～

That evening Jhani waited in vain for his sweetheart. She was neither to be seen at the marketplace, nor did she come to their trysting-bench at the park. All day he had been disconsolate. That night he was like a madman.

Early the following morning Kumar took his daughter away. He himself drove the car that carried her. Where they went nobody knew. But when he returned after a full week, he came alone.

During this period Jhani had grown more and more morose. No longer did he do any work on the farm as he was wont to do previously. No longer was he interested in anything—not even in himself.

Old Balaji had made several attempts to console him. It was quite useless.

'Jhani, why do you fret so? Did I not warn you to have nothing to do with these high-class people? The rich are proud because of their money. Never content with what they have got, they always try to get more. Not caring for a home nor happiness, they engage themselves in torturous schemes to make more money. They do not know the pleasure that is to be derived from honest, hard work, nor the place of a woman in the home.

'Come, cheer up Jhani. There are as many fish in the sea as ever came out of it. I will find a fine, buxom country-born lass for you who will make you a good wife and a faithful companion. Moreover, she won't be afraid of hard work.'

'But dad, my Loti was all those things and more,' Jhani had argued, 'Now that she has gone and I don't know where, I love her more than ever, nor do I want to look upon any other woman.'

A full month passed during which he hardly spoke. For hours in the evening he would sit on the front step of the verandah of their little home and gaze into space as the velvety shades of night fell. Where can my Loti be, he was thinking. It was with the greatest of difficulty that old Balaji could get him to give a hand towards doing any work on their land. Nor would he help with the cooking.

One day there was a great hubbub in the town of Bhind. There came the tramp of marching men and a whole company of armed police entered the market square. That night they camped under the large banyan trees that grew beside the bund of the tank to the north of the town and less than a mile out.

As was to be expected, the little township was agog with rumours and conjectures as to the reason for their presence. Little by little the story came out.

The notorious dacoit, Man Singh, had again raided and captured a prominent zamindar who lived about nine miles out of town. He had demanded a ransom of fifty thousand rupees for the captive's return. The money had been paid and the zamindar had been sent back, safe and sound.

Soon after another dacoit, whose name was Charna, and who was one of Man Singh's chief lieutenants, ambushed and captured a landowner while returning from his extensive estates with the rents he had collected.

Not content with looting all the rent money, Charna had held the landlord to ransom and had demanded thirty thousand rupees from his family for his safe return.

The family had hesitated to pay, and the stipulated time and place found the ransom unpaid.

Next morning a 'dhoby's' (washerman's) donkey was observed grazing placidly in front of the landlord's house. Tied to the back of the donkey was a bundle.

Passers-by noticed a repulsive smell coming from whatever was in the bundle, and they commented among themselves about it. By eventide the stench became unbearable.

Somebody with a stronger stomach than his neighbours, removed the bundle from the donkey's back and opened it.

Out fell the landlord's head. It had been skilfully severed with one blow from some sharp instrument.

A platoon of police had been sent out to try and capture this Charna. But not for nothing had he been called Charna, the 'Ferocious'.

The platoon had been surrounded and attacked as they slept by the riverside at night, after the sentries had been overpowered.

Everyone of them had been killed and beheaded after that. The corpses had been thrown into the river. The heads of the policemen, impaled on pointed bamboos, had been arranged in two ranks with their sergeant in front.

Consequent upon these atrocities, there had been a panic on the part of the wealthier class of people, nearly all of whom fled the area. Batches of armed police had been stationed at strategic outposts to act as spearheads for the all-out drive against the nest of bandits that was to follow.

But in the marketplace, and in the wretched hovels of the poorer people, the talk was always the same. On every hand one heard words of sympathy and of praise for the dacoit bands.

'By Krishna,' a Hindu said, 'if only there were more like Man Singh and his merry men in this land of India, groaning as it is under oppression from these rich landlords. Such bastards would be eliminated and there would be plenty of land available for the poor.'

'By Allah,' returned a Moslem, 'this Man Singh is a just man—and a brave one. Last month he made fifty thousand rupees as ransom on the fat zamindar from the Kohlibad area, and last week he sent half of it in donation to the new school for the blind, at Alipore'.

Jhani heard the stories in the marketplace and his whole attention became rivetted by them. They caused his blood to tingle. Here were men who hated the rich—just as he now hated them! Men like Kumar, who had blasted his life—and Loti's life! What if he could join such men. He would cheerfully devote the remainder of his days to helping to punish these monied classes who behaved so mercilessly towards the poor.

Well, why shouldn't he join them?

Hundreds had done so already. That was what had enabled the outlaw bands to grow so greatly in numbers. And if others had done it, why could not he?

That very evening Jhani made up his mind. He would seek out the bandit leader, offer him his faithful services, and devote the rest of his lifetime to killing the rich.

After their meal of wheat-gruel, cheese and chappatties, with boiled cauliflower, and washed down by tea, Jhani said to old Balaji, his father.

'Dad, I am going away for sometime. I cannot tell you where. I don't know myself. Nor can I tell you when I will return; that is, if ever I do return.

'I am sorry to leave you all alone, dad. I know I am not worthy to be called your son after letting you down like this. But I just have no interest in life after Loti went away. If I remain any longer in this place, every nook and corner of which holds such dear memories of her for me, I feel I shall go mad. So, dear dad, it's best I go.'

Like all people who live close to nature, Balaji had understood perfectly. He remembered his own feelings when his wife, Meerabai, Jhani's mother, had died. He had been inconsolable. Now Balaji thought Jhani was going away to search for his lost sweetheart.

'Go son; and may God be with you,' he had replied. 'Take the hundred rupees which I shall presently give you. It will help you on your journey. Only think of me and the old farm, sometimes. Remember we will be always waiting for you to return, son. And till that day, look after yourself, my boy. Trust in God, and He will not fail you.'

After that the old man had broken down and wept bitterly. So had Jhani.

Nevertheless he was up with the dawn next day. He rolled a few clothes into a bundle and took the solitary five-rupee note he had been saving up. It would suffice for his wayside expenses until such time as he could contact the dacoits.

With a brave face and dry eye, albeit his hand shook terribly, Balaji held out the hundred-rupee note he had hidden away for so long against a rainy day.

Jhani smiled, but declined to accept it.

'No, thank you dad. You need it and the farm needs it. I am young and strong and can work for my living.' And then the final moment of parting had come. They embraced and kissed each other on both cheeks.

Resolutely Jhani picked up his bundle of clothes, slung it over his shoulder, and walked away never once looking back. For if he did, the sight of the old farmlands so familiar to him since the days of his youth, and of his grief-stricken father standing weeping at the boundary of the fields—his own fields—and the thousand-and-one recollections of the town that held such precious memories to him of his beloved Loti, might cause him at the last moment to weaken and abandon his plan of adventure and revenge.

That must never be. He would devote his lifetime to punishing the rich, to scourging them, to robbing and torturing them, and to killing them; as many of them and as fast as he could, and in the most horrible manner possible.

For had not one of them taken away his Loti?

Jhani wandered for days after that, working where he could for his living and begging when there was no work to be had.

He crossed the Chambal River one morning and turned towards the ravines.

'Brother, whom do you seek?' asked the boatman curiously, as Jhani set foot on the further bank.

'I seek Man Singh and his men,' Jhani had replied briefly.

The boatman held his breath in amazement. Then he asserted, 'You are either quite mad, which I think to be 'the case; or you are very foolish; or you are very brave. I really don't know which.'

Then he pushed his long pole into the muddy bottom of the river and commenced the slow journey back.

Not knowing his way, Jhani moved forward in a direction at right angles to the river.

It was long after nine o'clock when something struck the ground in front of him, releasing a spurt of dust, before it sped onward with a vicious, twanging whine. Split seconds later, he heard the report of the rifle.

Jhani knew he had been fired at, undoubtedly by some dacoit sentry.

He did not hide or attempt to take cover. He just stood still and raising both arms, extended them high above his head, calling aloud in Rajasthani, 'Do not shoot me. I am a friend who comes in peace, voluntarily. I seek Man Singh.'

Another bullet hit the ground at precisely the same spot as had its predecessor.

Jhani knew that the marksman who could accomplish the feat of placing two bullets in exactly the same place, would not have missed hitting him—unless he had really intended to do so.

No doubt the hidden sniper had meant him to understand exactly that, which was the reason for the second shot.

He continued to remain quite stationary with arms held aloft and extended, while he went on shouting the same message that he had already yelled.

From somewhere ahead a voice hailed him, 'Keep advancing with your arms aloft. If you attempt to lower them, you are a dead man.'

Jhani did as he was told. He couldn't see anyone.

After a time his arms began to ache, but he knew he dared not drop them. The sniper no doubt had him covered all this time and would not hesitate to fulfil his threat if he attempted to put them down.

The ache increased, and Jhani was on the point of shouting aloud that he could no longer keep his arms aloft when, from the middle of a bush a little to his right stood up an unkempt figure, with a rifle to its shoulder pointed directly at him. The man had on a black skullcap and was wearing a torn khaki shirt and shorts.

'Who are you and what are you doing here?' the man called.

'Friend, I will tell you everything. Only permit me to lower my arms awhile. They are paining terribly and I cannot keep them up any longer,' pleaded Jhani.

'How do I know you are not carrying a "pocket-bundook" (a revolver)?' asked the ruffian.

'I am unarmed and come in peace. I seek Man Singh to offer my services to him. But please let me lower my arms while we talk. I am suffering agony holding them up like this.'

'Alright,' conceded the wild-looking sentry, 'but before doing so, remember this. One false move and the vultures will feed upon you this very day and the jackals tonight.'

But Jhani had already dropped his arms to his sides. He sighed in relief.

'You are a police spy, no doubt,' asserted the man flatly. 'That is why you are asking me to direct you to Man Singh. Do you think I am such a fool?'

'No brother, you are quite mistaken. I came here to join the dacoits because I want to wreak vengeance upon the rich who have done me a great wrong.'

'You will have to tell that story to my chief,' rejoined his captor. 'You cannot meet the Maharaj now, but I will conduct you to my leader.'

'I shall walk behind you with this rifle cocked,' he continued. 'Try any tricks and it will go off, immediately. Do you understand? Now, get going.'

So Jhani walked ahead with the bandit behind him.

They crossed two ravines and then a voice hailed them from the summit of the third nullah. 'Halt,' it commanded, 'and give the password.'

'Snakes come out at dusk,' shouted his companion promptly, from behind.

'Advance slowly,' advised the second sentry from the hilltop, at the same moment showing himself for the first time.

They climbed to the top of that hillock, intersected the next depression, and went up the fourth hill.

As they reached its crest they looked down on an encampment of some three dozen men who were squatting or lying on the open ground. Jhani noted that it was evidently a mobile unit that he saw before him, as there were no signs of tents or other equipment to indicate the dacoits were camped there for any length of time.

A big man with a black beard, the usual twirled moustache but no whiskers, sat a little apart from the main group. He wore loose white cotton trousers and a dirty grey shirt. On top of his head, appearing rather out of proportion in its smallness to the rest of his size, was a tightly-wound turban of brown cloth.

Prodding him with the end of the muzzle of his rifle, the sentry directed him towards the big man, who stood up as Jhani approached.

He was a hefty, muscular brute, standing well over six feet and a little taller than Jhani himself. He had cruel eyes, a long, predatory nose, and lips that were compressed into practically a straight line.

'What do you want?' His voice was loud and hard, and had that imperious note that indicated its owner was accustomed to implicit obedience.

Before Jhani could reply, the man with the rifle behind him, no doubt anxious to justify the capture he had made, chipped in.

'I saw this man wandering towards the ravines from my post, Charna Sahib. So I fired a shot to warn him. He started shouting back that he wanted to see our Maharaj and join us. So I brought him in.'

The big man so addressed did not answer the sentry, but continued to glare at the prisoner.

Jhani had heard the name by which the giant had been addressed and knew he stood in the presence of the much dreaded Charna, called the 'Ferocious'; the most terrible of all Man Singh's lieutenants; a man credited with superhuman courage, but no qualities of mercy whatever. He began to feel afraid.

'I have come, Sir, to offer my humble services to the great Man Singh. I have suffered a grevious wrong at the hands of a rich man, and

I want to wreak vengeance against him and all his class.' Impetuously Jhani had uttered the words while he met the cruel glance.

'What if you are a police agent?' asked Charna.

'Then you may kill me, at once,' returned Jhani promptly.

The dacoit chieftain looked him up and down for a few minutes. Then he asked, 'What is your name, and what is your trade?'

'My name is Jhani. I am a farmer. My father is Balaji and we own twelve acres of land close to the town of Bhind.'

'Be seated and tell me your story,' invited Charna, reseating himself, cross-legged, upon the ground a couple of yards distant.

Jhani accepted the invitation and then embarked upon a detailed account of his problem.

The dacoit listened till he had finished, and then smiled expansively, at the same time clapping his hand upon Jhani's shoulder in a friendly gesture.

'Silly boy,' he said, 'is that your only trouble? Why, it is no problem at all.

'That is what I like about farmers as a class of people,' he continued, 'they are simple and straightforward. Fancy getting so upset about all this! Why, the solution is easy. A good looking boy like you can get himself any number of girls.'

But Jhani shook his head, defiantly. He blurted out, 'I love this particular girl and want to marry her. Then he asserted in a tone of finality, 'I like no other woman.'

The dacoit laughed aloud at hearing this. 'So, because you have lost her, you want to become a dacoit like me?' he asked.

'I do,' asserted Jhani, 'and to kill the rich.'

'Well, that is fair enough with me,' conceded Charna, 'but let us see what the Maharajah has to say. We will be seeing him tomorrow.'

Jhani was given food and rested that day, and at dusk went with the band of men into whose company he had fallen, on a trek that led them some ten miles eastwards. They entered scrub jungle, and at about 10 p.m. came to a halt where the jungle gave way to ploughed fields. There they hid themselves in silence.

Charna called him a little after midnight and announced the band was going into action. He was told to remain in hiding until they rejoined him at this same place till about two hours time.

Soon after that the men disappeared and Jhani was left alone.

Sometime later he heard the sound of firing. This continued for a short while and then died down, to be followed by a reddish glow on the horizon about a mile away. Undoubtedly a fire, Jhani guessed.

A half hour or so passed, and then the dacoit band came back, walking stealthily and in single file. Jhani noticed that several of the men were carrying two and three rifles apiece. Three or four of them had tommy guns which had not been in their possession when they had set out. A number of the others staggered under the weight of boxes which they bore between them.

Rightly, he guessed that they had just made a raid on some military outpost or police chowki, and were returning with the booty they had captured. Doubtless the red glow he had seen had been occasioned by flames when the dacoits had set fire to some building or shed.

After they rejoined him the band continued in another direction which appeared to penetrate deeper and deeper into the jungle.

The raiders had evidently chosen their time well, as in a short while a late-rising moon helped them to grope their way among the trees and bushes as the jungle became more dense.

A little over an hour's walking brought them to a glade in the forest. At the border of this glade, Jhani heard a voice challenge them softly, to which Charna answered in his gruff tone. They then moved on, and soon found themselves in an encampment where many people lay, or sat beside dimly-glowing fires. At the further edge of the glade Jhani could make out the dim outline of a half dozen or so conical tents.

The party with which he had just arrived halted in the centre of the glade, and the men who carried two and three firearms apiece stacked them in a neat pile before one of the fires. There was whispered talk and hushed laughter as the newcomers recounted, in undertones, their recent adventure.

A little later Jhani noticed a fresh group of figures approaching them from the direction where the tents were pitched. An old man headed the party, closely followed by another with a tommy gun. Two more younger men brought up the rear.

When the light fell upon the old man, Jhani noticed his abnormally high forehead and the grey beard, whiskers and enormous moustache.

Charna addressed the newcomer, 'Salaam, Maharajah-Sahib. The gods have been good to us this night and we have seized thirteen service rifles, three tommy guns, a revolver and some boxes of ammunition without the loss of a single man. We caught the policemen playing cards by the light of their lanterns instead of keeping a careful watch, and wiped out both the sentries and the main body of men who were asleep, before they knew what was happening. Finally we set fire to the chowki.

'Good work, Charna Sahib; my congratulations,' replied the old man heartily, in a melodious voice. 'You have never failed me.'

Then with a chuckle he dug his lieutenant playfully in the ribs and said, 'The gods are always particularly good to you, eh? You rascal!'

Charna acknowledged the compliment with the happy smile of a flattered schoolboy.

Man Singh and Charna examined the booty together, and commented for some time after that on the quality of the present-day service rifles and their ammunition. Suddenly Charna looked around and his eye alighted on Jhani.

'Maharaj, I almost forgot,' he said apologetically, 'we found a boy wandering in the ravines who said he is looking for you. He wants to join us in order to kill the rich, because a rich father took away his daughter from this farmer boy who has fallen deeply in love with her.'

And Charna chuckled again at the thought of the foolishness of the thing called 'true love'.

Man Singh's piercing steely-eyes appeared to bore into Jhani. 'Come over here, boy,' he ordered softly, 'and tell me your story.'

Jhani stepped forward and poured out his tale in detail, while the old man listened sympathetically. Unlike the gruff Charna, he did not scoff or make fun of him after he had stopped speaking, but remained silent and thoughtful. There was a faraway, reminiscent look in his eyes.

Then he spoke, 'This old man, your father,' he asked. 'Tell me more about him and your farm. What did you say his name was?'

'Balaji,' answered Jhani. He went on to relate all about his father and the twelve-acre farm of which he was so proud, to the dacoit leader. Warming to his subject, he also spoke about his mother, Meerabai, and of how she had helped his father right up to the day of her untimely death after having been bitten by the cobra.

Charna turned away, while Jhani was speaking, and started examining some of the captured weapons. Obviously, being a man of action and of blood, he was not interested in such sentimental tales.

But Man Singh listened to him attentively throughout, and only after he had finished did the dacoit-king comment, 'What a sad and beautiful story.'

Then he patted Jhani on the back.

'Come with me, lad,' he said, turning towards the row of tents, 'I will give you a cup of tea, and at the same time, talk to you.'

Jhani followed him.

Man Singh led him inside the tent he occupied, accompanied by the bodyguard with the tommy gun. A lantern was burning dimly there.

The dacoit-leader clapped his hands and a retainer appeared.

'Bring 'cha' (tea),' he ordered briefly.

Then he sat on the ground and invited Jhani to be seated also. The man with the tommy gun remained standing. Not for a moment did he take his eyes off Jhani.

'Now Jhani,' said the old man with surprising tenderness, 'I am going to talk to you, not as Man Singh, the thief, but as a father and as if you were one of my own sons.

'For I have four of them and a daughter, too, you must know. Hence I understand what the love of a father is.

'You have asked to be allowed to join my band of villains,' and here he smiled good-humouredly, 'because you want to make war upon the rich.

'Jhani, you flatter me by volunteering your services to me. Never have I refused anybody who so offered himself to me, with but one exception.

'And that exception is you, Jhani. Because I am not going to allow you to do it.'

Jhani started in surprise as the old man turned and looked him full in the face. Words failed him in his great disappointment. Had he heard aright?

Man Singh's hand patted him on the knee as he added, 'Don't be upset, Jhani. I understand how you feel about matters. I will tell you why I won't allow you to join us, and I will also try to advise you what would be the best thing to do.'

Their talk was interrupted by the entry of the servant bearing a kettle of tea and two aluminium mugs. As he turned to leave, Man Singh ordered him to bring a third mug for his bodyguard.

The old man filled Jhani's cup, followed by his own.

Just then the servant came back with a third aluminium tumbler. This Man Singh himself filled and handed to his bodyguard, who sipped it, standing.

'Now Jhani, try to understand me,' he continued. 'You are a good boy, untainted by any evil, except that you have fallen in love, and that is not an evil thing. On the contrary, it is very natural.

'If I allow you to join us, you will grow into a thief and a murderer; a common dacoit like the rest of us here. No doubt you will fulfil your desire for revenge by killing a few rich people, but where will that get you?

'There will be a price upon your head, Jhani. It will be the price of violence and of spilt blood. It lies upon each of our heads, now.

'Eventually you will be killed, or you will be caught and put into prison.

'That would break the old man—your father's heart. Your beloved farmlands will never see you. What's more, you can never hope to meet your sweetheart, Lotibai, again.

'If I agreed to let you join me, Jhani, I would be making a murderer out of an innocent boy like you; while I would be breaking both your father's and your girlfriend's hearts. That I don't want to do, I had an old father once and I know what heartache he suffered when I took to this life of murder and violence. I, too, was a farmer like you. I can still picture my farmlands in my memory and long to be back on them if only for a few minutes. But that is denied to me, because I have made myself a fugitive and an outcast, forever.

'That is why I refused you, boy. Now do you understand?

'But I can advise you what to do, if you care to listen to me.

'Be a man, Jhani. Shoulder your responsibilities. Don't try to run away from them, or drown them in a bloodbath of revenge.

'An old saying tells us, "Revenge is sweet". But don't you ever believe it, Jhani. Revenge is a very very bitter thing, and brings only bitterness and frustration in its wake—forever!

'I know what I am talking about, Jhani. It was with motives of revenge and hatred in my heart that, like you now want to do, I left my father and farm and home and became a dacoit. I don't think God made me to hate and kill my fellow men. I think He wanted me to love them. That is why love still glimmers in my heart today, like it glimmers at this moment for you.

'But in my hot-blooded youth there was nobody to advise or restrain me like I am now advising and restraining you. I gave away to these feelings of hatred and vengeance. Just like you, I wanted to kill my enemies and take revenge upon them.

'And I did just that.

'What has it brought me, Jhani? Yes, I killed them it is true. But did their murder bring me any lasting satisfaction? No; and I repeat, a thousand times NO! It has brought the blood of a hundred men and more on my hands and the death penalty on my head.

'I have no house, no home, no father, no land, no farm, now, to call my own. I lay my head down to sleep on a stone at night never knowing but it may be my last, or hide in some hole or jungle or burrow. I am like a human jackal, forever on the watch, forever on the run!

'People think I am happy; but I am not, my son.

'It would be very wicked for me to assist you to follow in my footsteps, Jhani. Indeed it would be but another murder to my account. Your murder!

'For that reason I won't have you as one of my band.

'But listen to me a little longer, boy. Be a man! Fight your troubles, don't run before them!

'Go and join the army as soon as you get back. Be a soldier of free India. It is an honourable profession.

'Maybe God will grant your prayers at some future date. You may meet your sweetheart, Lotibai, again. Then you will be holding a respectable station in life. You can marry her without caring about anyone. She will be proud of you. Your father and your lands will be proud of you. I, for one, if I live to hear of it, will be very proud of you.

'That is my advice, Jhani. I, Rajah Man Singh Rathore, have spoken.'

Jhani was silent. Unshed tears glistened in his eyes as he wondered. Could this man, who spoke to him thus, be in reality the dacoit-king who was wanted in four states for murder, robbery and violence? Why, he had uttered words of infinite wisdom, spoken with a tenderness far surpassing the rough speech of his own farmer-father, Balaji.

Jhani's mind was made up. He would follow the old man's advice.

He jumped up, to bend low before the bandit-leader.

'Maharajah-Sahib, you have spoken as no father or mother yet spoke to me, and I cannot but follow your counsel,' he said simply.

'Good boy,' said the old man, getting up himself, 'I shall arrange for two of my men to accompany you this very night, by another route to the outskirts of the nearest village, six miles away.

'I know you will not tell anyone that you met and spoke to me or any of my band here. You are not that kind of boy.

May you be a soldier soon and perhaps a general in a few years. Who knows? Then perhaps it will be your duty to shoot this old dacoit, Man Singh, for the many evil deeds he has done.'

And he laughed heartily at his own joke.

But Jhani murmured, 'God forbid, your excellency. I could never do that.'

~

Kumar had taken Lotibai, his daughter, a long distance away. He took her to the city of Ahmedabad where lived his two sisters.

They had themselves married two brothers, both the owners of large cotton mills on the outskirts of the city. They had palatial houses and a steady revenue from the profits.

But both of them had no children.

In course of time the two brothers had died, leaving the two sisters very comfortably off. Being without children, ownership of the mills had reverted to their husbands' family (in accordance with Indian custom), while the two sisters continued to reside in Ahmedabad on very substantial monthly incomes from capital in the bank previously invested in their names, and a separate house for each of them.

It was to these two sisters of his that Kumar took Loti. He knew he could fully entrust them to not divulge the secret of the disgrace that had fallen upon him. He also felt they would be able to find a way of getting rid of the wretched farmer-boy's spawn if there was to be any, before it was born. Thirdly, as Lotibai was a stranger to Ahmedabad, he hoped that with her two aunts' backing and considerable influence, some man might be found, among the rich mill owners of the city, who would volunteer to marry her despite the fact that she was no longer a virgin; which would anyway have to be told to him in advance.

In the small town of Bhind where he lived and was so well-known, such a match would be impossible to arrange. On the contrary, the scandal would spread like wildfire and his name would become the laughing stock of the marketplace.

The two aunts, like Loti's father Kumar, their brother, were severe-looking individuals, much resembling him in angular features and compact, well-set build. The elder of the two, Kumari, who incidentally was older than her brother Kumar by two years had always bossed her husband one of the mill owners at home. This had caused the poor man during his lifetime to develop tyrannical characteristics at his mill where he had been most unpopular with his subordinates and the workers in general.

Fate had ordained that the younger sister, Parvati, who was junior to Kumar by three years should marry the more assertive of the two mill owner brothers, with the result that she had not been the ruling member of her household.

Now with the two brothers dead, Kumari had automatically adopted an almost parental if not distinctly dictatorial control over her younger sister, Parvati.

Soon after Kumar and Lotibai arrived at his elder sister, Kumari's residence, Parvati was called and in a conference between the three of them from which Loti was pointedly excluded, Kumar revealed the dark secret of Loti's condition.

Kumari, who had never been blessed with an offspring of her own, was most indignant.

'What were you about, Kumar?' she queried angrily, 'you should have horsewhipped the young blackguard.' Parvati, who was mildly thrilled by the romance of it all, asked. 'Is he a good-looking boy?'

Kumari pounced on her like a kestrel swooping on its prey. 'I do wish you would not ask such a silly, irrelevant question, Parvati. Is he good-looking; forsooth! The very idea! And suppose he happens to be? What has that got to do with it?'

'Won't that explain why Loti was tempted?' She put the question with matter-of-fact simplicity.

'Oh, do shut up, Parvati. As you grow older you appear to be getting more childish.'

With that rebuke Kumari turned to her brother, 'Let us have Loti in, so that we may talk to her.'

Lotibai was accordingly summoned, and Kumari did not lose any time in unburdening her contempt and feelings upon her unfortunate niece.

'You shameless girl,' she asserted, 'how could you allow a common farmer-boy to do this to you?'

Loti had begun to cry.

Kumar had left in his car the next day, with the strictest of instructions as to what was to be done with Lotibai.

The two sisters kept her under close surveillance; Kumari with critical watchfulness and Parvati with expectation, mixed with a secret sympathy she dared not confide to her austere sister.

Two months passed, and it was evident that Lotibai was pregnant.

Kumari summoned the family doctor, an old man, and asked him in the strictest confidence, as to his opinion.

The doctor examined Lotibai, and declared she was in the family way.

Parvati was rather excited when she heard the news. Oh; if only such a thing could have happened to her!

But Kumari spoke to the doctor in a low tone and for quite a long time at the corner of the verandah before he left.

Then she called Lotibai.

'As you must know yourself by now, girl,' she began, speaking with withering scorn, 'you are going to have a baby. This is the most disgraceful and shameful thing that has happened in our family, particularly when the father of the child is nothing but a farmer. At all costs the child must be destroyed. I have spoken to the good doctor and he has agreed to arrange for this to be done, but only as a very special favour and because he has known our family for so many years.'

This time Loti did not cry. On the contrary, she listened to her aunt with cold and calculated patience.

Then she spoke, and her tone was low and defiant.

'Listen, aunt Kumari,' she said, 'I love the father of the child that is to come and he loves me. He came the very next morning to marry me honourably, but dad prevented it. So it cannot be said he let me down.

'For that reason, I am going to have this baby, whatever dad or you may think, say or do to the contrary.

'And if you attempt to coerce me into causing an abortion, I shall go to the Commissioner of Police this very instant and tell him what you and your family friend, the good doctor, are about.

'You may have forced many people, many times, to do what you wanted them to do, auntie Kumari. But this time you cannot force me to have an abortion. What's more, you know it.'

Loti ceased talking and there was a poignant silence.

'Well said, Loti.'

A quiet voice had uttered the words. The voice of mild Parvati.

Aunt Kumari was furious. She trembled from head to foot with suppressed rage. Like all people accustomed to having their own way, she could not face a reversal, for she knew instinctively that this time, for once, she was up against it.

The girl had beaten her at the eleventh hour.

Then the floodgates of her wrath burst in full force.

'If you do not do as I say, you shameless slut, you can get out of my house at once. And I mean, today.' The words came in a torrent of fury.

'I will do that now, aunt Kumari,' answered Loti, and turned to leave the room.

'Just a minute, Loti.' It was the quiet voice of Parvati that spoke again. Turning to Kumari, she continued, 'This is our own niece, Kumari. Remember that. She is our own flesh and blood. I for one will not throw her into the streets.'

But Kumari was beside herself with rage. She leapt to her feet and her voice became shrill and vibrant with rage.

'Then get out, the pair of you, and never set foot in my house again.'

Within fifteen minutes Loti had gathered her few possessions; and then, her arm around the waist of frail, sweet Parvati—the little Parvati who had taken a beating all her lifetime till this day—they left the building together.

Lotibai had her baby. A bonny boy.

As she gazed upon him, lovingly, she saw in those sparkling eyes the same expression she had seen, and loved so much, in the eyes of his father, Jhani. Nor did the little man appear to have a care in this world, for without any urging, he turned instinctively to clutch her full breast in his tiny hands. He snuggled and sniffed till he found the nipple with his little mouth and applied himself assiduously to his first meal.

Parvati smiled contentedly as she looked down upon him. Even if God had not ordained that she should have her own baby, she was thankful to Him for giving her the courage that day to stand up to her sister, Kumari, who would have so heartlessly destroyed this little infant life in cold blood on the altar of their family pride.

∼

Nearly a year passed after that, and little Jhani, as Loti had insisted upon calling her baby, was growing up to become a very precocious little boy.

Even at that young age he was bursting with mischief, and Loti condoned all his naughtiness because it reminded her of his dear father, the mischievous little schoolboy who had insisted upon pulling her hair.

Aunt Parvati doted on little Jhani, too. The child filled the gap in her life that had always been there until his coming. Indeed, she looked upon him almost as her own son, and was at times jealous that she had to share his infant affection with his mother.

Lotibai had much to thank God for, and her auntie Parvati. Had it not been for the mercy of the Almighty and the courage and kindness of her frail little aunt, she would have been thrown on the streets.

But Lotibai had been thinking seriously within herself, also. She felt it was not right that she should continue to sponge upon this good woman who had stood by her at a time of need, for the rest of her lifetime. Now that her troubles were over, it would be but right that she should think of earning for herself so that she could support the little fellow independently.

The more she thought, the more determined did she become that she should do something about it.

And then Fate ordained the second circumstance that gave her the opportunity.

A Film Company from Bombay came to Ahmedabad to shoot some scenes in a picture about Gujarat, and were staying there for some time.

A girlfriend, whom she had come to know, was related to one of the producers of the company. One day this girl had said to her, 'Loti, you are so beautiful. Why do you live cooped up in a filthy hole like Ahmedabad? Why don't you become a filmstar? Any of the film companies will jump at you if you would only apply to them. If I was not the ugly wretch that I am I would have done this myself long ago.

'Look, my uncle is a Producer of the Bombay Associated Pictures Corporation. He is now in Ahmedabad in connection with this Gujarati picture they are shooting. If you agree, I shall fix up an appointment with him one of these days and introduce you myself.'

The idea was too thrilling for Loti to decide about there and then. Did she have any chance of success? Was there even a hope?

Lotibai promised her friend to think the matter over seriously and to let her know the next day.

That evening Lotibai had her bath as usual. Coming out of the bathroom, she stood before the full-length mirror on the door of her almirah, the Turkish bath towel still wrapped around her wet body.

Was she as beautiful as all that to stand a chance of being taken on in a film company?

Searchingly, Loti studied her own reflection as it gazed back at her out of the mirror.

Boldly, almost shamelessly, she allowed the bath towel to drop to her feet while she appraised the naked girl who now stood before her.

The breasts were as full and as firm as ever. Almost lovingly she lifted them together, one in each hand, noting with satisfaction the mulberry-hued nipples set against their slightly darker-coloured areolae that crowned the mounds of her firm flesh.

She saw with satisfaction the supple shoulders that narrowed, gracefully and symmetrically down her chocolate flanks to her compact waistline, which bulged in turn, sharply and broadly, to the contours of her hips.

She saw the round firmness of her thighs, and pinched them with her fingers to test that firmness. How prettily they bulged also, and then tapered commensurably down to her knees, only to swell again into a beautiful pair of calves that showed-off an exciting pair of legs.

Lotibai raised her eyes to appraise her face. Was there really anything pretty there or had her girlfriend only been flattering her? Perhaps there was; perhaps there wasn't. Anyhow, as she saw her face several times each day in the mirror, she really could not tell.

Nor did she sleep that night. She was thinking about the thrill of becoming a film actress.

Early next morning Loti sought out her friend and asked her to arrange the interview with her uncle.

The Producer sent word to say he would be glad to meet her the following evening at his office at 4 p.m. sharp.

Loti spent a long time in dressing the next afternoon. After some thought she decided to wear her white chiffon sari, bordered in blue and gold. It would not be too loud. At the same time, she knew it suited her well. Aunt Parvati and her friends had told her so.

Loti looked very very pretty as she stepped into the canary-yellow autorickshaw which would take her to the house of her girlfriend, Surendra. Then the two of them would go on together to the office of her friend's uncle, the Director-Producer.

Sathe, who was one of the producers of the Bombay Associated Pictures Corporation, prided himself upon being what he boldly termed, a self-made man. He had risen from one of the lowest positions in life to his present exalted status and wealth.

His father had been a bank clerk before him and Sathe had followed in father's footsteps. But Sathe loathed banking.

At home in the evenings he wrote novels.

Many of them were rejected by publishers to whom he sent them.

But he would not be discouraged. He persevered and wrote and submitted more novels.

And one of them caught on.

It was such a good story that it was snapped by a film company.

Sathe was offered a contract as an assistant to the Director who had been commissioned to shoot the picture based on his novel. He made so good a job of it that the Company retained him on its payroll as a sort of roving assistant.

Then the depression hit the film companies of India. This was in their early years, before they had become properly stabilised or recognised.

Many of them tumbled, and the question of closing down the concern in which Sathe worked came up for careful consideration.

That was the time Sathe stepped in and directed the picture of his lifetime. It was the best picture that had so far ever been made by an Indian film company.

It gave new life to the concern in which he worked. Fresh capital poured in from fresh shareholders and the organisation was formed that came to be known as the Bombay Associated Pictures Corporation. In recognition of his timely services, Sathe was made a Director-Producer in the company.

He was a short man, aged about forty-five years, always dapper, always neat and well-dressed. Filled with dynamic energy, his assistants knew him for a tireless worker. He did not appear to have ever heard of the word 'Cannot'; nor did he seem to know the meaning of failure. He would just go on and on and on, till he finished what he had set himself to do, and completed it successfully.

He had a bullet-shaped head of iron-grey hair that was turning bald at the top. Hazel-brown eyes, a sharp nose, a neat toothbrush moustache and rather full lips, went with a sharp jaw that ended in a slightly pointed chin.

Mr. Sathe flattered himself that he could tell at a glance whether the man or woman he interviewed was fit for the job for which they had applied and could make the grade, or not.

He looked up and smiled as his niece, Surendra, entered his office on the stroke of four o'clock that evening, followed by a very pretty, shapely girl of medium height in a white sari which contrasted, sharply, against her raven-black locks.

'Uncle, this is Lotibai, the girl I told you about,' introduced Surendra simply.

Sathe stood up and waved the two young ladies towards the half dozen or so chairs that faced him, across his table.

After they were seated, he looked at Loti searchingly. She could feel his gaze travelling up and down, exploring her. It almost seemed as if he was looking through and through her.

Then he spoke and his words had a searching frankness in them. They came straight to the point. 'What prompts you to want to join the films, Miss Lotibai? What makes you think you can act?'

It was a double-barrelled question, and it all but floored her.

Impulsively, she answered.

'I will be quite truthful, Sir, and hide nothing,' she said. 'Necessity to earn my own living makes me want to join. I have a good voice and am fond of music. And I feel I can act if I am given the chance.'

Sathe pouted his lips before he put his next question.

'Have you ever acted before?'

'No Sir,' answered Loti, truthfully, tears of disappointment forming in her eyes as she appreciated the unsatisfactory nature of her own replies, 'but please, please give me just one chance.'

Sathe pouted his lips once again.

What did these girls think film companies were, he wondered. Charitable institutions? Fancy having the audacity to want to join the movies without ever having acted before! It was a piece of cool impertinence, or nerve if you liked to call it that.

But Sathe liked nerve. He admired it. Did he not have nerve himself? Once a bank clerk, what the hell had he known about the films himself before he had joined? Sweet damn all! It was only his nerve and determination that had taught him after that, and built him up to his present position as a Producer.

Yes, he liked nerve and determination. For he had plenty of both himself.

And apparently this girl had, too.

Besides, she was a very pretty little thing and very prettily built, too. There was no denying that. He had already noticed the charming figure beneath the white chiffon sari.

And she was about to cry. He didn't like that. Were the tears put on, or genuine?

If they were put on—well, she was it bloody fine actress to make an artful old codger like himself wonder if they were real or not.

If they were genuine—well, what the hell!

Did it matter much, anyhow? Somebody had once given him a break in life, and he had taken it.

Why should he not give this pretty young thing a break now?

'Okay, Miss Lotibai,' he said, 'you're hired—as of tomorrow. Report for work here at nine o'clock sharp. We'll see what we can make of you.'

Loti stammered out her thanks. And this time there was no acting. Tears of sheer joy flowed down her cheeks. Unrestrainedly.

After dinner that night, Loti and aunt Parvati tucked little Jhani into bed together. Then they went to the dining room for a last cup of coffee.

'Auntie, there is something I must tell you,' began Lotibai, hesitatingly. 'I have kept it a secret all day, and I hope you won't be angry with me.

'You have been a darling, auntie Parvati. Kinder than a father and mother to me.

'But I just cannot go on living like this on your generosity, and be a burden to you, both in person and as regards the upkeep of myself and little Jhani any longer.

'So today I applied for a job in a Bombay film company—and got it. I start work tomorrow morning.'

Parvati was shocked. At first she felt annoyed with her niece for having kept all this a secret from her.

But she also thought she understood the reason behind it. If she had been in Loti's place, she herself would feel bad about living on somebody else's bounty indefinitely. She would have sought employment, just as Loti had done.

Aunt Parvati was an understanding soul.

Looking up, she smiled at Loti kindly. 'Congratulations, my dear,' she said warmly, 'may you become a famous film actress. But there is one compensation I demand. You must let little Jhani remain with me for some months at least, till you can establish yourself.'

Loti knew she could not refuse this kind-hearted soul who had stood by her for so long, although it would break her heart to leave the little chap behind.

∽

After Man Singh's two henchmen had left him on the outskirts of the nearest village, Jhani had worked his way by slow stages to Poona, where there was a Recruiting Centre for the Army.

He filled in the necessary forms and duly stood before the recruiting sergeant.

The sergeant gazed at him in the way all recruiting sergeants the world over, no matter to what army, nation, creed or colour they may belong, gaze at raw recruits from civilian life. There was open disdain in his eye.

'Now what the hell makes you think you will be a good soldier?' he asked.

'Because I want to be one,' Jhalli had replied.

'That's a hell of an answer,' commented the sergeant. 'And what were you in civilian life?'

'A farmer,' came the frank response.

'A farmer, by Lord Krishna!' breathed the sergeant, sourly, 'what next? Why don't you join the navy or the air force, and give those buggers the trouble of turning you into a soldier. A hell of a time we are going to have, teaching you your right foot from your left. A farmer! Oh hell!'

Jhani frowned. What the devil is wrong with this fellow, he wondered. At all railway stations and street corners, I see posters urging young men to join the army. Yet when I come here, this clot makes me feel unwanted. I must ask him.

And Jhani proceeded to put his thoughts into words.

'Look soldier,' he said, 'everywhere there are posters to be seen, inviting young men to join the Army.

'Yet when I come to do so, you ask me why I want to join the Army. May I ask why you put up such posters?'

The reply caused the sergeant to turn an ashy-grey beneath his dark skin. 'Wise guy, eh?' he commented. 'Okay; go through the door over there. The doctor will put you through the medical examination.'

Jhani was found physically very fit.

Next day he was sworn in and had become a sepoy or 'jawan' (private soldier) in the Indian Army.

Two days later he was given a railway warrant and ordered to proceed to Jubbulpore, where he was to join the regiment to which he had been posted for service. It was the 1st Battalion, the President's Light Infantry.

The next few days were hectic days to the farmer-boy. Accustomed to the routine of working on the land, getting up early to do it, and being his own master throughout the rest of the day, he found army life for the rookie very different; that is, in all ways except the 'getting up early' part of it, to which he was well accustomed.

Whereas the crow of the roosters would awaken him at home, here the strident notes of the bugler's reveille began the routine of the day; a routine far more exacting than any on the old farm.

Here everything was done to order, to time, to discipline. It was a case of hurry—and be quick—all the time, and any time. It started with brushing one's teeth and washing in the morning; rushing to the latrine; rushing to breakfast; rushing to don full kit and get on parade. These parades were endless and of varying sorts. Marching drill, arms drill, musketry drill. The training was complete. Small arms training, automatic weapons training, tactical training, field training.

The inspections very many. Kit inspection, barrack-room inspection, weapons inspection, and even health and physical examinations. Then there were duties to be performed. Barrack duties, camp duties, guard duties.

It was all very very different to the simple life of the agriculturist to which he had been brought up.

Jhani did not like army life at first. But there was one thing to be said in its favour. It did not give him much time in which to recriminate. Fleetingly he would think wistfully of Loti. Where is she at this moment, he would wonder?

Sometimes he thought of his old dad, Balaji, and of the twelve acres of hard ground that were his fields and farmlands.

He had been in the regiment one month when he wrote a letter home, informing dad he had joined the Army. As he wrote it, Jhani was thankful that the old man had spent the money to have him educated so as to be able to write that letter. He also wondered how his father was going to read it. For he was illiterate.

Then he remembered old Pushtoo. Yes, without doubt he would take the letter across to old Pushtoo, his neighbour. Pushtoo was considered a 'wise guy' in the locality. People would often come to him for help in reading or writing letters for them; and for advice on problems of a personal, family or other nature. The old man made some money out of this practice, also. He would charge half an anna for reading a letter; from one anna up to eight annas for writing it, according to subject-matter, length and the importance of the personage to whom the letter was addressed. Advice cost from two annas to perhaps two rupees. Minor problems were rated low. Advice on how to bargain to get—or to avoid giving—large dowries, might run from one rupee to three rupees. Weightier words of wisdom, on how to dodge the Revenue Tax Collector, the Income Tax Officer, and even the Police, required strenuous and deep thinking on old Pushtoo's part. That kind of advice would cost quite a lot.

Back came the reply to Jhani's letter within a fortnight. He smiled reminiscently to himself as he made out the village scribe's handwriting.

Dad said, 'I am very proud to hear you have joined the Army, son. Since the day you left, and not hearing from you, I have been worried to death over your silence, wondering where you were and what you were doing.

'The wheat crop is coming up fine this year and the well is full of water. The vegetables are not quite up to the mark, however, especially the carrots. Some underground insect seems to have attacked them. Perhaps the manure we put last year was not enough. The ducks are doing well, although I lost four of them lately. A civet cat burrowed its way in under the fence, and bit the heads off four of them, drinking the blood thereafter. All in the same night, too!

'So I borrowed the retired Police Jamadar's muzzleloading gun and sat up for the bugger the following night, hiding in the hay-rick. Along he came by eight o'clock, intending to kill more ducks no doubt. That muzzleloader is a good weapon. It blew him to bits.

'Look after yourself, son, and don't ever forget God. Try to avoid being sent to the wars if you can. But if you are sent, acquit yourself bravely and gain glory.

'And lastly, son, try to come back to the farm soon, please. These aged bones of mine creak at times, and I feel the work too strenuous. When I am gone there will be nobody to look after it and all the ducks will be killed. It is all for you, Jhani my boy. So, finish your soldiering and come back soon.'

There was a very, very painful lump in Jhani's throat when he finished reading that letter, and the lashes of his eyes were moist with tears. It brought the farm and his old father back to him so closely, and he felt very homesick.

Dad must have paid that versatile Pushtoo at least four annas for writing it, he soliloquised.

A year passed. Jhani was now a Lance Corporal. Liked by officers, sergeants and men, he had fitted in perfectly with Army life.

Six months later he took his first leave and travelled home on a warrant to see dad and the farm. Balaji wept for joy as he embraced his soldier-son, looking so smart in his khaki uniform. Proudly he showed him off to the neighbours and old Pushtoo.

Jhani noticed his father had turned more grey, and there was a slight stoop now in the sturdy, rustic figure. But it was only slight.

The farm appeared moderately prosperous, but as Jhani walked around the well-remembered boundaries later, his eye that had lost none of its skill, could tell that in places it was becoming unkempt and overgrown with the ever-encroaching thorny weeds that infested the area. He knew that the hard work was undoubtedly getting too much and too strenuous for his aging father to do all by himself, nor could he spare the money to hire help.

Jhani returned to his regiment after that and passed another fifteen months at its headquarters, in Jubbulpore. Now three chevrons on his upper arm indicated that he had risen to the rank of a Sergeant.

There was a cinema at Jubbulpore, known as the 'Garrison Theatre', which catered almost exclusively to the military personnel stationed there. During the days of of the British Tommy it had been a popular resort and means of passing away an evening when most of the local bars had been placed 'out of bounds'.

Then the Tommy left India for good, and was replaced by the Jawan. The cinema continued to cater to the military, but English pictures were rarely shown there now, giving way to the ever-increasing demand for the Hindi product, with films in that language.

Jhani himself was not over-fond of the movies and was only a periodic customer. But when he became a Sergeant, his social contacts expanded, and he went more frequently, in the company of other sergeants.

There was a young fellow in the regiment, also a sergeant, who had become a particular pal of his. This youngster's name was Moogan.

One evening Moogan said, 'Let's go to the "flicks" this evening, Jhani. There is a picture called 'Rath ki Rani' (the 'Queen of the Night') showing. It stars Battliboi and that new actress, Lotibai. I have seen her but once before, and she is quite a peach, I can tell you.'

Jhani's eyes took on a faraway look. 'Lotibai'—his Lotibai—where could she be? If only he could see her in the flesh, just once more.

'Well, what about it?' asked Moogan, 'will you come?'

But Jhani did not hear his voice. He heard only, instead, the swish of the rain and the crash of thunder. The barrack-room in which they were standing faded from sight, to be replaced by an old, ramshackled construction, without windows and with the moisture running down its decaying walls in streaks. It was almost dark in there—and growing darker each moment with the shades of approaching night.

In his arms he held a lovely creature, her hair and clothing soaked by the rain, her beautiful face with eyes closed upturned to his, the lovely lips half-opened as the heavy breathing of her lustful passion came in gasps and low moans of surrender.

'What the hell's the matter with you?' asked Moogan in surprise, 'you're daydreaming!'

Jhani shook his head as he forced himself to return to the present.

'Yes, I was dreaming,' he said, 'and it was a beautiful dream.'

Then he added, simply, 'My first sweetheart's name—and incidentally she was my only sweetheart—was Lotibai.'

Moogan laughed, a little surprised at his friend's serious demeanour.

'Do you mean to say you had only one girl? Hell, I've had half-a-dozen, and I've forgotten most of their names. However, we'll go to the flicks then. While you look at the actress, Lotibai, you can think of your old girl, eh? By the way, what happened to her?'

But Jhani did not answer that question. They arrived at the cinema a few minutes before six o'clock, when the show was scheduled to start. It was 6.05 p.m., though, before a bell rang somewhere and the lights went out.

The first item was an advertisement for Tata's 501 soap. The cakes of soap did battle with, and conquered the universal enemy, dirt, to the accompaniment of strains of the most martial music.

Then came an Indian newsreel, depicting the industrial expansion of the country, and showing the new Railway Engine Construction Plant, at Chittaranjan.

There followed a 'Mickey Mouse' cartoon, and two 'trailers' of pictures that were going to be shown at this theatre for the next change of programme, and the week after.

The bell rang again to announce to all and sundry that the main picture of the evening was about to commence.

It was heralded by a loud throbbing of tom-toms, accompanying the twang of Indian stringed instruments, followed by a fanfare of trumpets as the name of the main feature was thrown on the screen.

'Rath ki Rani'.

Jhani saw the Film Censor's certificate indicating the film had been passed for public exhibition. Next the words, 'Starring: B. Battliboi—and Lotibai'.

The sweet name struck another chord of memory as the first scene in the picture opened.

It was that of a woman arranging flowers in a vase.

Jhani looked very intently then.

For, the woman's face was—Lotibai's!

He gripped the arm of his chair as he stared at the screen before him. Could it possibly be true?

The girl on the silver screen spoke for the first time. She said, 'Prasad—is that you?'

It was his Lotibai's voice.

Jhani sprang from his seat, so that it's bottom fell back into place with a resounding 'clack'.

He made for the exit while still looking at the screen, with the result that he tripped over the legs of the other people seated in the same row.

'What the hell!' said one, angrily.

'Easy, Sarge, easy,' advised the regimental wit, a corporal.

Once out in the lobby, Jhani made for the Manager's office. Unceremoniously he flung open the door and butted in. The

Manager—a portly man—was leaning back in his chair with his feet on his table, complacently smoking a cigar.

'Tell me something, please,' asked Jhani in a rush, 'this picture that is now showing—where does it come from?'

'What do you mean—where does it come from?' countered the fat Manager, in surprise.

'I mean—what studios produced it? What is their address?'

Jhani's impatience was so great that he felt like shaking the bulky man.

'Oh, I see,' replied the Manager, taking his feet off his desk, 'why, the Bombay Associated Pictures Corporation of course. They are at Malabar Hill, Bombay. Why?…'

But the sergeant had already disappeared. It was something awful what too much drink could do to a man, the Manager mused.

Within twenty minutes Sergeant Jhani sprang to attention and saluted smartly as he entered the Orderly Officer's room.

'Sir, there is something I want. Urgently. I want one week's leave, beginning right now, to go to Bombay. It is a very important matter.'

The Orderly Officer looked at the young sergeant before him. He knew Jhani well. The man had a spotless record. But why all this urgency?

'What's happened?' he asked, kindly. 'Any bad news? I hope not.'

'I—I can't tell you, Sir. I—I mean I would rather not—if you don't mind, Sir,' said Jhani, swallowing hard. 'But please, Sir; I need it urgently. Please grant it.'

The Officer looked him straight in the face. The sergeant was actually trembling from head to foot. He was much agitated—there was no doubt about it.

All this was very irregular in the army. Leave had to be applied for through proper channels in advance, and sanction obtained from the O.C.; unless of course it was something extremely unforeseen.

But Captain Ratna was very human beneath his officer's uniform. He read the note of pleading in the sergeant's eyes, and he responded.

'Alright, sergeant. I will sanction it as a very special case. But be back at the end of the week. No extension, eh!'

'Thank you, thank you, Sir,' said Jhani fervently. Then he saluted, turned quickly, and made a dive for the doorway.

'Come back, man,' called the Captain, 'what the hell is the matter with you? Here, take this piece of paper and write out an application at least. And do you want a travel warrant?'

'There is no time for that, Sir,' said the sergeant.

Jhani borrowed the captain's pen and wrote the application hastily. Ratna looked at him, slightly worried.

Once more Jhani saluted and was out of the door within the next second.

I wonder what has upset the man, thought Ratna. He is almost a nervous wreck.

The giant wheels of the 'X. B. Class' locomotive that drew the mail train to Bombay that very night did not turn nearly fast enough for the impatient Jhani. The morning of the day after found him at the Victoria Terminus station at Bombay.

Almost running out of the building, he took a taxi to Malabar Hill, and within the hour stood at the entrance to the palatial studios of the Bombay Associated Pictures Corporation. The place had not opened for business yet, the time being just 8.15 a.m.

'Tairo! (wait),' he ordered the taxi driver, who was a Sikh.

Then he bounded up the front steps to the main doorway.

It was closed.

The night chowkidar, who was a Gurkha, was just going off duty. Being an ex-soldier himself, he appraised the sergeant's chevrons on the visitor's uniform.

Jhani turned to him almost pleadingly and asked in Hindi, 'The actress—Miss Lotibai—where does she live?'

The mongolian features of the Gurkha creased in an understanding smile. He replied, 'Somewhere in Santa Cruz; but I don't know the address.'

Jhani bounded down the steps again, dashed back to the taxi, and shouted 'Santa Cruz' to the driver.

It took a little more than an hour to reach the suburb. Jhani made frantic inquiries at the little post office. There he was given the address.

Ten more minutes, and he was pressing the doorbell of a little villa.

It seemed like an eternity before he heard the sound of the bolt being drawn on the inside. The door opened at last.

Before him, in the flesh, stood Lotibai—his Lotibai.

'Loti,' he cried, 'it's you; thank God.'

'Jhani, oh Jhani, my darling,' she responded, receiving him fondly into her wide-open arms.'

The Sikh driver of the taxi had never read classics. But as Jhani paid him and he slipped his vehicle into gear, he quoted a very famous text:

'Much ado about nothing.'

When they were through kissing and caressing each other, Loti told Jhani all about his son in Ahmedabad, and of how she had come to join the films.

He in turn told her how he had met Man Singh, and that it was the dacoit-leader's good advice that had kept him from turning into a murderer, to become a soldier instead. Then Jhani related how he had gone to see the picture! 'Rath ki Rani', which lead him to tracing her.

They were very happy all that forenoon.

After lunch Jhani asked, 'But what will we do now, Loti? I have to be back in Jubbulpore within the week, or I will be court-martialled.'

His sweetheart's eyes looked at him adoringly. Then came her tinkling laughter; the laughter he knew so well and had missed so much.

'Silly Jhani. Remember the answer you gave me that rainy evening on the way home from the moosafarkhana? I give you that same answer now. There is only one thing to do. We will get married tomorrow or the day after, at the Registrar's Office, by special licence.'

'But what about your film career?' he asked, dubiously. Loti grimaced. 'It gives way to the career I have always yearned to lead,' she said simply, 'as your wife.'

They were in time that afternoon to submit their application before the Registrar of Marriages, with a special fee, to be married as soon as possible. The wedding was fixed for the morning of the day after the next.

That evening Loti took Jhani with her to call on Mr. Sathe.

Shri Sathe received her graciously. He had never ceased congratulating himself on the very successful outcome of the gamble he had taken that evening at Ahmedabad by employing her. It was evident he was quite unprepared for the shock that he was to receive.

'Mr. Sathe,' said Loti in her direct manner, 'I have come to thank you for all you have done for me, and at the same time to beg of you to please release me from the remaining term of my contract. I want to get married to Jhani here, and join him in Jubbulpore.'

'Then she sketched their association briefly, ending up with how Jhani had found her.

Mr. Sathe tried to find a way out.

'Do you mean to tell me that you are gong to sacrifice your whole career on the screen, which promises to turn into a very brilliant one, just to marry a...a sergeant?' He could not help being so blunt, even rude in what he said. He wanted Lotibai to realise she was about to destroy the brilliant future that lay ahead of her as an actress.

'You must remember, Mr. Sathe,' Loti reminded him unaffectedly. 'He is the father of my son.'

Shri Sathe thought he understood, but was not too sure.

As he lay in bed that night, with Loti's fragrant hair spread in abundance over the snowy whiteness of her pillowcase, and the creamy chocolate-tint of her completely nude body clasped tightly to his own naked and slightly darker form, Jhani felt for the first time after many years, that it is good to be alive.

Noon on the third day found them man and wife. The ceremony at the Registrar's Office had been a brief one, and there had been only two witnesses.

One of these was Mr. Sathe, still not quite recovered from his disappointment. The other was her maidservant, whom Loti had brought along with her from her villa in Santa Cruz for the purpose.

That very night Loti left from the Bombay Central Station aboard the Gujarat Mail of the Western Railway, for Ahmedabad, from where she would bring young Jhani to Jubbulpore to meet his father for the first time.

And the same night 'big' Jhani—as Loti now fondly called her husband—left Victoria Terminus by the Central Railway to rejoin duty at Jubbulpore and quickly arrange accommodation for his wife and son.

The meeting between 'big' Jhani and 'little' Jhani was something that Lotibai would remember for her lifetime. It had made her cry openly with sheer joy.

She had told the little fellow when she had brought him from aunt Parvati's home, that she was taking him or a long journey by 'chook-chook train', at the end of which he would meet his daddy.

Little Jhani had often heard his mother mention his daddy as a big man and a sweet man, but had never seen him. He was agog with excitement and anticipation throughout the trip.

Finally the train clacked over the points in the yard, and began to slow down as it drew into Jubbulpore Railway Station. The smooth flagstones lining the platform slid by gently. Then, with a slight jerk of binding brakes it came to a halt.

Loti opened the compartment door eagerly. There, almost opposite her, scanning the windows of the carriages anxiously, stood 'big' Jhani—her Jhani.

'Jhani,' she hailed.

'Loti,' came the joyful answer.

Next minute, regardless of the curious gaze of the coolies and people jostling past, Jhani had leapt into the doorway and had Loti in his arms. Then it was that he felt a shy tugging at the knee of his trousers and a small voice asked, 'Daddy?'

Suddenly she remembered.

Loti looked down at the diminutive figure beside her and said, 'Beloved, there is your son.'

'Big' Jhani bent and scooped the little man to his breast. He kissed him on his cheeks and forehead as he said, 'Son—sonny boy—my son!'

The little chap said again, 'Daddy.'

There were tears of joy in the sergeant's eyes. They trickled down his rough cheeks and into the sides of his mouth.

Loti was crying openly—there had to be an outlet for her gladness. There just had to; for it was too great. The coolies and the people jostling by, stopped and stared.

They lived happily in the little cottage that Jhani had rented for themselves for eight months after that.

But Fate, untiring of the drama she had already enacted with these two people—this man and this woman—elected to spin the wheel of fortune and circumstance and weave the web of coincidence, yet once more, just to see what would happen.

The activities and fame of Rajah Man Singh Rathore, king of dacoits, had spread by this time far beyond the fastnesses of his ravine hideout on the farther bank of the Chambal River.

It had reached to the four quarters of India. Man Singh was spoken about in England, the U.S.A., and even Europe.

In India, thousands of policemen had been deputed to try to stop him; catch him; kill him.

They had all failed.

Now the military were called upon to take a hand in the game.

The yearly festival at the Bateshwar Nath temple was due to be held in exactly ten days' time. The police knew that it was a function the dacoit-king had never failed to attend, year after year in various clever disguises. Year after year they had been there in force themselves. They had scanned the pilgrims almost individually; questioned hundreds of them. Man Singh's description had been broadcast circulated, studied and learnt by heart by the thousands of policemen searching for him. Yet they had not caught him.

And there was a reward of fifteen thousand rupees on his head!

This year the police knew that Man Singh would attend the temple on the festival day as usual to have darshan (puja; worship). They determined to try once again to catch him.

Some Big Brass thought it would be a good idea to call in the military to help the police to do this.

No. 1 Company of the 1st Battalion, the President's Light Infantry stationed at Jubbulpore, was chosen for the duty and were entrained with the temple as their destination, a week in advance.

Sergeant Jhani belonged to No. 1 Company.

The day of the festival dawned bright and cloudless. By nine o'clock in the morning the sun beat down mercilessly from a clear sky.

The vicinity and outskirts of the temple were thronged with thousands upon thousands of pilgrims who had come from distant places to attend the festival. They walked about; or sat, ate or slept in the blazing sun. Vendors of sweetmeat, fruit, and cold drinks—mostly coloured water of red, green and blue hues with sugar added to it—were doing a roaring trade.

A thin pall of fine dust covered everything and everybody, raised from the parched sand of the earth by the moving feet of the restless thousands. Pariah dogs ranged among the throng, singly and in packs, snatching at morsels thrown to them in charity by the people who were hungry themselves. Occasionally two dogs would grab for the same small piece of dried chappatty. Then a dog fight would start. Other curs in the immediate vicinity would join in. A seething pack of half-a-dozen rending, biting dogs would run hither and thither, snapping at any moving thing; man, woman, child or other dog, that came in their way.

Over all and everywhere, myriads of blue bottle flies hummed restlessly, settling with impartial disregard on sweetmeat, fruit, chappatties, people, dogs—and even on the armed policemen and soldiers as they moved about among the crowds.

In addition to the policemen and soldiers mingling with the pilgrims and whose business it was to scan every face closely and talk to every and any suspicious character, there was a far-flung circle of armed police and military pickets that surrounded the whole area in a ring of steel.

Man Singh's description had been dinned into his head, and into the heads of all the men in No. 1 Company. But Jhani remembered it well enough.

Because Man Singh had been his benefactor.

For once in his service, and for the first time since his days as a rookie, Jhani hated soldiering.

He had taken an oath to be faithful to his duty. Yet could he betray his benefactor if he should meet him? The man who had actually given him a fresh lease of life.

As a sergeant, it was Jhani's task to be on the alert all the time. He had to check the pickets and be with those others on his men who were moving among the crowd. He was also expected to keep a sharp lookout himself for anyone remotely resembling the dacoit-leader.

And so it came to pass that, towards midday, the sergeant wended his way towards one of the public latrines that had been put up to meet the exigencies of the occasion.

It was just a 'tattied' affair; meaning by that that the four walls were of temporary erection, being of bamboo matting.

Each of the latrines had two sections; one for men and one for women.

As most of the pilgrims would be illiterate, this differentiation of the sexes was indicated to all and sundry by crude paintings in green and white; that of a man in white shirt and dhoti, with green turban, being tied to the bamboo mat at the entrance to the latrine for men; and that of an ogre-like female in a green sari, at the entrance to latrine for females.

The passage and flooring of both enclosures had been hastily cemented for the occasion to prevent swamping of the earth by water and excreta. Large zinc pans were installed in the closets for the latter.

Jhani entered the men's latrine.

He came out after ten minutes. And then an accident occurred.

Someone had thrown a banana skin on the cement flooring, just outside the entrance.

Jhani was wearing army regulation boots (somewhat disdainfully referred to in India as 'ammunition' boots, or 'kuttaks').

And anyone who has ever worn 'ammunition' boots will know that the heel is shod with a U-shaped, horse shoe-like iron piece surrounding its outer edge, while hobnail studs are hammered into the soles.

He trod directly on the banana skin.

The very next second, Jhani slipped violently, all but falling upon the floor on the broad of his back.

To recover his balance he flung out both arms violently, and skidded obliquely, to crash head-on into an aged crone, almost bent double and tottering on a wooden ' staff, who had just come out of the adjacent latrine for women.

The brass badge on Jhani's right shoulder caught in the thin piece of sari cloth covering the old hag's head and part of her face. As his weight lunged him against her the badge went with it, to wrench off the cloth and leave the old woman bare-headed.

Recovering his balance, Jhani turned around to apologise.

He found himself gazing into the piercing, steel-like eyes, of Man Singh.

The sergeant's jaw dropped in amazement. No; there was absolutely no doubt about it whatever. The eyes held that same merry twinkle of challenge; that subtle expression of apology for fear of being misunderstood; that expression that begged no offence be taken; that expression that radiated kindness and good will.

There was no beard, moustache, or whiskers; but without shadow of doubt it was bis benefactor, Rajah Man Singh Rathore who stood before him, disguised so perfectly but for that unforeseen accident that had given him away.

Jhani recovered himself quickly.

There were no pangs of conscience whatever to becloud his mind now. His spoken oath gave place to the far greater moral oath that bound him to this man in its firmer, much more sacred, grip. This man who had saved him from becoming a murderer; and had made it possible for him to rejoin Loti and his son, honourably.

'Maharaj Sahib; go in peace. I shall not betray you,' Jhani breathed the words, 'no; not for any reward in money or all the gold on this earth.'

'Thank you, Jhani my son. Did I not know I could trust you?' Man Singh had whispered back. 'Congratulations on becoming a soldier—and a sergeant, too! I am very very proud of you.'

Jhani could not restrain himself from adding a few hurried sentences. 'I have found her, Maharajah Sahib. We are now happily married and have a son. And one thing more, oh benefactor to whom all three of us owe our present happiness, and for which we are humbly grateful to you. My father has written a letter inviting us and in a fortnight's time we are going to the farm to spend two months with him.'

'I am so glad to hear it; God bless you all,' came the reply. 'And tell Balaji your father—see how well I remember his name—that I am so happy to have saved him from the pangs of sorrow that I caused my own father. Give him this as a personal message to him from Rajah Man Singh Rathore, the dacoit.'

The old hag rejoined the pilgrims; and the sergeant his company.

'The great man recognised even humble me. He remembered my name, even dad's name. He said he was very proud of me. He said he was very happy over all that had happened.'

These thoughts sang joyfully in Jhani's mind.

While the authorities were again greatly disappointed on that festival day. For once more they had not caught Rajah Man Singh Rathore.

Chapter Three

The Policemen who Sought a Reward

Bhind is an area of land comprising some thousands of square miles in the state of Madhya Pradesh, the most extensive state in renaissant India. Its largest town, the capital, bears the same name. The district itself is mainly covered with thick jungles, and human habitations are few and far between. It is a land of legend and folklore, fables and ghost stories told by the dancing flicker of firelight; most nearly approaching the India of bygone days. Men's wants are few and simple, because money is hard to get. And due to its absence in too-large quantities, people are free and happy. Moreover, they are guileless and untainted for the most part by the vices of civilisation.

The men of Bhind require but few material possessions to make them contented. In the hot summer nights when people gasp for breath and perspiration trickles in rivulets between the breasts of a sleeper and bedews his forehead where, one drop uniting with another forms sufficient to drip down upon, and sodden his hard, dirty pillow, the canopy of the star-studded sky above may be the only roof over his head, a free gift to all her sons from Mother Nature for a shelter. When the rains come and the frogs croak in millions in the surrounding swollen streams and ponds; and wood-crickets chirp in their thousands; and fire flies scintillate and synchronise their elfin lamps to bejewel the night with a throbbing, pulsating phosphorescence; and snakes crawl out of their flooded holes to swallow the frogs and seek for drier abodes; and mosquitoes buzz and hum and dive and sting in hundreds; a man requires a little hut built of wattles with grass thatched roof, to afford some protection from the weather and the snakes.

But be the season dry or rainy, a man needs the presence of a woman, wife or concubine, to cook his food, be a companion to him and administer to his creature wants.

Then he will require a few annas a day to buy wheat flour for making his 'chappatties' (these are flat, circular cakes, a foot or so in diameter by perhaps one-fourth of an inch thick). It is the only form of bread known to the people of the area and comprises the staple diet and item of food.

Clothing is a simple matter and presents no problem whatsoever. A long cotton shirt, hanging over a cotton dhoti which is tied around the waist and passes between the legs; a length of cloth loosely wound around the head to form a turban; and a pair of rough, leather sandals to keep the sharp thorns from penetrating his feet; are the only articles worn by a peasant throughout the year. A coarse black blanket is an extra item, used in the chilly winter months from November to January.

Cultivation is scarce, the monsoon unreliable, and farming difficult. People are sometimes desperately poor, but everyone devoutly believes in a God that will supply all his daily necessities, and perhaps throw in a few extras as well.

But luxuries in any form are mostly quite unknown. Occasionally, God would appear to have grown angry with His poor people. A monsoon would fail and the subsequent drought kill all the standing crops. Then there would be no grain, no money, and consequently, no food. Or an epidemic of sickness would ravish the land and thousands would die beneath its spell. At such times of misfortune, even the stoutest hearts quailed from fear and people would sometimes wonder why they had ever been born.

To make matters worse would come the landlord or the servants of the local zamindar, demanding rent for the land that had yielded nothing, with threats of eviction if the money was not paid at once.

How could they pay money when they had none to pay? Their

crops had failed and they had nothing to sell. A good number of them were already in debt, for they had not paid for the seed they had sown or the manure they had put down, all for no purpose, in their fields. Surely the landowner understood their plight?

But the landlords and the zamindars and their servants would molest and beat them, threaten to evict them; perhaps even throw them out physically, by force. They would face dire starvation by the roadside, for no man would give them anything, even if they begged.

Yes indeed; often would a poor peasant wonder why he had been born. Famine and pestilence would sometimes stalk the land and make them think like that, and despair. They would lift up their eyes to heaven and weep, and hope that God had heard their supplications.

But say; was there not one last hope of deliverance left to them on this earth? In the name of Rajah Man Singh; lover of the poor, the down-and-out and needy; benefactor and guardian; deliverer and saviour in time of need and distress. Beloved Man Singh, leader of his dacoit band and succourer of the benighted and starving.

Last year the little hamlet of Rampur had been on the verge of famine and starvation, its crops withered and parched and died beneath a merciless sun without a drop of rain to even moisten them. The rent-gatherers had been more than ever petulant and demanding. Life had held out no hope, and the people of Rampur had called on God to take them away swiftly, and spare them from the pangs of slow starvation and torture and death.

Then suddenly into the village one morning had rumbled eight bullock carts, their oxen tugging and straining under a top-load of gunny bags that reached right up to the eliptical grass roof of each vehicle. The bags were filled with wheat and the leader of the cartmen delivered them to the villagers of Rampur together with a simple message, 'A gift from Man Singh'.

That gift had saved the village from disaster. Before it had been exhausted relief came from the Government in the form of abundant supplies of food. The situation was now well in hand, and the subsequent monsoon had been as plentiful as its predecessor had been scanty. But the inhabitants of Rampur never forgot Man Singh and his timely aid.

There was a reward of Rs. 15,000 offered by the Government for the apprehension of this notorious individual, who was charged with over two hundred murders and dacoities untold. Yet nobody claimed it. Because, nobody gave information against beloved Man Singh, or betrayed him.

The eight cartmen were closely questioned. They stated a man had hired them a week earlier to drive their carts to a railway station 40 miles away and load bags of grain that would be waiting there in a goods wagon. He had paid them Rs. 160 for the double trip at the rate of Rs. 20 for each cart. He had also whispered the name of Man Singh to them, and had said that, if they did not complete their part of the bargain and deliver the bags of grain to Rampur within the week, none of them would live to see the sunset on the first day of the following week. So they had delivered the bags on the sixth day.

The cartmen also added that when they reached the wayside railway station to which they had been told to go, the stationmaster there had affirmed that a goods wagon had arrived two days earlier, laden with bags of wheat, and had been kept on a siding awaiting their arrival to unload.

The wagon had been booked in the name of some individual calling himself Man Singh. After all, it was quite a common name in that district.

One summer evening the sun dipped itself in a ball of blood-red fire behind the serrated tops of the tall sal trees that stretched to the western horizon. A narrow, dusty roadway ran through the dense forest, hemmed in on both sides by the close array of the trunks of sal trees. One could not see far between them because of the gathering dusk. The still air yet throbbed with the heat of the day that was done.

Two men who had been striding rapidly along the road, came to a halt beneath a large tree bordering the wayside. One was a tall man, having a beard. The other was of normal height and well-built. They both wore khaki tunics and shorts, putties, service boots and khaki turbans. And they both carried .303 service rifles. For they were policemen.

There is hardly any dusk in the tropics, and there would be none in this densely-forested area. In a few minutes heavy darkness would descend upon them, leaving only the twinkling stars in a slate-blue sky above.

A ball of something soft and brown sailed overhead, flitted around for a moment on silent wings, but soon settled soundlessly before them to be lost to sight in the dust of the roadway. It was quiet for a minute, and then emitted a queer sound, resembling a pebble being thrown and bouncing along the surface of a flat rock. It sounded like 'Chuck—chuck—chuck—chuck—chuckooo'.

The policemen recognised the sound and the bird that was making it. It was a 'night jar'. Indeed, darkness was upon them and they were very apprehensive.

And they had every reason to be. For they were in the very heart of the domain of the notorious dacoit and bandit-leader, Man Singh Rathore. In fact, they were but one of many groups of policemen who had been sent out armed, and in pairs, to try to collect information about and, if possible bring in that infamous brigand.

What was worst of all was the thought that large numbers of policemen had been shot, stabbed or had their throats cut by this fearsome character and his followers in the past. Just last week, nine constables and a sergeant had been ambushed while asleep on the riverbank, decapitated, and their bodies thrown into the river. The ten heads had been left behind by the dacoits at their last encampment as a gift to the posse of police that were pursuing them.

The taller of the two policemen unslung his rifle from his shoulder and resting it against the tree trunk, addressed his squat companion. 'Arre bhai! rath hogya' (meaning, 'Oh brother; night has fallen!'). Continuing in Hindustani, he said, 'We had better climb into the branches of this tree. There we will be safe from wild animals; and if we hide ourselves well, should the shaitan (devil) Man Singh and his gang of robbers pass this way they will not see us. What say you?'

The shorter of the two policemen looked up to assess the height and comparative safety afforded by the overhanging boughs of the big tree. With the rapidly falling darkness, its leaves and branches clustered blackly against the steely-blue of the sky above, in which he noticed the stars had begun to twinkle one by one. Withal he was not impressed. He commenced to quarrel with his taller companion.

'This is what comes of listening to you, you fool,' he stated bitterly. 'When I advised camping at the last village you assured me that the town of Kampampoli was but three or four miles further, where we could get a good night's rest, food, and perhaps a woman to share between us. Since that time we have walked at least ten miles, and this blessed road seems to have no end. Nothing but jungle, everywhere; not a signpost or hut of any kind. And now you want me to spend the night in a tree, like a monkey. Idiot that you are!'

The tall constable appeared momentarily taken aback by his companion's vehemence. Then he started to remonstrate.

'Come brother,' he placated, 'why do you quarrel with me? Such hardships are but part and parcel of our lives as policemen. I only suggested it is safer at night in a tree.'

'Not nearly as safe and as comfortable as we could have been at that last village,' retorted the squat man. 'If Man Singh or his band finds us now, our heads will join those of our ten colleagues who lost theirs last week.'

'Don't be afraid,' rejoined the tall man, whose name was Dass. 'Man Singh is nowhere near us. Even he would not hang out all night in the midst of a forest like this.'

His speech irritated Hariram, the shorter of the two still further. He mouthed an oath as foul in Hindustani as its English translation.

'Who is afraid, Dass?' he almost shouted. 'You, or me? Who first suggested climbing into this blasted tree? You, or me? Who spoke about wild animals and Man Singh? You, or me? You can climb the tree yourself. As for me, I am going on. This damned road must lead us to some place, eventually.' So saying, he reslung his rifle across his shoulder and made to proceed.

Dass lost his temper. As with most men of his nature when foiled, his ire vented itself in personal abuse and invective.

'You short, fat pig,' he hissed, 'I have listened enough to your arrogant words. We are both constables, but as the senior in service, I order you to remain here with me till daylight. After all, if anything should happen to you, I will be held responsible, although as a matter of fact even the jackals would not touch your carcass, far less Man Singh.'

'You be damned,' retorted Hariram, who appeared to feel that what he lacked in height he made up for in weight and muscle, 'you are just an ordinary constable like me, and not my senior. I am going on, and I would like to see you try to stop me.'

Their plight had filled both men with apprehension; terror of the jungle, the darkness, wild animals and of Man Singh. The quarrel that had just broken out had been a diversion to keep their minds off their real problem, which was fear of what might happen to them.

They faced each other, breathing hard and with set faces in the manner of angry men. It was quite dark now. The stillness and gloom around them seemed to scream a message of warning, as if from a thousand muted tongues.

Then they heard the sounds. Footsteps padding along the dust of the road before them; drawing nearer to them, ever nearer.

Could this be the dreaded dacoit and his band of followers? But the footfalls denoted there were only two or three men approaching them, and not a large band.

By now it was too late—and too dark—to attempt climbing into the tree in a hurry. As if by mutual consent, the policemen stepped behind its trunk and waited anxiously. Nor had they long to wait. In a few seconds two figures loomed in the murkiness and came to a halt almost opposite them.

'Why do you hide behind the tree, brothers. Come out, we will not harm you.' The words were uttered in a soft tone by a melodious voice that seemed to carry with it a hint of sarcasm and of amusement.

Dass had been angry before. Now he became furious. He strode forth from behind the tree and approached the two figures. Hariram followed a pace or two behind him.

'What the hell do you mean by saying we are hiding and are afraid,' he shouted at the top of his voice. 'We are policemen and are afraid of nothing!'

'I see,' answered the same voice quietly. 'Then why do you stand behind the tree trunk?'

Dass sized up the two men before answering. It was difficult to make out details in the gloom, but as far as he could see, the man who had spoken must be a fairly old fellow. His flowing beard and heavy moustache and whiskers could easily be made out, and even in the darkness they appeared to be completely grey. He was dressed in the usual manner, in a long shirt and dhoti, while an enormous turban enveloped his head. His companion was younger, very straight and tall, and appeared to possess a distinctly military bearing. With all that, Dass felt that he and Hariram could deal with the young fellow if occasion arose. The old man was not worth taking into account should a fight ensue.

'Stop your insolence,' he grated, 'we heard footsteps approaching and hid behind the tree trunk to see if they were caused by the man for whom we are looking. And...'

'And for whom are you looking?' the old man inquired, mildly.

Dass swallowed hard. This old devil was annoying him, and would have to be taught a lesson.

'Never mind,' he snapped, 'and who are you both?'

'Farmers,' came the quick answer.

'Farmers?' interjected Hariram incredulously; 'in the middle of the jungle; at night! Funny sort of farmers, indeed. You appear to me to be more like suspicious characters. Farmers, forsooth!'

At hearing these words the old man shook with laughter, while a wide grin spread from ear to ear over the erstwhile stony countenance of his sturdy companion.

'That is a good joke indeed,' he cackled, 'you calling us suspicious characters, while you go hiding behind trees yourselves! Ha, ha, ha.' He fairly bounced with merriment.

'Enough of your insane laughter,' broke in Dass sternly. 'Have I not just told you that we hid ourselves thinking you might be the man we are looking for?'

'And who may he be?' wheezed the bearded old man.

'That rascally dacoit, Man Singh.'

'And why do you want him? Has he done you any harm?' asked long-beard querulously.

'What a stupid question to ask,' broke in Hariram. 'Are you blind that you cannot make out our uniforms: We are policemen, while Man Singh is a dacoit. Every policemen in these four states is looking for him.'

'Besides,' added Dass, 'what is more to the point is the fact that there is a reward of fifteen thousand rupees for his capture, dead or alive, and I want that money very badly. Say, can you give me any information about this rogue?'

'Do you need this money so much that you would give away this Man Singh for it, provided you came to know where you could find him?'

For the moment Dass was nonplussed for a ready answer. He never imagined that anyone could be as dull as this old fool. Then he blurted out, 'Look here, old man; I cannot stay here all night answering your silly questions. For the last time let me assure you that I would give away Man Singh and even my own superior officer in exchange for fifteen thousand rupees. I need the money badly. I have a daughter who has matured, and I must find a husband for her. No husband will agree to marry her without dowry money. And I am a poor man who has no money. If I get this reward I will be able to offer a reasonable dowry to whomsoever agrees to marry my daughter and have a good sum left over for myself.'

'I understand,' said the old man, apparently satisfied.

He was silent awhile, then added, 'Folk round about here say this fellow, Man Singh, has helped many people in straightened circumstances with money. I wonder if you should ask him.'

'Now I know you are really mad,' Dass replied contemptuously. He took a beedi from the pocket of his tunic, put the end in his mouth, lit the other end with a match and inhaled the smoke into his lungs gratefully.

As a joke he said to the old man, 'Perhaps you will be good enough to tell me where this character hangs out, in order that I might ask him. In any case, it is all a pack of lies. I don't believe these stories one hears about that devil's supposedly good actions. Personally, I think he is a crafty, murderous pig, and that's about all.'

To add emphasis to his denunciation, Dass spat scathingly on the sandy road.

'I am Man Singh.'

With a mighty start the two policemen straightened themselves. The hitherto feeble-looking old man looked feeble no longer. He appeared to grow before their very eyes both in height and girth. His companion, who had been a strapping-looking individual seemed to assume the proportions of a giant.

There was a faint gleam in the starlight as the giant whipped the naked blade of a footlong wicked-looking dagger from his waistband, and held it menacingly in his right hand, its point resting against the pit of Dass's stomach.

Man Singh remained nonchalant. The two policemen were too thunderstruck to be able to speak. They just stood inarticulate. Slowly an expression of abject terror came into their eyes. They sweated and trembled in fright.

'Give me your name and address, constable, and I will teach you what kind of person Man Singh is.' The words were spoken quietly and without anger. But there was a peremptoriness in them that brooked no delay.

'My name is Ganga Dass, police constable No. 451 of the Bhind town police. I live in Block No. 276 at the Police Lines there.' The words came tumbling out of the policeman's mouth, almost mechanically.

'Go home, Dass, and find a husband for your daughter. Three thousand rupees will be paid to you before this week has ended at your very door in the Police Quarters. It will suffice for a dowry and none of it is to be kept over for yourself, do you hear?

'Tell your friends that Man Singh is sometimes merciful. Your heads and your bodies might have otherwise suddenly parted company.

'And one thing more. The whole amount is to be spent for your daughter's dowry. None of it is for you. I will inquire later, and if you have broken this injunction you will surely die! Goodnight.'

Turning to his younger companion, Man Singh said, 'Come, son, let us be going. Our suppers will be getting cold.'

The next instant they were no longer in sight. Three or four seconds later and their footsteps had faded from hearing in the powdery dust of the roadway.

The two constables remained petrified. Their service rifles hung across their shoulders, suspended by their slings. In their pouches each man carried 20 rounds of live ammunition. Yet the idea of firing at Man Singh or trying to arrest him had never even occurred to either of them once.

At last the spell was broken. 'Shaitan ka batcha!' (spawn of the devil!) ejaculated Dass, as he took to his heels in the opposite direction.

Hariram followed suit. But in spite of his best efforts, he could not catch up with his running companion. Perhaps that man's legs were longer, because he was taller.

Or was Hariram just a bit too fat?

There were two days left and the week would be over. Man Singh had not yet fulfilled his promise. The money had still not been paid.

When Dass and Hariram had eventually reached a village after running what had seemed to be endless miles that memorable night, unthinkingly they had both gasped out to various and astounded audiences garbled versions of what had happened.

They had altered the facts considerably, though. According to them, they had been waylaid by a dozen members of the gang, overpowered, tied hand and foot, and then questioned by Man Singh. They stated they had boldly admitted to the bandit that they were searching for him in an attempt to gain, and share, the reward offered. Dass had said he needed his portion of the 'reward money to offer as a dowry for his daughter's marriage, when Man Singh had undertaken to send him 3000 rupees within the week, to his address at the police quarters.

The tale spread like wildfire and next day reached the ears of the Commissioner of Police.

That Officer knew that Man Singh had hitherto never failed to keep his promises and would therefore assuredly attempt to pay the money within the stipulated time at the given address.

He determined to catch him when that happened.

An armed guard was placed, night and day, at the entrance to the Police Lines, while pickets surrounded it with instructions to shoot to kill any person entering or leaving under suspicious circumstances, or who did not answer a sentry's challenge. Passes were issued to the residents of the police quarters.

The armed cordon was soon complete. For the next week it would be impossible for any unauthorised person to enter or leave the vicinity without being closely scrutinised.

P.C. Dass was in a bad mood.

He had enjoyed the publicity that had come with all these events. But now he had begun to realise he had been a fool to have mentioned anything about it. Maybe Rajah Man Singh had really meant to keep his word and give him that much-coveted amount of Rs. 3000. But now it would be humanly impossible for him even if he had meant to do so.

If only he had kept mum about the whole incident.

Of course he blamed P.C. Hariram for letting the cat out of the bag. Hariram had done most of the talking even if he, Dass himself, had been the first to speak about it upon reaching the village that night.

Then another day passed and there remained but one more. If Man Singh did not pay the money by midnight that night, he would have failed to keep his promise.

Excitement was keyed to fever pitch.

The Commissioner decided to be on hand himself in the event the dacoit-leader should determine to be bold enough to try to carry out his word and come in person.

So he sat in his office long after working hours that evening hoping that something would happen. Hardly a furlong away was the entrance to the Police Lines.

Police Constables Dass and Hariram had been strictly ordered to remain in their respective quarters all day and not to attempt to stir out until further instructions had been given them.

Dass's 13-year-old daughter, Laxmi, who had recently matured and who had been the cause of all the trouble and excitement, although quite unwittingly, was not as happy and excited as she otherwise might have been. The reason was that her pet dog, which answered to the name of 'Tiger', could not be found since noon. Indeed, he had not come for his midday meal; something he had never missed all his lifetime.

He was only a nondescript, black mongrel, with straggling long hair. But Laxmi was devoted to him and the dog had never left her before. That morning he had followed her as usual to the marketplace and there he had mysteriously disappeared. She was anxious and began to cry.

At 8.30 p.m. the telephone on the Commissioner's desk shrilled loudly. He grabbed the receiver and placed it against his ear. A pleasant voice spoke in Hindustani. 'Police Commissioner Sahib, this is Man Singh speaking. Hasten quickly in your jeep to Quarter No. 276, in order that you may be there to witness the payment of the money I have promised to constable Dass.'

Then the line went dead at the other end.

With a loud oath the Commissioner banged the cradle of the telephone and then yelled to the operator at the Exchange, 'Trace that call, immediately.'

Then he sprang to his feet and made for the doorway of his office, grabbing his leather belt from the peg in the wall from which it was hanging. Fixed to that belt was his holster containing his .38 revolver which he had loaded earlier that very evening.

Outside was the jeep with his orderly-driver lounging at the steering wheel. The glowing end of a beedi dangled from his lips, the acrid taint of its smoke reaching the police officer.

In three strides the Commissioner had arrived at the jeep and was clambering into the vacant seat to the right of the driver, who had just time to throw away his beedi.

'Drive quickly to the Police Lines,' he shouted, 'and stop at the entrance.'

A couple of minutes later they were there.

Seeing the Commissioner suddenly arrive, the sentry had no time in which to 'turn out' the guard. But he hastily sloped arms and then came to the 'present'.

'Never mind the bloody drill formalities,' shouted the irate Police Chief, 'why the hell don't you challenge me and ask me to show my pass?'

The sentry was taken aback and did not know what he should do next. Stoically returning his rifle to his shoulder at the 'slope' position, he demanded almost casually, 'Halt! who goes there? Show your pass please,' adding as an afterthought a rather timorous, 'Sir'.

'Oh, go to hell, growled the Commissioner, and then to the driver of the jeep, 'Drive like blazes to quarters No. 276.'

His orderly let in the clutch and the jeep bounded forward.

Hazily, the sentry wondered whether or not he should obey orders now and shoot the Commissioner dead. For he had been definitely instructed to shoot to kill anyone who entered or left the lines without showing his pass on demand. And the Commissioner had just done that.

The Chief himself suddenly remembered his own orders and involuntarily flexed the muscles of his back, momentarily expecting to feel the sentry's bullet in that region. It was just the sort of thing a dim-witted sentry, like the dolt he had left standing there, would do—shoot his own Commissioner—he mused.

But fortunately nothing happened and the jeep arrived in a cloud of dust at No. 276. The Commissioner bounded through the open front door, shouting, 'Police Constable Dass; where are you?'

The constable, who had been reclining on his bed bare-bodied and with only a dhoti, scrambled up hastily and stood at attention. 'Here Sir,' he stuttered.

'Has anything happened? Has the money been paid? Speak up, man, and don't stand there staring at me like an 'oolu' (owl).'

'Nothing whatever has happened, Sir,' answered the surprised constable.

The Commissioner was relieved. Thank God it had only been a hoax and not a reality. If the money was to be paid that night right under his very nose and in spite of all his precautions, he would be the laughing stock of the entire Police Force throughout the length and breadth of India. He would probably be compelled, through shame, to volunteer for retirement from active service although he had a couple of years left before that time came.

Just then a nondescript black mongrel entered by the front door behind the Commissioner. The girl, Laxmi, who had been standing at the other doorway at the rear, and wondering what all the confusion was about, spotted the dog and ran to him with outstretched hands.

'Tiger; you naughty dog! Where have you been all day?' she greeted affectionately.

The animal stopped and gazed up at her with loving eyes, his awkward black tail wagging vigorously and causing his hindquarters to wag along with it.

'And what have you got tied to your collar?' asked Laxmi, indicating what appeared to be a six-inch long black cylinder neatly fixed to the collar at both its ends.

Regardless of the risk he ran of being bitten, the Commissioner grabbed the dog by its collar and tried to wrench off the black cylinder.

But it had been wired on firmly at both ends.

'Take the damned collar off', he shouted at Dass, irritably.

A couple of minutes later the cylinder lay on the table. It was of thin tin, painted black. In his excitement the Commissioner wrenched off the top with his bare hands.

Inside were thirty new one-hundred rupee currency notes, and a short message written in pencil in Hindi, on a piece of cigarette paper. It read, 'Rajah Man Singh Rathore always keeps his promise'.

Dass looked at the money. Then his eyes closed, and in spite of the near presence of his senior most officer his lips were heard to mutter the words, 'Ram, ram; Rajah Man Singh Sahib.'

Within hardly two months time his daughter was married. And she procured a respectable husband, too. The dowry of three thousand rupees offered with her made sure of that.

And Police Constable Dass kept none of it for himself; for above everything else he certainly did not want to die.

Chapter Four

The Invasion of the Ravine Kingdom

'The Old Man is creating hell and something has got to be done about it.'

The District Superintendent of Police (D.S.P.) was speaking, and there was an air of finality in his voice.

The 'Old Man' to whom he was referring was by no means really old. And the term had by no means been applied in a disrespectful sense. Rather, there was a hint of apprehension and awe in its use.

For the D.S.P. was referring to his immediate superior, the Deputy Inspector General, who had summoned him just the Tuesday before. That officer's words were as fresh in his memory as if they had only been uttered the moment before.

'It is a damned disgrace, Chandra,' he had thundered, banging the office desk before him with the palms of both his hands simultaneously. 'One single man out there in the blue, leading a handful of nondescript ruffians; and nearly two thousand policemen after him for almost three years! And yet they cannot catch him.

'Come, man, do you realise it?' he asked, warming to his subject. 'The whole of India is laughing at us. Every bloody policeman, in every bloody police force, in every bloody state in this peninsular is asking, 'What the hell are two thousand policemen, from four states, about? They cannot catch one hairy brigand!

'Our name stinks to high heaven. The governments of these four states write me D. Os. practically every ruddy week, asking me for a full report on what progress we have made. Progress, my left foot! These bastards at headquarters appear to have no other work to do.

They just sit on their fannies at their desks and dictate silly letters to some little bit of fluff they call their stenographer.

'But let us face the fact, Chandra my boy. We have absolutely no progress to report to them. Every week I pass the buck and write the same reply, but in different words: "Investigations are proceeding satisfactorily and we expect to be able to raid Man Singh's headquarters very shortly."

'But no raid takes place. Because it can't; for the childish reason that we don't know where the bugger's headquarters are.'

The D.I.G. was working himself up to a fine pitch of rage. His name was Sen Gupta, and he was a Bengali. One of the smartest officers in the Calcutta Police, he had been assigned to the special task of eliminating Man Singh and his dacoit bands, with 1700 policemen and officers under his command to achieve this result.

That result, however, had not materialised.

Sen Gupta was an intelligent man, and he was an officer who expected—and got—ruction from his subordinates. He drove them and lashed them with his tongue, till they did something about it.

His rather large head was covered with short, stiff hair, with no signs of grey in it despite his fifty years of age. It was the sort of hair that always refused to be combed or brushed, and so he left it alone. A close-clipped, black toothbrush moustache sat above his upper lip and added to his stern appearance. Grey-green eyes glittered from almost hairless eyebrows. A longish nose; thin, selfish lips; and a square, slightly protruding chin, combined with the moustache and bristly hair to give him decidedly formidable aspect.

Slightly above average height—he was exactly 5 foot 10½ inches—he was a heavily-built man who touched the scales at 200 pounds.

Above all, he was decidedly short-tempered, and when he became angry he would snort like a bull, breathe in gasps, and hammer his unfortunate desk or whatever article of furniture came within reach with the palms of his hands; and he would go on hammering, harder and harder.

He was doing that just now.

Almost idly, Chandra wondered as to which of the two were suffering more—the D.I.G's hands or the D.I.G's table.

Sen Gupta stopped gasping suddenly, and went on in a dry voice, selecting his words.

'Do you know, Chandra, when I was at school in Calcutta, my second language was Latin. God knows why they taught it and why I learnt it. I have forgotten the whole ruddy subject except for one phrase which stuck in my head. And for that one phrase I shall be always grateful to the language of the Caesars.

'The phrase is, "Faeces taurus sapientum sedit". And it means, "Bullshit baffles brains".

'And that is exactly what I have been doing in my reports all these weeks, Chandra my boy. Baffling the brains of these blighters at headquarters; that is, if they have any brains at all, which I doubt—with my bullshitting reports.

'But the game is played out and cannot go on any longer. Even the dimwits there have woken up to the fact that my weekly letters are just parrot-like repetitions and don't mean a damned thing.

'The people in New Delhi consider us the choicest set of nincompoops out of all the policemen in India. I don't know what the outside world thinks. But, if they have heard of what is going on, I, as the head of these operations, must be considered to be on a level of intelligence comparable with Donald Duck.'

Throughout the tirade, Chandra had not said a word. He had been through several of the sort before, and knew that if he dared to interrupt the Old Man would probably explode altogether, and burst a blood vessel and die.

So he wisely kept silent.

Sen Gupta went on and on in the same strain for a while. Chandra was thinking: What the hell! This fat bastard keeps yapping by the mile. Why doesn't the bugger get off his bottom and do something himself, instead of crying on my shoulder.

Chandra was a tall, lean man, and very dark. He came from the city of Madras, in southern India. Comparatively young—he was

35 years old—to hold the rank of a District Superintendent, he had put in meritorious service in his earlier years with the Madras Police among the criminal tribes of that State; and had also spent some time pursuing dacoits in the area around Bastar State and the central parts of the Godavari River where outlaws, although of a minor character, had operated for generations on end.

In fact, any police officer or policeman who had had some knowledge or experience in the pursuit of dacoits, or outlaws of any description, major or minor, throughout India, had been drafted into the special force that had been organised, and placed under Sen Gupta to liquidate Man Singh and his notorious followers.

Eventually the D.I.G. was silent. Having given vent to his emotions, he began to feel somewhat less pent-up. Just then, Chandra was saying, 'All you state is true, Sir. But what do you suggest be done?' It was a tactless question, put too soon after his recent outburst.

Sen Gupta bristled afresh.

'A damned silly question to ask, Chandra,' he said, shortly. 'Damned silly, indeed! That is exactly what I am asking you, man. So what the hell is the good of asking the same question back to me? Why, do something of course. You have a hell of a lot of men under you. Cross the Chambal River and comb out every ravine on the other side systematically. Rather simple when you come to think of it after all, what?'

Chandra grew angry beneath his dark skin, and his face took on a somewhat ashen hue. What the hell, he thought again; as if Man Singh and his gang will be sitting tamely on the other side, just waiting for us to come and catch him.

'I will have a shot at that, Sir,' was all he commented.

The Old Man had not even bothered to look up at his junior officer. He was staring at the new sheet of blotting paper on the pad before him.

Then he took up the pen on his desk, dipped it in ink, and drew a face roughly on the blotter. It was a face with an absurdly-long, twirling moustache and a huge beard.

Although he had drawn it himself, the face seemed to leer up at him, mockingly.

Sen Gupta jabbed the point of the nib at the drawing. The 'Relief' nib struck the paper and the point bent backwards. But the caricature appeared to smirk as much as before.

The D.I.G. flung the pen across his desk and yelled, 'Orderly! Idher haow! (Come here).'

A police constable marched into the office at a terrific rate; jerked himself to such an abrupt halt that his body leaned forward on its own two feet with the impetus of the speed he had been walking at, and saluted vigorously, the fingers of his right hand vibrating in the region of his temple.

'Bring 'cha,' ordered the D.I.G.; and then to Chandra, 'won't you have a cup of tea?' he invited.

'No thank you, Sir,' Chandra answered rather stiffly; and then, hesitatingly, 'if that is all, I will get back to my people and see what can be done.'

The D.I.G. nodded, absent-mindedly.

And thus the interview had ended. Chandra had clicked his heels and saluted before turning about and walking out of the D.I.G.'s large and airy office.

Sen Gupta had merely nodded again.

Now it was Saturday, and Chandra was sitting at another desk. This one belonged to the Inspector of Police stationed in the town of Bhind. The Inspector's office itself was an annex to the Police Station. Overhead the punkah (long fan made of plaited tatty or cuscus roots) swayed to and fro at a regular rhythm, pulled by means of a rope passing through a hole in the front wall and over a pulley. The 'operator' squatted on the verandah outside. He was an almost naked cooly.

As a token of deference towards his senior officer, the Inspector had surrendered his own chair to Chandra, who now sat on it at the Inspector's table. The latter sat on another wooden-bottomed chair opposite the D.S.P. at the other end of the table. Chandra had been telling him of the interview he had had with the D.I.G., and had closed his account with the assertion that really something had got to be done about it.

The Inspector was anxious to appear cooperative and efficient. But he had been in the district longer than Chandra and longer than the D.I.G., and knew the problems involved. He was a Rajput named Gulab Singh, who had served in the Army and been transferred to the Police, subsequently. Some 45 years of age, wizened in look and wearing the usual Rajput whiskers and beard, he was as tough as nails. Many a time previous to the advent of his two present officers, he had accompanied punitive expeditions of police across the Chambal to try to search the ravines. From every one of those sorties they had returned empty-handed, and from not a few with less policemen than had set out. Some of these policemen had been shot by snipers hiding behind boulders or in caves or among the cliffs with which the ravines abounded. At other times the whole, party had been ambushed and many killed before they were even aware of danger. So, the D.S.P.'s anxiety for action and the D.I.G.'s impatient annoyance did not succeed in arousing much enthusiasm in Gulab Singh, the Inspector.

'Huzoor,' he told Chandra in Hindi, 'there is a proverb which says, "The foolish clamour for deeds and sometimes wise men suffer thereby". To enter among the ravines with a large number of men by day is quite futile. If the police force is big, the dacoits just vanish. If it is small, we will be fired upon and some of us killed. I have seen it happen over and over again, many times.'

Chandra did not reply. He was thinking deeply. What the Inspector had just said was quite true, and he had to admit it in spite of the D.I.G's impatience. To take a body of policemen across the Chambal in broad daylight would produce no result whatever. Either they would see nobody all that day, or they would be shot at, unexpectedly.

Nevertheless, something just had to be done.

So the D.S.P. continued to think, and the Inspector continued to regard him stonily, lost in his own meditation.

Suddenly Chandra stiffened involuntarily. An idea had come to him. A good idea. The more he thought about it, the more he liked it. A slight smile played about the corners of his mouth.

'Inspector Sahib,' he spoke with deliberation. 'You have said that it was futile to take a force across the river and into the ravines at daytime as the outlaws would see us coming?'

'That is so, huzoor,' replied Gulab Singh, patiently.

'Then what if we take them across secretly at the dead of night and hide the other side during the day?' The Inspector's eyes opened a little wider in astonishment. What silly scheme is this, he wondered. 'Man Singh's spies are everywhere, Sir. The river is watched at night. They would see us crossing.'

'Not necessarily, Inspector, not necessary,' continued Chandra, indulgently. 'We would choose a dark night for the undertaking; and a time when nearly all men are asleep, including the sentries of friend and foe alike.' Here Chandra smiled very confidingly, as if to indicate to his subordinate that he knew all about the vagaries of sentries all the world over.

Gulab Singh did not reply.

'Please hand me that wall calendar, Gulab Singh,' continued Chandra after a while, 'and please fetch the large map of the area that has been issued to all police stations and chowkies and should be hanging on the wall. Where is it?'

'Here Sahib,' said the Rajput, rising from his chair and walking across the room to an ancient wooden almirah standing in the corner. He unhooked the front latch and the door of the almirah swung crazily open. Chandra heard the hinges squeak, even at that distance.

Reaching his hand up, Gulab Singh felt along the topmost shelf and brought down a roll of paper, almost a yard long.

He took it to the desk, removed the pen-rack and ink bottle that stood there, placing them on the window sill, and put the roll of paper before Chandra. It was the map.

Chandra unrolled it.

The edges began to curl up again. The Inspector noticed this. He walked back to the window and returned with the pen-rack and ink bottle, placing the former on top of the left-hand edge, and the ink bottle on the right edge of the map. The two bottom corners he prevented from rolling themselves up by the simple expedient of opening the desk top slightly, pushing the bottom edge of the map inside, and then reclosing the top.

For there was no paperweight in his office.

The Inspector then walked across the room, removed the large calendar hanging by a nail on the wall opposite to his desk, and placed it on the map before the D.S.P.

Chandra studied the calendar in silence, while Gulab Singh sat down again on the wooden chair opposite him and relapsed into thought.

It was the 10th of the month. The new moon would be on the 15th.

'How many policemen have we stationed near the river who could be moved under cover of darkness, quickly?' he asked.

The Inspector considered the question for a few seconds.

'There are twenty-four armed constables, two sergeants, and a Sub-Inspector at Raoti,' he answered, 'and it is four and a half miles from the river.'

'Hmmm,' mused Chandra. And then, 'That's all?'

Before Gulab Singh could answer, he continued, 'Not much; but still, not too few. They will have to do the job. To march more men, either in the daytime or at night, would give the whole show away. People would know something is afoot and that the police were making a move of some kind. Man Singh would be informed.'

'And what arms have these twenty-seven men got?' he next inquired.

'As you know, huzoor, all the police squads in this area are specially trained men. They are either of ex-army stock, or come from the Armed Reserve. And every detachment is accompanied by an automatic weapon unit, with two tommy guns. The rest of the men will have service rifles; and of course the Sub-Inspector will have his revolver.'

Chandra could not help smiling at the meticulous reply furnished by his subordinate.

'And can we get boats to cross the river without telling the owners in advance, or asking their permission? That is most important, Inspector Sahib. As you know, this badmash (bad man) has his agents everywhere; I have no doubt even among the boatmen. They would inform him if they had the slightest hint as to our movements.'

Gulab Singh thought again. Then he said, 'There will be two or three small boats always tied up at a place called Kenchen. It is a point half-a-mile upstream. The river takes a bend there and becomes narrower. You will see it if you look at the map, Sir.'

Chandra began to study the map on the desk before him.

Then the Inspector added, 'But they are small boats, huzoor, and might hold ten men at the most—certainly not twenty-seven.'

'How many boats are kept there normally?' asked Chandra.

'Maybe two or three,' said the Inspector. 'I can find out exactly, if your honour wishes.'

'Tch!—don't do that,' Chandra replied, testily. 'Your inquiries would probably excite suspicion. We will have to chance our luck. If there are less than three boats, we will have to come back for the men who are left behind. And there won't be only twenty-seven men, Gulab Singh,' he continued, meaningly, 'there will be twenty-nine. For you and I are going on this little jaunt. I intend to see this thing through, myself.'

There was another silence as Chandra looked alternately at the map and at the calendar.

'Today is Saturday, the 10th,' he mused aloud. 'We have five days to go before the new moon which will be on Thursday, the 15th, according to the calendar. So we must act on the 12th, 13th or 14th, eh. The Old Man wants action soon. In fact, the sooner the better.

'Suppose we fix Monday the 12th?' he queried, looking up at his subordinate as if expecting a reply.

'What is in your mind, Sir?' asked the Inspector, innocently.

A look of annoyance flitted across Chandra's countenance momentarily. Then he remembered he had been thinking and talking to himself and not to Gulab Singh. So he started to elaborate on his plan aloud.

'Now listen attentively, Inspector. Nobody should be told in advance about this move, do you understand? Not even the Sub-Inspector and the policemen who are to accompany us. Their tongues might wag and the information leak out. If that happens, the expedition is doomed to failure. Worse still, we might be ambushed,' and he looked up meaningly. 'Therefore, only you and I, and no other living soul, knows about this.'

'Now tomorrow, which is Sunday the 11th, you and I will start on a tour of inspection of all out posts in this area. It will be just a regular inspection and nothing else. But we will call it a 'surprise check'. We shall arrange to reach Raoti somewhat late on the afternoon of Monday the 12th. There, we will carry out a rather thorough inspection. We will check the men, their equipment, their camp, their uniforms, and even inquire into the quality of the rations they are being given to eat.

'We will do all this leisurely. I will be exceptionally strict and ask a dozen questions. You do the same. Between us, we will make it too late to push on to the next outpost that evening.

'So I shall call the Sub-Inspector, berate him for the several faults I have managed to unearth, and blame him for being the cause of detaining us. I shall say to him something like this, 'Sub-Inspector, because of all these things that I have found, it has become too late for the Inspector and me to move on tonight. Due to you, and you alone, we must stay here till morning. So, pitch a tent which the Inspector and I will share tonight. And prepare dinner, for we are hungry. And don't forget to wake us up at crack of dawn tomorrow. We must be on our way before sunrise.

'Having said all this to discomfort that unfortunate officer, we will have dinner and retire early.

'But not to sleep, Inspector.

'At exactly midnight, I shall call you. You, in turn, will awaken the S.I. and bring him to our tent. Then, and only then, shall I acquaint him with what is to happen.

'By two o'clock we should have the men ready, with arms and ammunition, and prepare to move.

'The problem of preparing and taking food with us for the next three days is decidedly ticklish, Gulab Singh. I mean the three days for which I plan the expedition to last. We dare not tell the camp cook overnight to prepare chappatties. His activities would excite suspicion and he may talk. We could chance it that there might be something in the eating-line ready in the kitchen. But it would be quite insufficient for one thing; and knowing these cooks as I do, I doubt there would be any eatables on hand. You must bear in mind that the men will have to hide in the ravines all the next day and move again at night. And continue doing this for the following two days.

'Yes, this question of food is one hell of a problem, Inspector. Does any solution occur to you?'

Gulab Singh racked his brain. After some minutes, he said, 'There appears but one way out, Sir. We shall have to get the police cooks here, at Bhind, to start preparing chappatties right away—hundreds of them. Sufficient for twenty-nine men for three days. These chappatties we will have to take along with us in the back of the jeep when we set out tomorrow. We shall have to keep them hidden in the jeep till the last moment and then distribute them among the men to put into their haversacks before we actually set forth to cross the river.

'The chappatties will become stale, Sahib, and be as hard as tinplates. The men will be mutinous and probably chuck them away rather than eat what will seem like cardboard, after three days.

'You will surely turn into the most unpopular D.S.P. in the whole of India after that.' Gulab Singh could not restrain himself from uttering this last sentence with a mirthless laugh.

'I know, Inspector Sahib,' admitted Chandra, speaking earnestly, 'yours is an excellent suggestion and incidentally the only solution to the problem, for which I am grateful. Unfortunately, we Indians don't like tinned rations.

'But don't worry,' he went on to add, 'I shall give the men a short pep talk before we actually set out, explaining that it was impossible to have done anything else if we wanted to observe complete secrecy. I shall also promise double promotion to each man, and the equal division of the reward of fifteen thousand rupees which is going begging for the apprehension of this Man Singh, among the twenty-eight of you people.'

Gulab Singh acknowledged the implication in his superior officer's last statement with a slight nod of his wizened head and a flitting smile.

'How many chappatties are the cooks to prepare, Sahib?' he asked, instead.

'I intend to eat the same as the rest of you', replied Chandra. 'Let us do some mental arithmetic, then. Twenty-nine men, for three days, at, say ten chappatties a day for all meals. What does that work out to?'

He did some silent calculation.

'Eight hundred and seventy chappatties; my God! Do you think the cooks could prepare that much here in the short time left to them? They will have to work like hell; and all night.'

'Surely, Sahib; and the sooner we start them off, the better. Are there any more instructions your honour wishes to give before I go along and set the cooks to work?'

'Let me think a minute,' said Chandra, slowly. 'The general idea is to cross the Chambal that night; hide ourselves in the ravines next day while keeping a sharp lookout for any of the dacoits on the move; creep forward again the following night and hide once more the next day; and repeat the same thing on the third day.

'By then, if our luck is any good, we may stumble upon something or someone. Even if we do not succeed in finding their headquarters, should we capture one of them we might be able to bribe him—or, if necessary, force him to lead us to where this Man Singh himself hides out.

'But we won't be able to stay for more than three days I suppose, with those chappatties becoming drier each day, Oh,' and he looked up, remembering something, 'don't forget to make the men fill their water bottles before we start. They will certainly be needed. In fact, we may run short of water.'

Chandra stopped talking and mopped the perspiration that was streaming down his face with his handkerchief.

'Damned hellhole!' he muttered darkly, 'if it is like this now, what must we have to endure when summer comes? I wish to God I had never been sent to this bloody place.'

It was, indeed, oppressively hot.

Gulab Singh himself had suddenly found the room very sultry. Then he noticed that the punkah above their heads had stopped moving.

'The punkah has stopped, huzoor,' he explained, 'the wretched cooly must have fallen asleep.'

Both men walked out on to the verandah. The punkah-cooly, dressed only in a loincloth about his waist, was curled up on the bare stone floor, sound asleep.

'Wake up, you swine!' said Chandra, prodding the recumbent figure with the toe of his boot. 'Is this the way in which you do your job?'

The man sat up and blinked his eyes against the glare of the sun outside.

'Balah,' admonished Gulab Singh, 'I have warned you many times before not to sleep at your post. I shall fine you eight annas for this.'

The cooly seized the end of the punkah rope in both his hands and started pulling it for all he was worth. There was an expression of injured innocence on his face. The pulley creaked with the movement, and the punkah swayed jerkily.

The chappatties took till noon next day to complete. Gulab Singh wrapped them in pages of newspaper, which in turn were packed into tarpaulin groundsheets and then tied up.

It took three such small tarpaulin sheets to hold the lot, and filled the rear seat of the jeep to capacity.

The D.S.P. and he then set out on their inspection tour. It was nearly two o'clock by the time they left.

They inspected two outposts that evening, camped the night in a Travellers' Bungalow, and continued their inspection the following morning, which was Monday, the 12th.

Three more units were checked. Then followed Monday's midday meal. It was 3.30 p.m. exactly when the jeep came to a halt at Raoti.

The Sub-Inspector in charge of the police unit turned out of his tent, half-dressed, to greet his superior officers. The visit had been entirely a surprise.

'Good afternoon, Sub-Inspector,' greeted Chandra in his most official manner, 'I have come on a surprise check. Get yourself dressed, and the men. I shall give you ten minutes.'

'But I received no intimation that your honour was coming,' complained the S.I., indignation and apprehension vying each other, plainly, in the expression on his face.

'Exactly,' answered Chandra curtly, 'that is what I meant when I said "surprise check" just now. So, hurry up.'

Gulab Singh turned aside to hide the smile that he could hardly suppress. The Sub-Inspector's obvious discomfiture at their sudden visit, was almost pathetic.

Ten minutes later the men had fallen in in three ranks with their rifles. The Sub-Inspector stood before them.

'Squad, "shun!" he ordered.

The policemen sprang to attention.

Then, 'Slope arms!'; and finally;

'Present arms!'

The D.S.P. returned the salute and made the appropriate approach by walking up to the paraded men; Inspector Gulab Singh following in his rear.

The Sub-Inspector saluted, and Chandra returned the salute.

'All right, Sub-Inspector', he ordered, 'I will now inspect the men.'

'Squad, slope arms!'

The men sloped arms, and Chandra began walking down the front rank. Behind him followed Gulab Singh; and behind him again, the Sub-Inspector.

Under such conditions, it was not difficult for a martinet to find fault. And Chandra proved himself to be a real martinet, that day.

'When did you last polish your buttons?' he asked one constable.

'Whose uniform are you wearing? It is much too big for you.'

'Boots are meant to be polished. Do you ever do that?'

The rear ranks fared even worse.

When the parade had finally been dismissed, Chandra held an armoury inspection, a kit inspection, a tent inspection, and finally a ration check.

It was after five o'clock when he had at last got through. The unfortunate Sub-Inspector had been wishing for the past hour or so that the earth would open suddenly and swallow him up; or, better still, that this bastard of a D.S.P, would drop dead.

But neither eventuality happened.

'A very poor show; very poor, indeed,' said Chandra, pursing his lips and looking witheringly at the exhausted S.I. 'That is why I always conduct surprise checks. They show up faults that would never otherwise come to light.'

The tired S.I. did not comment.

Chandra then looked at his watch and allowed his countenance to register alarm. He shook his wrist and then held the watch to his ear.

'Great Heavens,' he exclaimed, aghast, 'my watch shows a quarter-past five o'clock! Is that right, Inspector?'

Gulab Singh made a show of consulting his wristwatch in turn. Then he said plainly, 'That time is correct, huzoor. The inspection has, indeed, taken very long.'

'I should bloody well think it would,' retorted Chandra, quickly, 'with everything wrong or improper in some form or the other.'

Then he turned to the S.I., and glared at him.

'Sub-Inspector Tulak Ram', he spoke, acidly, 'it has become too late for me to move on tonight, because of all this delay; and you are responsible for it, entirely.

'Have a tent pitched. The Inspector and I will share it. And prepare khana (food) for both of us. We will rest here and move on tomorrow at dawn. Call me without fail at five o'clock.'

If the S.I. had looked disconsolate before, his face was now a study in dismay.

My God, he was thinking, is this accursed man going to stay here all tonight?

'Well?' Chandra's question broke in, icily, upon his thoughts.

Tulak Ram struggled manfully to recover his composure.

At last he said, 'There is no spare tent,' adding hastily, 'but you will flatter me, Sir, if you and the Inspector would be pleased to occupy mine. I will sleep with the sargeants tonight. And khana shall certainly be prepared.'

It took hardly ten minutes for the S.I. to remove his belongings from his tent. Gulab Singh drove the jeep up and parked it near the entrance so that nobody would nose around and wonder what the tarpaulins at the rear might contain. Then he entered the tent, after Chandra.

'Poor devil,' the latter was saying in an undertone, 'he must be hating me, like hell.'

'I have no doubt he is wishing your honour was dead,' commented Gulab Singh in a matter-of-fact voice.

And they both laughed.

Dinner was served in the tent punctually at eight o'clock.

Half-an-hour later, Tulak Ram dutifully presented himself at the entrance.

'A hot bath has been prepared and is ready for both of you, Sirs,' he announced, 'may I instruct my orderly to bring it to the bathroom at the rear?'

'Thank you,' said Chandra gracefully, 'that was thoughtful and kind of you, Tulak Ram, but I hope the water in these parts is clear.'

The S.I. did not acknowledge the thanks with even a smile; while the look he gave the D.S.P. was distinctly hostile.

They both bathed, in succession.

Soon after nine o'clock, the S.I. came again and inquired if there was anything more they wanted. Chandra said, 'No, thanks.'

At 10 p.m. the police bugler sounded the 'Last Post' and the camp fell into darkness.

There was only a single camp cot—the Sub-Inspector's—in the tent, on which Chandra lay down. A rope charpoy borrowed from one of the sergeants, had been provided for the Inspector.

'Take a nap, Gulab Singh,' Chandra whispered across to his companion on the other charpoy. 'I am not feeling sleepy. I shall call you at midnight.'

The Inspector was tired and fell asleep almost at once. It seemed to him hardly five minutes later when he felt a hand shaking him by the shoulder.

He opened his eyes. It was pitch-dark. Then he remembered where he was. Standing over him he could feel somebody shaking him; gently but persistently.

It was Chandra, and he was saying, 'Gulab Singh, wake up; it is ten minutes to twelve o'clock.'

The Inspector sat up on the charpoy, yawned, and stretched both arms above his head.

'Now go to the other tent and fetch the S.I. And as you are about it, you might as well call the two sergeants who are sleeping with him. I will outline the plan to the three of them when they get here.'

Gulab Singh got up from the charpoy. He slipped his feet into his boots for fear of treading on a cobra or saw-scaled viper in the darkness, but did not lace them. Then he left the tent.

He walked across the few yards that separated them from the neighbouring tent occupied by the sergeants where he knew Tulak Ram was sleeping, entered, took out his matchbox from the breast pocket of his khaki tunic, and struck a match.

He could make out a figure sleeping on a charpoy. Two others lay on the floor.

The man on the charpoy appeared to be having a nightmare. He was muttering incoherently in a high-pitched key. Gulab Singh thought he recognised the S.I.'s voice.

Probably he was dreaming of some demon, with the face of the D.S.P. hotly pursuing him. Gulab Singh smiled to himself at the thought.

The match he held between his fingers commenced to burn him. He threw it down, struck another, and approached the dreamer.

The flickering light revealed that he had been correct. It was indeed Tulak Ram. And he was undoubtedly having a nightmare.

And then the second match went out.

Gulab Singh reached downwards and shook the S.I. gently. It took some minutes to wake him up.

Then the Inspector struck a third match and whispered to the astonished Tulak Ram that the D.S.P. wanted him and the two sergeants to come to his tent immediately.

The S.I. could contain his indignation no longer. He muttered aloud, 'What! In the middle of the night! Can't the bugger even sleep? This is unendurable. I shall tell this bugger tomorrow morning that he can stick this job where the monkey stuck the plum. I'm resigning; first thing in the morning.'

Gulab Singh chuckled aloud.

'Okay; okay,' he spoke soothingly; 'but see what he wants, first. Maybe you will change your mind after that.'

'No bloody fears,' retorted the S.I., now thoroughly exasperated, 'this D.S.P. is the kind of feller I would like to meet on a dark night on a lonely road. He won't be fit after that, in a hurry, for any more of his blasted surprise checks. Damn his bloody eyes!'

But he got up, and woke both the sergeants, one after the other.

The four of them trooped across to the D.S.P.'s tent in a bunch. The lantern had been lighted and was burning dimly.

They found Chandra seated on the edge of the camp cot awaiting them. Tulak Ram made a mental note of the fact that the wooden rod of his camp cot, upon which the D.S.P. was sitting, was actually bending under his weight and in momentary danger of breaking in two. Would this pig pay for it if it snapped? Assuredly not. Beneath his breath he cursed the officer afresh.

He also saluted, half-heartedly.

'Be seated, boys,' Chandra spoke affably, 'you may smoke if you wish while I let you into a little secret.'

Look at this blighter, Tulak Ram was thinking to himself. He sends the Inspector in the middle of the night to wake and call me, and then has the nerve to tell us to smoke if we want. Who the hell thought of bringing cigarettes, anyhow?

As if he was able to divine the hostile thoughts that flowed from his subordinate, Chandra stuck his hand into the pocket of his bush-coat and fished out a packet of Gold Flake cigarettes, followed by a round, nickel-plated army lighter, and offered them to his subordinates in turn.

They each took a cigarette. Chandra helped himself also. Then the lighter was passed from hand to hand, and within a minute the narrow confines of the tent was filled with the haze of tobacco smoke.

The secret is just this. My visit of inspection last afternoon was no inspection at all. It was only done to provide an excuse for my coming here late in the afternoon, and for remaining overnight with you.

'Particularly to you. Sub Inspector Tulak Ram, do I owe an apology for my churlish behaviour all afternoon. But I had to make it appear that everything was wrong in the camp in order to delay my inspection to the point that it grew too late to depart and I would be forced to spend the night here. Actually, Tulak Ram, you have a fine show here and have organised matters very creditably. I shall make a report to this effect just as soon as I get back to headquarters.

'The D.I.G. is raising hell about this Man Singh feller because he is still at large and we cannot catch him.

'So, as soon as I am through outlining details of the plan to you now, we will silently awaken the men, issue arms and ammunition, and start off on an expedition which is to last for three days.

'We will go down to the Chambal River and cross it in boats which, the Inspector tells me, will be moored at the point where the river takes a bend—Kenchen, is it not, Gulab Singh?'

The Inspector nodded his head in the dim light and Chandra went on.

'We will cross very silently and penetrate as far as possible into the ravines. But at the first indication of dawn we shall hide ourselves in some ravine or cave. Before that, we will post a couple of men to watch carefully during the hours of daylight that follow.

'Without being seen themselves, they should keep a careful lookout for bands of dacoits moving in any direction or towards any particular place.

'Our whole purpose is to try to discover the lair where this Man Singh character hides out, make a lightning raid on it, and capture or kill him.

'If nothing happens that first day, we will advance again a little farther in among the ravines the second night and hide once more when daylight comes. And so also for the third night and day.

'If we have seen no one, or captured nobody during those three days, we will return on the fourth night. Secrecy won't much matter then. When we reach the river we will have to swim two or three of our men across to return with the boats.

'That is the scheme, in general.

'There are some details which we must now go into.

'The first is this. After we have all crossed tonight, two or three men must go back with the boats. It will not do for the owners, next morning to find that their boats have mysteriously crossed the river during the night. They will raise an alarm which might get to Man Singh's ears, and he will be astute enough to know a police party had effected a crossing.

'This is a point we completely overlooked hitherto, Inspector,' added Chandra, addressing Gulab Singh. 'Since you said a boat would not hold more than ten men, we shall need three boats, and that will require three men to bring them back to the mooring place. And we cannot afford to delay on the further bank waiting for the three men to swim back to us. So our party won't be twenty-nine strong as we thought originally, but will only have twenty-six men.

Turning to the Sub-Inspector, he continued. 'It was not advisable, for reasons of security, to inform you in advance, Tulak Ram. The same holds good as regards the preparation and taking of food with us. So the Inspector and I have brought 870 chappaties, prepared by the police cooks at Bhind, along with us which you will find stored at the back of the jeep. This is the ration for the full three days and was to be divided among the twenty-nine of us. Now that there will be only twenty-six, we will have a couple more of them to go round.

'I know that they will be very stale and very dry, by the third day. But that cannot be helped.

'However; I can assure you of this, Sub-Inspector. If we succeed in capturing or killing Man Singh within the next three days, every man jack of us will receive a double promotion. Also, I will see to it that the reward of Rs. 15,000 that stands for the arrest of Man Singh or the surrender of his dead body, is evenly distributed among the twenty-eight of you.

'Now, Tulak Ram. You must first pick out the three men who are to bring back the boats tonight. And also ensure that there are three good swimmers amongst the other twenty-three, for those three men will have to swim across to fetch the boats to us for our return journey.

'Distribute arms, and at least 100 rounds of ammunition each, to the men who are to cross, including the tommy gun unit who must have ample reserves. Inspector Gulab Singh will give you the chappaties, which should be issued thirty-three to a man. And everybody should carry a full water bottle. That is very, very important.

'No noise is to be made in waking the men—no talking—no explanations—no lights—and the least possible delay.

'It is now past 12.30 a.m.,' Chandra said, consulting the dial of his wristwatch. The men must fall in and be ready to march, fully equipped, by two o'clock. The three men who bring back the boats will come back to the camp and assist the permanent chowkidar to look after the things that are here till the expedition returns.

'I will address the men briefly for a few minutes and explain what is afoot before we start off,' Chandra added, 'by 2.05 a.m., on the dot, we must move, Sub-Inspector. So go to it at once; and you, Gulab Singh, please help him.'

It was past 2.10 a.m., however, before the D.S.P., had finished addressing the assembled constables in an undertone and explaining the whole plan to them.

They moved off after that in single file, to minimise making a noise, each man walking close behind the one in front of him.

The Sub-Inspector led, as he knew the way. Then followed the D.S.P., the Inspector, and the two tommy gunners with one of the sergeants. After that the twenty-two constables were strung out, including the three men who were to return with the empty boats. The remaining sergeants brought up the rear.

They moved diagonally cross-country in the direction of their embarking point at Kenchen, rather than make directly for the river.

After about an hour's walking, they came to a footpath that, Tulak Ram whispered, led from the village of Raoti, some five miles away, to the very point of crossing, at Kenchen, for which they were making. Progress was a bit easier after that, and more silent.

Not twenty minutes later the S.I. halted them, and then crept forward himself silently to the landing stage, to ascertain how many boats were actually moored there, and if anyone was watching them.

Ten minutes after that he was back with the good news that five small boats, in all, were moored to the bank, and that not a soul was with them. A glowing tribute, indeed, to the absolute trust and regard that existed between the owners and Man Singh and his followers.

Chandra congratulated himself on the extreme precautions he had taken to keep the whole expedition a secret—down to the ridiculous point of preparing 870 chappaties in advance and having to cart them along with him from Bhind.

What chance would there have been otherwise, when such feelings of good-fellowship existed between the local folk and this crafty gangster? They would assuredly have conveyed to him every single move made by the police party if they had come to know of it. Small wonder previous expeditions had failed, or ended in disaster! No doubt the officers who had planned them had not attended to such small details personally and as closely as he had. Not taken such infinite pains to keep their movements a secret till literally the very last moment.

The Old Man would be very pleased with him, Chandra thought. And Chandra was very pleased with himself.

The party approached the moored boats.

All five of the craft were identical in construction and capacity. Just ordinary river boats crudely made from cut planks put together almost anyhow. And they certainly would not hold more than ten men in each.

Three of the boats were untied and pushed into the water, and the three men who were to pole them back were assigned accordingly, one to each boat.

Then the three police officers, one sergeant, the two tommy gunners and three constables got into the craft which was to cross first; nine constables got into the second boat; and the remaining sergeant and seven men into the third boat.

In that order they commenced crossing the river, each boat being poled along silently by means of the long bamboo with which it was equipped. Less than ten yards separated the craft from each other.

It was very very dark, and the water looked black and forbidding.

They were within perhaps twenty yards of the opposite bank when it happened, swiftly and all of a sudden without any warning whatever.

As if from they very depths of the river itself, a giant octopus seemed to reach up and seize each craft on its port side, with many tentacles.

And that was the side from which the current was flowing.

At least, that is what it appeared was happening, as Chandra watched for a split second while the boat he was in heeled over dangerously to the left.

As the gunwale of the boat on that side was forced still closer to the river's surface, the mystery of the apparent octopus was explained.

The tentacles that had come out of the water and had looked so black were human arms. As the boat canted still closer to the water human heads came into view, bobbing out of the river in a line—about twenty of them to each boat, at least.

There were men in the water. And they were all pulling upon the sides of each of the boats—and on the same side, to port. The boats would capsize in a second or two.

One word rang in the D.S.P.'s brain—it was 'Dacoits'!

Hastily, Chandra grabbed his revolver from its holster and fired at point-blank range at one of those heads. The head disappeared beneath the surface of the river.

And simultaneously the boat he was in turned over and they were thrown into the water.

Of what exactly happened after that, Chandra had little clear recollection.

He heard yells of pain and curses of rage all around him. The water churned and frothed with intense activity. He caught glimpses of steel as knives flashed aloft and screams of agony followed when they descended. There came the dull thud of blows being administered and the sickening crack of human skulls.

Something heavy descended on his head with terrific force, and he remembered no more.

It was broad daylight when Chandra regained consciousness. There was an acute pain at the back of his skull. He tried to raise his hands to discover what was wrong, but found he could not, for both hands were tied behind him.

He was alone and there was no sign of any of his companions.

Chandra looked about him. He was lying under a glade of trees beneath which tents had been pitched. Men were sitting in groups beside them, talking. Around him, in a circle, appeared a continuous ridge of rocky cliffs and boulder-strewn hillocks.

Then a voice rang out.

'Look brothers; the policeman is awake.'

A group of men surrounded him, and he at once knew them for what they were.

Dacoits of Man Singh's band.

As he gazed at them, their circle at one end broke and two men strode forward.

The first was an outstanding figure. He was an old man with a high forehead. He had a flowing beard, whiskers and huge moustache.

Often enough had Chandra read that description of its owner upon whom he was now gazing—and over and over again had he studied and memorized it. He knew he was face to face with the redoubtable Rajah Man Singh, himself.

The other man who walked behind the leader was carrying an army-model tommy gun in the crook of his right arm. There was nothing outstanding about this second man, beyond the fact that he scowled fiercely down at the police officer.

'Salaam, D.S.P. Sahib,' greeted Man Singh in his musical voice. 'You wanted so much to see me, and here I am.

'Incidentally, Sahib, you are the second policeman to ever reach my secret hiding place. I congratulate you both; you are brave men.

'The first died; shot, whether you care to believe me or not, by a policeman himself and not by one of my men. Of course it was an accident. But I came to like that man. His name was Katar Singh, an Inspector in the C.I.D.

'Now, you too must die, Sahib; and in your case you will have to be shot by one of my followers. For it is forbidden for a policeman to look upon my secret headquarters, and live.

'But, because you are an officer and a brave man who did his duty well, you shall not be tortured, Sahib. You will be killed outright. After all, each one of us must die at some time or the other, and my own turn will follow when it has been appointed to take place. You merely go before me, Sahib; that is all.

'Before you go, I will let you into a secret. Your plans were perfect, and no doubt you must be wondering how we came to learn of them in advance and were able to ambush you.'

Then Man Singh turned, and called aloud twice, 'Balah! Balah!'

A little individual broke through the group of encircling men and advanced timidly. He wore a dirty cotton waist cloth and was bare-bodied.

Gazing down upon the D.S.P., he salaamed respectfully.

It was Balah, the punkah cooly, who had stopped pulling the punkah because they thought he had fallen asleep.

As if to clarify any doubt, the almost naked small man said, 'That's why I couldn't pull the punkah, Sahib; because I was at the door, listening.'

Chandra mused—so, his spies are stationed at police Inspector's offices—perhaps there is one even near the D.I.G.!

But further cogitation was interrupted by a short burst of fire from the tommy gun in the hands of the bodyguard who had accompanied Man Singh.

And Chandra never knew the answer to his thoughts.

Chapter Five

The Rich Landlord and the Poor Maiden

Lalita was her name; and it is a beautiful name, no matter in what language it may be spoken. Lalita was a Hindu girl, and she was as pretty as her name.

She was only sixteen years old. But girls mature early in India due to the climate, often at the age of 11 years. (Their parents seek a mate for them then, entering into protracted negotiations with the father and mother of the prospective bridegroom. The boy and girl concerned have themselves nothing whatever to do with it. Their consent is not asked, or taken. They have only to obey their respective parents' behests in the matter of matrimony, and the choice of a mate for them.

The boy who rebels against this custom is ignominiously turned out of the home and becomes an outcaste from his family forever. The girl who offers objection is in still worse plight. Frequently, she is beaten into submission.)

Despite the apparent disadvantage of this system, it also brings its own benefits. Flirtations and promiscuous love between boy and girl is rarely known. The type of woman available to any man for sex before his marriage, and even thereafter, if it should to that, other than his legal wife, is the professional prostitute. And this last type of women are very few in compared to the population of women as a whole and the total population of the land.

Secondly, it ensures that a husband has a virgin for a wife on his wedding night. This is something that is often uncertain in other lands.

The Indian wife who, on her honeymoon night, is found to be unchaste, is invariably turned out by her husband the following morning.

Thirdly, the parents on both sides, in the interests of their respective offspring, aim to procure the best possible partner for their daughter—or son—available the circumstances as regards social status, respectability financial background, personal appearances, education general abilities.

Fourthly, the couple when married, realising the tremendous amount of effort, search and negotiation that went into the arrangements before their marriage become a fait accompli, invariably make the best of circumstances, prompted by the fear of offending parents and the remaining members of both the families should they behave otherwise, and mutually strive to make the marriage a success.

Separations and desertions are very rare, and divorces practically unknown.

Unfortunately, in Western countries with their complete freedom of individual thought and action, it is very different; and broken homes are becoming an increasingly common feature.

Another factor that appears to act very powerfully keeping the home together in India, is that the husband is accepted as complete master of the household, and wife is subservient to his wishes and command. The emancipation of women has not become the menace it might well prove to be when they get over-emancipated! Very rarely, indeed, is an Indian housewife to be found who dares to act differently to her husband's ideas and injunctions.

No doubt Western readers, particularly of the fair sex, who may scan these lines, will hold up their hands in horror and express their unstinted disagreement with and disapproval of these Indian customs. Please remember, fair ladies, I am just telling you about things as they are in India, and am not entering into any argument with you about the right or wrong, fairness or otherwise, of these practices. So, please don't quarrel with me over it. You are entitled to your opinion and the Indians to theirs. For the matter of that, so am I to mine. But you would not be interested, anyhow, in the latter.

THE RICH LANDLORD AND THE POOR MAIDEN

Let no one think that the negotiations undertaken by a girl's—or a boy's—parents, in seeking a mate for their child, are simple and easy. Very very far from it on the contrary. There are so many things to be considered.

The girl's parents have to prepare themselves to bestow a gift of money, jewellery, or land in the form of a dowry, with their daughter. It is not very hard for you to imagine that, the greater the dowry the more eligible must the bridegroom, whose parents are attracted by it, qualify himself to be. If the boy is in Government service, it carries a very high degree of desirability to procure him as a husband and son-in-law. For one thing, he will draw a pension for his lifetime when he retires at the age of 55 years. For another, he cannot be sacked or retrenched. Dismissal from Government service only arises under two contingencies. The first of these is dishonesty. Under this heading may be clubbed embezzlement, robbery, the acceptance of bribes and other financial chicanery. The second is the commitment of physical assault, with violence. For instance, a Government servant may be sacked if he should hit the boss, or his co-worker, over the head with the office stool. Even then the constitution of the country, which seeks to protect the underdog from exploitation in any form, provides an elaborate system of chargesheeting, and the opportunity for explanation, and so forth. The offender, with some astuteness, still has chances to go free if he can prove the boss fell on the stool, and not the stool on the boss. So, a Government servant for a bridegroom, is indeed a marvellous 'catch'.

But should such a prize not be readily available, the next best substitute is sought in the person of the son of some rich man who is in business, or owns houses or land.

Another all-important factor in selecting a suitable partner is that of caste. Both husband and wife should invariably belong to the same community and caste. This is a very practical outlook, for a wife of higher caste would look down on her husband, and vice versa.

Then comes the horoscope. The exact moment of the birth of each Indian child, be it boy or girl, is very carefully and accurately recorded. According to the time, day and month of birth, professional experts cast a 'horoscope' in keeping with the principles and precepts of Indian Astrology. The planets are said to influence every moment of that child's lifetime, from birth to death. His or her lucky days are foretold; the whole future carefully forecast and recorded. This practice is followed in the case of every baby; boy or girl; of all except the very poorest classes.

Now it is not difficult to realise that the horoscopes of the pair to be married should agree, for it would never do to unite a couple whose 'bad' and 'good' days were different. Indeed, it would be absolutely disastrous for a wife's stars to be in the ascendant at the very time those of her spouse were on the wane, would it not? The Indians are, indeed, a practical people!

On the boy's side; apart from trying to procure a bride who brings with her the maximum dowry in cash or kind his parents try to find the qualities of education, fair complexion, good looks, modesty housekeeping abilities, and all other virtues combined in the girl of their choice. Every Indian girl is a good cook by training from very young so that the culinary aspect presents no problem in particular.

Very naturally, all this takes some looking for—and finding—on both sides.

I have taken you a long way from the main theme of my story and pretty little Lalita, but it is necessary that those of you who read these lines and have never lived in India should both understand and realise the root cause of the trouble with the girl.

Lalita had everything it takes by Western standards to make an attractive wife. She was a pretty girl, with unusually brilliant grey-green eyes, enchanting eyelashes, and delightfully provocative slightly thick pink lips. Her budding young breasts strained rebelliously against the confinement imposed by her cotton jacket, and appeared as if they would at any time burst their bonds. Their softly rounded fleshy curves and the deep cleft in between the jutting hillocks made passers-by stop and stare; the young men with hope and anticipation, and the old with regret that Father Time had been so exacting with them.

Each morning Lalita would carry her heavy brass water-pot to the community well in the centre of the village, fill it and then balance it gracefully against her hip. With a swaying, rhythmic motion she would wend her way to the little hut she shared with her mother and two younger sisters, empty the water-pot, and then return to the well for a second supply. The youths would eye her lustfully on such journeys and the women in envy of her natural charm and grace.

Above all, Lalita had a vivacious and determined disposition.

But by Indian standards, at least so far as a 'respectable' marriage was concerned, Lalita was not so well off.

To begin with she was a Harijan, one of the 'untouchable' or low-caste community who, up to quite recent years had been considered social outcastes of the baser order, and who were not allowed to marry above their own status.

Secondly, she had two elder sisters, and in providing the necessary dowries to get them married, her father had dissipated his slender resources as a petty merchant in a tiny, box-booth store.

Then he had died, leaving her mother in debt and herself and her two younger sisters unprovided for, with no hopes of any money to afford even the meagrest of dowries for any of them when their turn came to get married.

Well did Lalita remember her mother weeping over the dead body of her father, bemoaning his sudden demise, and loudly expressing her wish that she had died instead, rather than be left behind with three female children and the prospect of house rent to be paid to the landlord each month with no money coming in.

Bukthi, the landlord was a rich man; yes, very very rich indeed. Not only did he own over a quarter of the number of houses and huts in the village of Alamgarh itself, but he also owned some hundreds of acres of land surrounding it. He rented the houses, and the lands, to the villagers, and was most exacting when it came to the question of collecting rents from them. He would accept no excuse for delay should the monsoon fail and the crops die and the ryots be unable to pay him. Bukthi would just summon the band of hired ruffians he called his servants and instruct them to bodily throw the defaulter out on the road. The question of the farmer and his family thereafter starving to death was no concern of his.

The same principle applied to the tenants of the many houses owned by him. No tolerance or mercy was ever extended. The defaulter was put out on the street the very day after his rent became due if he could not pay it. If he dared to complain, Bukthi's servants would beat him, half to death.

When Lalita's father, Mendhe, had died, the house rent had become due. After paying for his ceremonial cremation her mother, Sita, had just been able to clear it. Thereafter, she had struggled hard to keep abreast of her debtors, but had slowly succumbed to the unequal contest.

Last month, for the first time, the rent had fallen into arrears. Bukthi had come to collect, and he now stood at the door.

He was a fat man too, yes very, very fat. His double chin gave his small head the impression of being connected to his barrel-shaped body directly, without the presence of necessity of a neck at all. His huge belly overflowed the waist band of his dhoti and covered it in folds of flabby flesh. His breasts, even bigger than a woman's, were two sagging appendages, black hair between them and dank with a layer of perspiration, for the morning was warm and Bukthi was angry at not having been paid his rent which was due. A thin, muslin dhoti encased his elephantine thighs and was wound in between. So fine was the cloth as to be almost transparent in the bright sunlight. The darker shape of his gross body could be shamelessly seen through the thin material, for it was the only article of clothing he wore. He was bare-footed. Horizontal caste marks across his forehead from temple to temple proclaimed his superior lineage and social standing.

'Oh, miserable woman, where art thou?' he bawled, standing outside the door of the little brick-and-mud hut, and shouting lustily.

Sita heard and recognised the voice and her heart missed a beat for fear. Was it not cruel enough to lose her husband without being left penniless in addition? This fat monster would no doubt now order her and her three daughters out on to the street. She trembled and felt weak at the knees as she stooped her head under the low lintel of the doorway and went outside.

She was a frail woman of about fifty years of age; thin and with hair liberally streaked with grey. But her longish finely-chiselled features and grey-green eyes revealed the source from which Lalita had inherited her beauty. A sari, that had once been blue but was now faded to a dirty ashy colour could hardly detract from what would have been a stately appearance had she been dressed better.

'Why do you keep me waiting outside like a dog.' Bukthi thundered. 'I have come to collect last month's rent due by you.'

'I came the first time you called. Sir,' began Sita by way of apology 'but…' and her voice trailed to a halt in despair.

'There are no 'buts' with me,' barked the fat man. 'Either you pay your rent, or out you get. I am not running a charitable institution.'

Tears welled in the poor woman's eyes, brimmed over to her careworn cheeks and trickled down the furroughed skin. One fell, as a drop of moisture, on to the ground where it was immediately absorbed by the parched earth.

Unconsciously, the thought crossed her mind that even the soil in this land is cruel. It grabs at my tears and asks for more. But then, the earth was dry and in need of moisture. This fat man before her had lakhs of rupees; yet demanded the paltry sum she owed of twelve rupees.

'Please. Sir, be kind to us and have mercy,' she pleaded, the tears running faster now. 'When my husband, Mendhe, was alive he paid you regularly every month and never once defaulted. I have no source of income or support now. Please, please give me another month's time in which I and my daughter may seek for work. Then we will pay you the rent for both months due'.

The scowl on Bukthi's face grew deeper. It was clear he was in no mood to have mercy, or even to listen to her.

'Miserable wretch!' he almost spat out the words. 'What care I for you or your troubles and woes. I want my rent that is due for last month, and what is more, I want it now. NOW, do you understand?' His voice rose to a frenzied scream as his fat belly vibrated with the vehemence of his words, and his double-jowls set up a queer trembling that he himself could not control. Bukthi would have appeared a comical sight, indeed, on a stage setting, had only the circumstances connected with the whole affair been less tragic than they were in reality.

Sita could find no answer to that outburst. She commenced to cry unrestrainedly.

Lalita had taken her brass water-pot to the village well, and having filled it was just that moment returning with the pot balanced as usual on her shapely right hip. She had apparently walked faster or perhaps filled the pot to the brim. Whatever it was, some of the water had splashed upwards and wetted the thin cloth of the white jacket, speckled with red dots, that she was wearing. The sodden material clung even more tightly to her jutting right breast and revealed its contours intimately.

Lalita had heard Bukthi's raised voice and her mother's weeping, long before she drew level with them. She knew the fat landlord, both by sight and reputation. She also knew that the previous month's rent for the hut that Bukthi called a house, had not been paid. She guessed that he had ordered her mother to vacate, and being of a decidedly determined and forceful disposition, she made up her mind to tell this loathesome fat creature just what she thought of him. They had nothing to lose in any case, as he would undoubtedly turn them out that very instant.

These thoughts passed rapidly through Lalita's pretty head, and by that time she had reached her mother. Very carefully and deliberately she lowered the heavy brass vessel with its contents to the ground, and then turned to face Bukthi with flaming eyes.

'You fat bully,' she hissed between clenched teeth without any preliminaries, 'if you have anything to say, say it to me. Cannot you see my poor mother is exhausted enough, as it is, and sick, too, that you have to shout at her, you fat lout.'

The virulence and unexpectedness of this quite unforeseen counter-attack fairly took the wind out of Bukthi's sails. For some moments he was at a loss for words. His heavy jowl dropped and his mouth hung open in the manner of a stranded fish, gasping for air.

The sight tickled Lalita's sense of humour. She began to giggle; and then laughed openly.

Her mocking laughter stung Bukthi to violent fury. By now his eyes fairly popped out of his head. 'You little slut,' he stuttered, 'mind your business or I will lay my hands on you and break your neck this moment.'

The laughter died in Lalita's throat. In turn, her eyes flashed fire and her under-lip trembled uncontrollably with a woman's desire to cry with anger, and her own determination not to give vent to her feelings.

A crowd of villagers had been attracted by the altercation and were by now surrounding the three participants in a wide and interested circle. Among them were a good number of children and these were laughing.

Bukthi lost control of himself entirely and went berserk.

Striding forward, he swung with open palm at the girl before him. Being a woman and unaccustomed to actual fighting, Lalita failed to dodge or parry the blow. It caught her a thudding welt across her face. Her ears sang with the impact and for a moment everything vanished before her, to be replaced by a reddish-white mist.

Then she remembered what had happened. Sobbing with fury, she reached up and tore with her sharp nails at the leering fat face above her, scratching furroughs of red through Bukthi's dusky fat skin. With both hands she tore, and scratched, and mauled. The blood began to trickle down his face. He backed in self-defence, while Lalita pressed forward her plucky attack.

The onlookers howled with merriment and appreciation of what was going on before them. Not one of them had any love for the fat landlord, and this spectacle of him getting beaten up by a sixteen-year-old girl was something that they were enjoying to the maximum.

As she attacked, Lalita abused her opponent roundly. And not only him, but in the usual Eastern fashion, all his ancestors that had gone before him. 'Bastard-fat son of a pig and descendant of a family of swine,' she screeched, 'you would dare hit a woman! I will show you what one of my sex can do. Take this–and this–and this.'

The crowd were laughing even louder.

In desperation Bukthi grabbed at the furiously-attacking figure of the girl before him. His hand clutched her right breast. He felt the pulsating softness of the flesh beneath, barely restrained by the thin wet cloth of her jacket. Meanwhile, his face burned from the deep scratches she had inflicted with her long, sharp nails. In retaliation he gripped the mound of her breast in his hand and tugged at it with all his might.

Lalita screamed with pain, while the flimsy material of her jacket tore asunder under the strain, to reveal a completely naked breast, topped by the plum-coloured protrusion of her nipple surrounded by its dark-brown areola.

'What goes on here?' demanded a voice of authority.' And then the Sub-Inspector of police, who had been passing by on his bicycle and been attracted by the crowd and the hubbub, broke through the circle of spectators.

Bukthi looked an ugly sight with the blood streaming down his lacerated face. Tears of temper ran down his cheeks. Lalita was also crying, her feelings a mixture of rage, pain and shame.

A dozen tongues started wagging simultaneously as the crowd tried to acquaint the police officer with what was happening.

'Hold your tongues,' he commanded; and then, turning to Bukthi whom he already knew and did not like, said, 'Now Sait-jee, what explanation have you to offer for this disgraceful scene?'

'I was but asking for the rent that is due to me and has not been paid,' Bukthi pleaded meekly, 'when this vixen attacked and started scratching me.'

'That is a lie,' countered Lalita between her tears, 'he hit me first.' A voice from the crowd spoke up. 'That is true, police Sahib. I myself saw Bukthi strike her first.'

The Sub-Inspector turned to the landlord. 'It surprises me to see a gentleman of your status engaged in a street brawl with a mere girl. You had both better come with me to the police station, where I will file a case against the pair of you for causing a disturbance to the peace.'

Bukthi saw the further humiliation that lay ahead of him should the police book a case. He would become a laughing stock before the Magistrate when accused of brawling with a woman on the street. Besides, he felt the Magistrate did not like him very much, already. Twice he had prosecuted tenants who had owed him money on lands they had rented from him. Instead of making them pay, or punishing them, this Magistrate had shown leniency towards the ryots by allowing them more time. If this case came to court, Bukthi felt the Magistrate would really take a very dim view of it.

Like all bullies, he suddenly went to pieces when thwarted.

'Oh, please Sir,' he begged of the Sub-Inspector, 'kindly excuse me and let me off. She is to blame and I am not at fault.'

The Sub-Inspector's lip curled in contempt. 'So, she is to blame, eh?' he mocked, 'and you are quite innocent, I suppose?'

Then he looked at Lalita, who had stopped crying. In the excitement of the moment she had quite forgotten about her right breast which was still exposed. The police officer glanced at it momentarily; then rivetted his attention upon it.

Appreciatively, he sucked in his breath.

'Sir,' Lalita said, 'for the matter of that, we are both to blame equally for fighting in public. He struck me and I struck him. So take us both to the station and lock us both up.'

A glint of admiration displaced the dim film of lust that had been coming into the Sub-Inspector's eyes. 'Well spoken, girl,' he commented. Then, turning to Bukthi, he said in tones of deepest derision, 'Truly, fat man, you should be thoroughly ashamed of yourself. Not only do you strike a woman publicly, but you cringe for mercy and try to lay the blame on her. She, at least, accepts her part of it; but you have not even got the guts to do that. You...

bastard!' he muttered under his breath, repeating the word with a very bad epithet before it to qualify precisely the nature of 'bastard' Bukthi was.

Then he resumed talking, 'Either you will apologise in my presence and in that of this crowd, to this girl, or you will come with me to the police station. I will allow you exactly one minute in which to make up your mind.'

Bukthi stared dumbfounded. How could he, the great and rich landlord, possibly apologise to this little Harijan she-devil who had so disparaged him? But then he thought of the Magistrate, and what further disgrace lay in store at his hands.

'Well, time's up,' broke in the Sub-Inspector, 'come along with me; both of you.'

Bukthi made up his mind quickly. 'Just one minute, Sir; I will apologise'. Then, turning to Lalita, he quickly mumbled the words, 'I apologise,' ungracefully.

He looked at the police officer after that, who said crisply, 'Get out.'

Bukthi turned and walked rapidly away. Feelings of shame, mortification, rage and frustration tore at him, and vied strongly with each other for supremacy.

But through and above them all, he seemed to see a small, protruding, plum-hued, erect object. It was the nipple on Lalita's right breast which had been laid bare when he had torn away her jacket. There and then he made a resolution. He determined to humble the owner; by possessing her!

Another month passed, and strange to say Bukthi had done nothing more about his threat to evict Sita and her three daughters. He had not even gone near the hut they occupied.

Sita had tried hard to find employment for herself. Remarkably, there seemed to be none in the whole village. That appeared to be most unusual, as other women, older than herself secured jobs in houses and places the occupants of whom had just told her they had no vacancies. At last, she confided her concern to an old woman friend.

'Amlabee,' she said one evening, 'why is it that I am born so unlucky? Why is it I cannot even get a job? Others go before me and after me. They get work. But when I ask, it is always the same answer, "Sorry; no vacancy."'

Amlabee, the old crone addressed, smiled darkly, 'It is not your bad luck that prevents you from being employed. It is that man, Bukthi.' Then she leaned across confidingly to Sita. 'Only two nights ago the grocer, Ramdass, was here talking to my husband. I overheard him saying that Bukthi had openly circulated instructions far and wide that neither Sita or her daughter, Lalita, should be given work or financially helped in any way. I intended to tell you this before, Sita, but refrained for fear I should hurt your feelings. He is the one who is the cause of you being boycotted and debarred from being given a job.'

This news appalled Sita. She pondered about it for some days, and then decided to seize the bull by the horns and tackle Bukthi about it directly, without telling Lalita.

Next morning, she hung around the main gateway of the mansion of a house that was Bukthi's personal residence. At about ten o'clock, he came out of the gate clad in a tight-fitting tussore-silk coat, buttoned high at the neck. He wore the usual thin muslin dhoti, and a small black cap on his head.

Now or never argued Sita to herself. She accosted him, salaamed respectfully and then came out with what was in her mind. 'Huzoor, why is it that you have told so many people not to give me or my daughter employment? Rather, if you would but help us to get work, I will not only gladly pay your house rent, but the arrears of money I already owe you in this respect.'

Bukthi halted in his tracks. For a moment it appeared as if he would erupt into a towering rage. But his expression of anger slowly became supplanted by one of cunning as if an idea had suddenly come into his mind. With a sly look in his eyes and a totally unusual smoothness of speech, he replied.

'Don't be so silly, sister,' and then, glibly, 'whoever told you that? Why should I try to stop you from getting work? I realise that only then will you be able to pay my rent.'

He paused awhile. Then went on ingratiatingly, 'Look here. I am sorry about that quarrel we had. I am afraid I lost my temper. Most remiss of me, I am sure. But I will tell you what. To prove I bear you no ill-will and am genuinely regretful about that incident, I will not only wait some time more for the house rent but I will also lend you one hundred rupees, interest free, to tide you over your present difficulties. How will that suit you?'

To say the least of it, Sita was amazed. Could her ears be deceiving her? Or was Bukthi mad, or drunk?

She looked into his face, earnestly trying hard to fathom what was in his mind and lay behind those jet-black eyes. For once, her woman's instinct failed her. She saw nothing.

Perhaps it was because she had plenty of other misfortunes to remember and think about. Not only had she failed to pay the rent, but she was heavily in debt all over the village. Only the day before she had tried to borrow the small sum of five rupees from the local moneylender. But he had laughed at her when she asked him.

'Do you think I am mad to throw away money to a destitute widow without a hope in hell of ever getting it back?' he had chided. 'Go on, get out of here. If you really want the money bring some security, such as a gold ring, nose ring, earring, or some other trinket worth at least fifteen rupees.'

'But I have nothing whatsoever left,' she had wailed. 'That's exactly as I thought,' he had cut in, 'so, get out; and stay out.'

And now Bukthi was offering her a loan of one hundred rupees, without security and without interest, and further time to remain on in his house.

It was unbelievable.

But the question was; should she accept, or not.

Indecision weighed heavily upon her. On the one side was the prospect of sheer starvation both for herself, Lalita, and, the two younger girls. On the other was a lurking doubt. Could this be really true?

'Well,' queried Bukthi beningly, 'do you want the money, or not? You must tell me quickly. I have a business appointment in another ten minutes or so.'

Faced with the temptation of immediate financial relief and a square meal for herself and her three daughters that night, Sita agreed.

'Come on back with me to my house for a few minutes,' Bukthi invited, 'and I will hand you the money.' Obediently she followed him, and waited silently in the verandah, while he went inside.

He was not long in returning, though. Within a few minutes he was back, carrying some ten and five rupee notes in his left hand. In his right hand he held some sort of printed form.

'This is merely a formality,' he told her, kindly. 'Just sign here,' and he indicated a place near the end of the form, 'and I will fill in the particulars that I have lent you the sum of one hundred rupees today, free of interest, repayable shall we say,' and here he again smiled benevolently, 'within two years. Will that be sufficiently long?'

Once again, and for the last time, Sita hesitated. Bukthi appeared to grow angry. 'Please don't waste my time,' he reminded her. 'I am already late as it is and cannot delay a moment longer. Do you want the money, or not?'

For fear he should change his mind at the last moment, Sita hastily scrawled her signature at the spot indicated, using the Parker 51 fountain pen he offered her for the purpose. Bukthi carefully allowed the ink to dry for a moment, folded the form and tucked it into the left hand breast pocket of his tussore-silk coat, remarking that he would fill in the details himself later, as he was in a hurry.

Then he counted out eight ten-rupee and four five-rupee notes, which he handed to her.

Sita took the money gratefully, bowing low in a salaam of thanks. And so she did not notice the gleam of satisfaction that came into his eyes, above her lowered head.

Another two months passed, but still Sita and Lalita found it very difficult to obtain steady employment. They did, each, get one or two temporary jobs which lasted a few days. But then they were out of employment again. Meanwhile the hundred rupees which Sita had taken from Bukthi, and of which she had not breathed a word to her daughter, were dwindling fast.

Yet another month passed, and the money was all gone.

Once more, in sheer desperation, Sita approached Bukthi, and this time, almost but not quite as readily, he volunteered to lend her another fifty rupees on the same terms as on the first occasion. And once again he contrived to make her sign a blank pro-note form.

Still another two months passed and the fifty rupees were also gone.

Steady employment eluded mother and daughter yet, while misfortune appeared to dog their footsteps. And that was the time when Bukthi chose to play his ace card.

He had come to learn of Lalita's daily visits with her water-pot to the communal well very early every morning and one day instructed his servant to accost her there and tell her he wanted to speak to her. The servant did as he was told and delivered the message. Lalita who knew nothing about the loans her mother had taken from Bukthi, promptly told the servant to tell him to go to hell.

The servant duly delivered her reply.

Bukthi fumed within himself, muttering darkly, 'You wait till I get hold of you you little bitch. I will make you squeal for mercy and I will show you none.'

A couple of mornings later, he waited for her himself, around the corner of the street down which she would have to walk to reach the hut she and her family lived in, at the lower end. Every little while he peeped to see if she was coming.

At last he saw her, the brass pot balanced gracefully on the right side of her swaying hips, walking towards him. He drew back in the shelter of the wall till she had turned the corner and stood face to face before him.

'Well, my beautiful one, we meet again,' he said banteringly. 'I have some words to say to you.'

'Get away, you fat pig,' Lalita muttered defiantly, before I throw my pot, with its contents, in your face.'

Bukthi stepped backwards hastily. He had suffered a painful experience once already at this vixen's hands, and knew what she could do at close quarters when aroused. He did not want to risk another encounter.

Putting his hand in his breast pocket, he drew out two printed forms.

'Listen, girl,' he grated harshly, 'do you know what these are?' And then, before she could answer, he went on quickly, 'they are caned 'pro-notes'. One of them indicates that your mother has borrowed one thousand rupees from me. The other shows she has borrowed a further five hundred. Altogether, one thousand five hundred rupees! She asked me not to tell you about these loans at the time she took them. Look, if you don't believe me. There is her signature.'

Then, stepping a further pace backwards out of all possible reach by this hell-cat, he held up the documents in his left hand, indicating with his right forefinger Sita's signature upon each of them.

Despite the distance, Lalita could clearly recognise her mother's handwriting and signature. Her heart seemed to miss a beat.

'Now, do you know what I am going to do?' he queried, harshly, 'I am going to hand over both these documents to court. Your mother will be arrested and thrown into jail for not paying her debts, beside her house rent which is now due for six months. I will even pay for her upkeep in the debtor's cell; but go to jail she shall!'

Bukthi waited a minute to let the full significance the threat he had just uttered sink into this defiant girl.

Then he continued, 'But there is one way of saving her. And only one person can do it. That one way and one person, is you.'

Lalita still did not fully comprehend what he was driving at. With mouth half-opened in astonishment and eyes that began to fill with tears, she listened to him.

Enjoying every moment of his triumph, Bukthi continued with evident relish, working up to the climax in the form of the dramatic announcement he was about to make.

'Spend one week with me. Let me enjoy your body fully and to my satisfaction. Let me do everything I want to with it. At the end of that time, and provided you have been very, very nice to me and have done all I shall ask you to do, I promise you that I shall not only destroy both these bonds before your very eyes and forget about the six months' rent your mother already owes me, but I shall allow all of you to go on living, rent free, in my house for the rest of your lives.'

Only then did the significance of his words and his threat sink fully into Lalita's consciousness.

Her eyes flashed fire, while the teardrops, like stars, twinkled in the corners of each. Three words escaped her lips, 'You unutterable swine!'

Never had she seemed more beautiful or more desirable to possess. Bukthi hugged himself in a paroxy of anticipatory delight.

'I will allow you up till tomorrow evening to decide whether you want to save your mother from jail, or to sacrifice her,' he continued. 'After all, it is not much that I am asking of you, a mere wisp of a Harijan girl, in return for such a large sum of money and so many other benefits in addition. Don't breathe a word to your mother or anyone else. If you do so, she goes to jail. Tell her you are going to the next village to seek a job and come to my house tomorrow night at exactly eight o'clock. Come to the back door and not to the front gate, as the neighbours should not see you. I shall be expecting you. And remember, finally, that if you do not come, the very next morning your mother goes to jail. That is all I have to say, except to once again remind you of the fact that you, and you alone, are the only person who can save your mother from imprisonment.'

With these words, Bukthi turned abruptly to walk away, and in doing so almost tripped over a crippled beggar who had appeared as if from nowhere and squatted on the road behind him.

'Alms for a poor cripple, your honour,' he whined. 'Pray give me half-an-anna.'

'Get out of my way, you idiot!' barked Bukthi, irritably, 'I almost fell over you.'

So saying, he walked past the beggar without looking at him again, and disappeared around the corner.

They were alone. The beggar and Lalita.

No sound was to be heard, except for her convulsive sobbing. She was too simple a girl to consider whether it would be altogether possible for Bukthi to carry out the threats he had uttered.

'Do not fear, lady,' the cripple interrupted softly, 'you will be saved. I swear to you, on the word of Rajah Man Singh Rathore. Do not mention a word of all this to your mother, or another soul. And go to the back door of his house tomorrow night, at exactly eight o'clock as he has asked you to do. Enter boldly. No harm shall come to you. Once more I swear it, on the word of Rajah Man Singh. Do not fail to go.'

With those words the beggar dragged himself laboriously across the road and vanished from sight, without once looking back at her.

Lalita felt an overwhelming relief.

Even she, humble Harijan girl that she was, had heard of the countless instances of chivalry the great dacoit-king had shown towards insignificant people like herself, in the past, at their hour of greatest need, and how he had rescued so many from the jaws of impending calamity.

That very instant she made her decision and she made it irrevocably. She would not worry who the cripple was; from where he had come; how, in that terribly-maimed condition he could possibly contact the bandit leader in his hidden lair in the jungle or among the ravines so many miles away; or how she would be rescued from the clutches of the fat Bukthi the following night before he could rape her.

But she would obey, implicitly, what she had been told to do. She would, tell no one; and she would go to the back door of the landlord's house at exactly eight o'clock on the night he had told her to come.

It was three minutes to eight the following night when Lalita stood irresolutely outside the rear entrance to Bukthi's residence. It was a moonless night, but the stars overhead twinkled serenely in a cloudless sky as if oblivious to the cruel fate that awaited her behind those closed doors.

Not a soul was in sight. The nearest street lamp shone bleakly about a hundred yards away. The doorway was in darkness and the door was shut, although a ray of light penetrated below it from the interior.

The clock on the tower of the town hall, nearly a quarter of a mile away, solemnly struck the hour of eight as Lalita timidly knocked upon the door. Glancing down the street as she did so, she noticed a solitary bullock cart turn the bend in the roadway, its only light a dim lantern, and approach towards the house.

Evidently Bukthi had been certain she would come and was awaiting her arrival, for within a few seconds of her knocking the door opened and she saw his obese frame silhouetted against the light from the room inside.

'Good evening, Lalita, I was expecting you. It is nice of you to have been so punctual. Do come in.'

His tone was suave and gentlemanly, and he stepped aside to allow her to enter.

She went inside.

Bukthi closed the door behind her.

And then, in an instant, his manner changed. Gone was the polished gentleman of a moment before. His features assumed a strained expression—the expression of concentrated lust. The tip of his tongue protruded from his mouth, and in anticipation wet his upper and lower lips. His eyes bored into her sari and appeared to undress her till she was stark naked before him. The perspiration of pent-up passion poured from the pores of his forehead, and made his face look greasy and glistening.

With both hands he grabbed for her breasts.

THE RICH LANDLORD AND THE POOR MAIDEN 183

At that instant, Lalita realised that she was all alone with a sex-mad beast, and she screamed aloud.

As his hands touched her there came a loud knocking at the door, and a muffled voice announced urgently, 'Telegram.'

Bukthi stopped in mid-stride. He was breathing heavily and trembling with unleashed passion.

'Go away, damn you,' he shouted, 'bring it again in the morning.'

'Cannot,' came the muffled reply. 'Urgent telegram. You have to receive it now.'

With a vile oath at being disturbed at such a time, Bukthi pushed Lalita into a corner of the room and flung open the door. Four men, instead of the one telegram messenger he had expected to see, stood outside. Before he knew what had happened, they were inside the room, and had closed the door behind them.

Bukthi opened his mouth to protest, when things happened fast. The tallest of the four men, a veritable giant, leaped upon him, pushing a handkerchief into his open mouth. His three companions pinioned his hands behind his back and tied them together with a cord they had apparently brought for the purpose. Then they bound his legs also.

The giant quickly replaced the handkerchief he had forced into Bukthi's mouth with a cloth gag which was knotted fast behind his head.

Unceremoniously he was thrown to the ground.

The four men looked around and the leader's eyes alighted upon a costly Persian carpet. This he took up from where it was lying on the floor, and the men commenced to roll Bukthi into it.

All this time they had been undisturbed. Evidently in anticipation of an evening with Lalita completely at his mercy, Bukthi had sent his servants home and was alone in the house.

When they had entirely wrapped the landlord in his Persian carpet, the tall leader cautiously opened the door and peered outside. Obviously he found the coast clear, for in a few seconds he beckoned to his three companions. They staggered under the tremendous weight of the fat man as they bore him outside, rolled up inside his own carpet.

Then, for the first time, the leader appeared to notice Lalita and spoke to her. 'Come along, girl. I offer you security in the name of Rajah Man Singh. Soon you will be returned safely to your home. Have no fear whatever.'

Not for one moment did Lalita hesitate, so great was her trust in the bandit king's honour. She followed the three men, staggering beneath their burden, outside. The giant came behind her and closed the back door of the house as they left it.

Lalita was surprised to notice that a covered bullock cart stood beside the kerb on the roadside. It was drawn by two bullocks. Suspended to the wooden shaft that passed between them. A dimly-lighted lantern flickered faintly. At the front of the cart squatted the shrouded figure of the cartman.

Suddenly she remembered the cart she had seen approaching as she had entered the house. Man Singh's henchmen had timed their arrival correctly to the split second.

By this time the three men had pushed the carpet, with its human contents, into the cart. One of them got in with it. The tall leader wordlessly motioned for Lalita to enter the cart, also. She did so.

With a faint click of his tongue the driver of the cart started the bullocks and the cart creaked and rumbled down the roadway, the tall man and his remaining two companions falling into step behind.

To an onlooker, it was just an ordinary bullock cart, proceeding on an innocent journey. Inside of it were some members of a party of travellers. The rest of them walked behind. It had all been so simply but efficiently arranged, and looked so very commonplace.

Lalita admired the ingenuity of Rajah Man Singh and his men.

In course of time they left the township far behind and journeyed on and on. Despite the excitement she had been through, Lalita began to feel sleepy. Her head lolled forward and she dozed fitfully. Every hour or so the men would change about, and one would take turns to ride in the cart while the other three walked behind.

At about midnight they had heard muffled sounds coming from the interior of the roll of carpet. They had stopped the cart and unrolled it. Evidently, just in time. Bukthi was almost dead from suffocation and his clothes were sodden with sweat, caused by the terrific heat brought about through the carpet that was wrapped around him.

So the leader had decided not to replace it, but kept Bukthi bound and gagged on the floor of the cart.

Soon afterwards the road entered the forest and everything became as black as pitch. Giant trees, growing in close array, were interspersed with smaller ones, the whole joined and laced together inextricably by vines and jungle creepers, presenting as it were a solid and impenetrable fortress wall on either side of the road, extending high up to the tops of the trees. Only directly overhead, and following the contour of the road beneath, was a ribbon of sky, clearly differentiated from the black phalanx of the forest on either side by the myriads of stars that twinkled and scintillated unceasingly, throwing off hues in their brilliance that bore all the colours of the spectrum. Other twinkling lights flitted about in the darkness of the foliage on either side of the road. But they were living lights; the phosphorescent lamps of fireflies, as they flashed their elfin glow now here, now there; now singly, now synchronising in hundreds; momentarily illumining the outline of the trees, only to plunge them again the very next second into a deeper, more impenetrable, gloom.

The lantern suspended on the shaft to which the two bullocks were yoked cast but a feeble light hardly two yards agead of them. The moving shadows, thrown by the legs of the oxen as they strode patiently along, seemed living things, demons of the jungle night that haunted them on their journey; steadily, inexorably, to an impending doom. The three men, walking close together behind the cart, appeared ghostlike phantoms forming a rearguard against any attempt at escape by the inmates of the vehicle.

It was shortly after 3.30 a.m. when Lalita, who had been dozing again, heard voices and felt the cart in which she was sitting come to a sudden halt. Then she saw the three men who had been walking behind, draw respectfully aside as other figures approached.

'Mohan, are they all here?' a rather melodious voice inquired. 'The fat man and the girl?'

'They are here, Maharaj Sahib,' replied the tallest of the three men whom Lalita remembered as the one who had evidently been in charge of the kidnapping assignment.

'You have done excellently, Mohan. Thank you,' said the owner of the melodious voice. Then, turning to his other companions who had not yet come into view due to the elliptical roof of the cart coming in the way, the speaker said, 'Carry the fat pig to the camp.'

Addressing Lalita, he said, 'Girl, you have nothing whatever to be afraid of. Please get down and follow me.'

Normally, any adult woman would have been terrified under the circumstances. She guessed that she was among the members of a dacoit band. But Lalita felt no fear whatsoever. A strange assurance of complete safety came over her, with mingled feelings of gratitude and respect for the great leader who had saved her from an awful fate.

Could this, indeed, be the redoubtable Rajah Man Singh?

Without a word, she eased herself off the hard wooden floor of the cart and on to the ground.

Then the mysterious man who had been giving the orders led the way motioning with his hand for Lalita to follow closely. She did so. Out of the corner of her eye she noticed four men lift Bukthi to their shoulders and start walking behind her. In the rear of them were yet other men. They commenced to walk through the jungle in single file, along some path evidently the leader knew well, as did his companions. In a few seconds the dim lantern from the bullock cart was lost to sight behind the stems of the trees.

Now the darkness became intense. Strain her eyes as she might, Lalita was unable to see the pathway at her feet. She stumbled. The leader halted and turned around. In the gloom she felt his hand groping for hers. She clasped it. He continued walking, leading her by the hand.

She never knew what distance they had covered. But suddenly the path took a turning and they converged on what was clearly a glade

THE RICH LANDLORD AND THE POOR MAIDEN

in the forest. The dying embers of half-a-dozen camp fires glowed around her.

The party came to a halt.

'Oh comrades,' spoke he of the pleasant voice, 'pile wood on the fires, for we are about to hold court. But first, let some 'cha' be served to the newcomers.'

The four men laid Bukthi, still trussed and gagged, upon the ground and squatted down around him. The leader said to Lalita, 'Sit down, girl, and be comfortable till the cha is served.' Then, turning to one of his followers he added, 'Bring a blanket for the girl; she is sure to feel the cold.'

From somewhere a blanket was offered to her. Lalita draped it around herself and brought the end over her head, for the night air was decidedly crisp and her sari was already damp with the dew.

Then she sat down on the ground.

The dacoit leader followed suit.

By this time the fires around them had recommenced to blaze, reinforced by the logs of dry wood that had just been piled on by the members of the band.

In the flickering light, momentarily growing brighter, Lalita turned to look at her benefactor.

He was an elderly man, light-complexioned and with a snowy white beard, moustache and whiskers. He wore the usual dhoti and bandi. She noticed that, despite his age, he sat erect and had the bearing of a soldier with long years of military training. He had a surprisingly broad forehead which was smeared with wide chalk marks. A heavy string of amber beads hung around his neck.

But what was the most impelling feature about him were his eyes. They were steely-hard and piercing. Cruel as a Kestrel's, they yet seemed capable of turning as soft as any mother's as she gazed lovingly at her babe.

In a few minutes hot tea was served all around in enamel mugs, Lalita receiving her share immediately after the chief. Bukthi got his quota too, as soon as the gag had been removed from his mouth and his arms and legs released.

When they had finished drinking, the old man began to speak. And he smiled as he spoke. A curious smile. It appeared placating, apologetic, and yet seeking to be understood. It gave the impression of coming from a good-natured and kindly judge; yet one who knew he had an unpleasant duty to perform and was determined that justice should be served.

'We all do wrong and sin at times,' he said, 'for to err is human. It is bad if the sin we commit causes ruination to ourselves. But, if that sin is planned, diabolically, to encompass the destruction of another person, particularly if that other is innocent, then the sin is very great indeed.

'We shall now hold court to decide whether our brother here, one Bukthi by name who stands accused, has committed such a sin; and if he has, whether he should be punished or not; and what form that punishment should take.

'There are fifty-two of you here present excluding the girl, the accused and myself. I will cast no vote in the matter. I want you to judge fairly and before God, whether this man Bukthi is guilty or not; whether he should be punished or acquitted; and if you feel he is guilty, in what manner he should be punished.

'I don't want anyone here to try to please me by punishing him. I tell you here and now that such punishment will not please me in the least. Rather, it will grieve me. But if you honestly decide that justice should be meted out; assuredly it will be done.

'Now I will state the charges against the accused, one by one. You, Bukthi, will be given every opportunity to explain yourself and refute the accusation if you want. Only you must speak the truth and nothing else. You will be given a patient hearing with no interruptions.

'Alright then; let me begin with the first question. Are you a landlord owning several houses and a good number of acres of land? Just answer "Yes" or "No" please.'

'Yes,' Bukthi's voice was scarcely above a whisper.

'Do you collect rents from your tenants?'

'Yes,' said the fat man again.

'How much money do you collect a month in this way? Now, before you answer, bear in mind that I already know. If you speak the truth it will be in your favour. If you should tell a lie, a hot ember shall be put on the sole of your foot.'

Bukthi commenced to tremble violently. Then stuttered, 'A few thousand.'

'We know that already, fat man. But, how many thousand?'

'About three thousand rupees,' came the reply.

'That is a lie, my friend. Altogether you get six thousand and seventy rupees a month. Am I correct or not?'

The landlord looked startled. There was silence for nearly a minute. Then he said, 'Yes'. 'Has this girl's mother paid the rent she is due you?'

'No,' Bukthi returned vehemently. Then he began to passionately plead his case. 'She has not paid for six months, your honour.'

'I am not "your honour",' said the old man, quietly; and then continued. 'And how much does she owe you, altogether? Now remember to speak the truth, for we know the answer.'

'Seventy-two rupees,' claimed Bukthi hotly. 'At twelve rupees a month for the past six months, she owes me seventy-two rupees.'

'I see; that happens to be correct, as I already know. Now, what proportion is this twelve rupees to the six thousand and odd rupees you get each month?'

'I—I don't know,' stammered Bukthi.

'You don't know, eh. But it is quite a small proportion, is it not?'

No answer came from Bukthi.

'Come, friend,' said the old man impatiently. 'If you won't answer a simple question, perhaps the fire will make you.'

'I suppose so,' admitted Bukthi, surily.

'Used to be paid regularly before?'

'Oh yes,' replied the landowner, with alacrity.

'Then, why did she stop paying you?' came the next question.

'How should I know?' Bukthi was becoming increasingly rebellious. 'In any case,' he continued, 'who are you to ask all these questions? I am not bound to answer them.'

'My name is Man Singh,' said the old man, 'possibly you have heard of me before.

'It is also possible that you may have heard I have ways and means of making people answer, if they refuse. I really don't want to employ them on you. So, I strongly advise you to reply; and reply truthfully.

'Now what was that last question? Oh yes; why did this girl's mother stop paying you suddenly?'

Bukthi decided to humour this devil. So he said, 'Well, she said her husband had died and left behind no money.'

'Is that true?'

'He died alright. But how am I to know he left her no money?'

'Fair enough,' said Man Singh, 'you have a point there. She may have been lying to avoid paying rent. Now let me ask the next question.

'Is it a fact that you instigated your friends not to give her, or her daughter, employment, or work of any kind, when they sought for it?'

No reply.

'And is it true you were kind enough to loan her one hundred rupees, and later another fifty rupees, free of interest?'

'Of course,' said Bukthi, spontaneously.

Then he realised his mistake; but it was too late.

Man Singh snapped his fingers to attract the attention of a rather short man of particularly dark countenance and clean-shaven, who stood among the crowd of onlookers, and then said to him, 'Please show me those bonds, Mustafa.'

The short man addressed delved in the pocket of the black coat he wore over his long shirt, and brought out two pieces of paper which he handed over to the old dacoit.

Bukthi and Lalita recognised them simultaneously. They were the two pro-notes bearing Sita's signature with which he had threatened her a couple of days before. It was evident that, after the kidnapping of the fat landlord, quite another party of outlaws must have been deputed to search his house for these documents. Lalita admired Man Singh's thoroughness, while Bukthi's bloated face drained to a pasty hue. His eyes bulged in fear.

Man Singh unfolded the documents and studied both the sheets for a moment.

'Since you admit you lent her a hundred rupees and then another fifty rupees free of interest, how is it these bonds are for one thousand rupees, and five hundred rupees, respectively?'

No answer.

'I submit you are guilty of chicanery. I accuse you of lending this woman one hundred rupees first, followed by fifty rupees, and then adding a zero in each case and writing pro-notes for one thousand rupees and for five hundred rupees, respectively, to get this poor woman and her daughter hopelessly enmeshed in your clutches. Are you guilty or not?'

Man Singh's voice was flat and toneless. But it was penetratingly clear and precise.

Bukthi did not answer.

'And what did you say to this girl when you met her the day before yesterday?'

Again no answer.

'Surely you remember, great landlord? There was also a witness to what you said. Do you recollect the cripple you stumbled over? He heard you distinctly. And what is more my friend; I was that cripple.'

Lalita could hardly believe her ears. The accused's mouth hung open foolishly.

Man Singh continued, 'However, as I am not taking part in this trial by offering testimony against you, let us hear what the girl herself has to say.'

He turned to Lalita, 'Girl, what exactly did he tell you?'

In a low, but clear voice, Lalita told them everything.

Once more, turning to the half-swooning fat man, Man Singh continued inexorably.

'When this girl came to your house last night, what did you do?'

'N—n—nothing,' stammered Bukthi.

'Girl, is that true? You need not be ashamed to speak. We are your friends here.'

Slowly, but clearly, Lalita said, 'No sooner did I enter, than he shut the door and began to molest me. In fact, had your men not come in the nick of time, I am certain he would have raped me.'

A stony silence came over the assembly for some minutes.

Man Singh got to his feet. Lalita noticed he seemed taller than he had first appeared to be. Addressing the squatting group of men, he said.

'Comrades, you have heard the charges. To each charge the accused was afforded an opportunity to reply and defend himself. Now, be very fair in your judgements. What say you? Is he "Guilty" or "Not Guilty".'

There was a unanimous murmur of 'Guilty' from fifty-two throats.

'Should he be punished, or not?'

'He must be punished,' they intoned.

'What form should his punishment take?'

To this question there was lively difference of opinion.

'Flay him to ribbons,' advised one. 'Cut his throat,' suggested another. 'Bury him alive,' said a third.

And then a short, rather thin man, stood up. Lalita noticed that he had sharp features which gave him an intellectual appearance.

'Maharaj,' he began, 'it is my opinion that we should not kill him outright because he has not actually caused the death of anyone as yet. Further, if we do so, nobody will know of his misdeeds. Therefore, we should punish him in such a manner, without killing him, as to be a lesson that will deter other blackguards like him from doing such things in future. We should also write a letter to the Commissioner of Police Sahib, acquainting him with the charges and reasons for which we have punished him.'

There was loud and continuous approval of this suggestion from the throng.

'And how should we so punish him, Ali?' asked the dacoit leader.

'Maharaj Sahib; I have thought of that, also,' replied the astute Ali. 'We should cut off the tip of his tongue as a deterrent against telling such lies again; and we should burn the fingers of his right hand, for holding the pen that wrote these false documents and that later tried to molest this helpless girl.'

'Bravo,' shouted the dacoits in high glee, while a voice somewhere at the back yelled, 'Ali, you should have been a judge and not a thief.'

There was loud and prolonged applause and laughter, at that.

Man Singh was silent and appeared thoughtful. He glanced at Lalita; then at the cringing Bukthi; and finally at Ali.

The smile he had been wearing throughout the proceedings suddenly faded from his face. His countenance became stern and implacable. He turned to the accused.

'I pronounce judgement,' he said solemnly. 'The tip of your tongue shall be cut off, and the fingers of your right hand burned in the fire. Ali, you shall supervise the sentence being carried out. But take care that it is not more than just the tip of his tongue, and only the fingers of his right hand.'

Turning to Bukthi, he added, 'And for my part, you shall never again demand rent from this girl or her mother, nor the return of the money you have given them. And you will not harass them anymore. Disobey me, and the next time you will die.'

'Mercy, mercy; have mercy on me,' wailed the unhappy prisoner, grovelling on the ground. 'I will never ask the woman for any money, but spare me; please, please.'

'Girl, come along with me,' commanded the dacoit chieftain. He held her arm firmly, but gently, as she got to her feet, and then led her away into the darkness of the jungle.

No words passed between them for the next fifteen minutes.

Lalita heard Bukthi's screams die in his throat with a horrible, gurgling sound.

Shortly later, there was another outbreak of incoherent moans and the smell of something burning.

Then Man Singh said simply, 'Justice must be done.'

He led her to another part of the clearing, where she was given two blankets and told to sleep.

The next morning she saw no signs of Bukthi. Lalita was given food and told to rest herself, and that she would be taken back safely soon. Till then she was on no account to attempt to escape. She remained a virtual prisoner for the next three days.

On the fourth night she was put in a bullock cart that took her to the outskirts of the town in which she lived. She noticed that a second cart was being driven in front of the one that carried her.

It was four o'clock in the morning when the two carts were stopped about three miles out of town. She was told to get out and walk home quickly. She commenced to do so.

Lalita observed another figure walking along the road before her. It was the figure of a very fat man. But he appeared bent, as if from old age or the effects of a serious illness.

Bukthi could not speak distinctly any longer. Nor could he use his right hand to sign documents again.

And one more thing. He never asked Sita or Lalita to pay him house rent or return him any money. In fact, he never spoke to either of them after that.

Chapter Six

The Three Travellers and the American Journalist

There is, somewhere in the south of India, a large industrial concern which is expanding rapidly. It builds aircraft, constructs railway coaches, and even makes buses to modern design.

This organisation has branches in many parts of India, and not long ago had opened a depot as far north as Srinagar, the capital of Kashmir.

The episode I am about to relate to you came to pass through a simple decision—the decisions by the parent organisation in the south of India to send one of its buses to its newly-opened depot at Srinagar—a journey by road of over 2500 miles.

A regular driver was assigned to drive the vehicle, and an officer of the company was deputed to accompany it. Also two mechanics were allotted to travel with the bus in the event of a breakdown, and to be of general help.

This officer's name was Othi. He was a North Indian, and came from the Punjab. A man of genial disposition and good heart, he felt the assignment would prove a tough one if undertaken alone. So he decided to throw open the invitation of a free bus journey to the enhanting land of Kashmir to two of his bosom friends, both of them also officers serving in the same organisation.

Of course, since these two officers were not travelling on company's duty, they were obliged to apply for leave for the occasion and obtained special permission to travel in the bus going to Srinagar in their private and unofficial capacities.

The younger of the two officers was an Indian Christian; a tall, handsome youth whose name was Percy Rahu. The remaining officer was a middle-aged and stocky orthodox South Indian Brahmin, a person who came from a highly-placed and respected family, and who made it very clear from the start that he was fully prepared to share in the adventure wholeheartedly on one strict proviso; namely, that he cooked his own meals or ate exclusively at Brahmin restaurants. Absolutely cosmopolitan in every other respect, he strictly clung to his orthodox Brahmin custom of only eating food prepared by one of his own caste and community, failing which he would prepare it himself. This man's name was Seshagiri.

The disposition of Othi, who was carefree and wanted to enjoy life to the maximum, matched well with that of Rahu, the handsome youth who had an eye for the ladies and felt that, as life was lived but once, it should be enjoyed to the fullest extent. Seshagiri sometimes had proved to be a brake on their exuberance in the past, but at the same time, Othi and Rahu recognised that their more sober companion would be a valuable asset to the party, if only to keep them out of getting into too serious trouble at times, and to remind them of the fact that they had to complete the present assignment of delivering the bus at Srinagar on schedule, and then return to their home station by air, and on time.

We are not concerned with their adventures on the way, which is another story; but one afternoon found the bus halted at the ferry-crossing on the Chambal River. The time was 3.45 p.m., and the ferry-boat, a flat-bottomed, raft-like affair, was away at the opposite bank of the river, having just taken across a load.

There was nothing to it but wait till the ferry-boat returned.

The nearest road bridge across the river was over fifty miles away. The party might have driven the bus that way and had the benefit of crossing over by the bridge, but for the fact that all of them were strangers to the roads and had never been to this part of India before, road signs had been few and far between, and they had been inquiring their way all along. Hence they had been directed by short-cut routes and had finally come to a halt where the road had terminated and the river rolled smoothly past before them.

'Now what do we do?' asked Seshagiri, whom his friends called 'Sesh' for short, blankly. 'How do we cross the river from here?' By nature he was always a bit of a pessimist.

'Arre baba, don't let that worry you,' spoke up the optimistic Othi, 'there must be some way.' And then, turning to Rahu, who had been driving, he said, 'Percy, hop out and try to find somebody, and ask him how the hell we are to cross this river.'

Percy switched off the ignition, stuck out his long legs before him, leaned back and stretched his arms. It took a lot to worry Percy.

'Nothing doing, Othi old boy,' he replied at length, 'I cannot speak this lingo in any case. You come from this part of India or at least from the north, so you do the finding, and talking—provided there is somebody to talk to. I can't see a soul anywhere.'

'Arre baba,' Othi complained again, as he heaved his great bulk out of the second seat and descended to the ground. Then, 'There is nobody here,' he announced, 'I shall walk up yonder hillock, a hundred yards away, and see if there is anyone in sight.'

'Do so, laddie, do so,' agreed Percy, 'while Sesh and I take a nap. I have been driving this cumbersome rattletrap for the last two hundred miles and am feeling drowsy.' With these words, he got down from the driver's seat, walked to the rear of the vehicle, got in again and laid himself out on the bunk that ran along the full length of the bus.

The regular driver and the two mechanics got down also, sat by the riverbank, and commenced smoking beedies.

Seshagiri remained alone in the front of the vehicle. Some minutes later, he turned around and addressed the recumbent Rahu.

'I say, Percy, I don't like this at all. Where has that fool, Othi, gone to? Isn't this the area we have been reading so often about in the newspapers where dacoits abound controlled by somebody by the name of Man Singh, who has been called the 'king of dacoits', or some such name?'

But Percy had fallen asleep.

Seshagiri faced towards the driver and the two mechanics, all three of them South Indians like himself, and called out in Tamil, 'Do you know fellers, that this area is infested with dacoits who raid at night and cut one's throat from ear to ear?'

Nobody waited to answer that question. All three of them scrambled to their feet and hastened back into the bus and slammed the door behind them.

The noise of the slamming door awoke Percy.

'Can't you blighters allow a man to have forty winks, without getting out and then scrambling in again, like blue-arsed flies. Make up your minds for heaven's sake. Stay in; or stay out.'

And with those words, Percy turned on his side and prepared to fall asleep again.

But Sesh saw his chance and put his question afresh, 'Wake up, Percy,' he called from his seat in front, 'do you know we are in the area where Man Singh and his dacoits hang out?'

'Wasser that?' mumbled Percy sleepily, without moving.

'Wake up, you lazy bugger,' said Seshagiri once more, 'I am trying to tell you, for the third time, that this is the area where Man Singh and his cut-throat ruffians, hang out.'

Rahu sat up and ran a hand through his tousled hair. 'Do you mean the Man Singh we read so much about in the papers?' he queried, incredulously.

'I certainly do,' replied Sesh emphatically, 'him, and nobody else.'

'Oh boy, what luck!' exclaimed Percy, now thoroughly awake. 'I do wish I could meet the blighter. It would be an interesting experience. I believe he has many wives.'

'Who would cut your throat,' finished Sesh, sarcastically.

'From here—to there,' put in Percy, not to be outdone.

Their further conversation was interrupted by the return of Othi, who was accompanied by a tall, old man. He was a commanding figure, with high forehead, long beard and whiskers, and a most truculent-looking moustache. He wore trousers that were tight-fitting below the knees and baggy above. A faded brown cotton coat covered his dirty shirt. And he had a piercing pair of steel-grey eyes.

'I found this feller sitting on the other side of the hillock,' announced Othi with triumph. 'He says he is a Sikh, and that a 'ferry boat will take the whole bus across. He told me it has gone to the other side, and will return in half-an-hour.'

Then, addressing the old Sikh, he asked in Punjabi, 'What did you say your name was Singh-ji?'

'Ranjit Singh,' replied the old man.

His voice was melodious and strangely firm for his age.

'Get in, Ranjit Singh-ji,' invited Othi hospitably, 'Would you care for some tea? We have a little left in the thermos flask.' The old man politely refused the tea, but got into the bus.

Othi went on to explain to him in Punjabi, 'All my friends are from southern India and hence cannot understand this language.'

'Then we shall speak in Hindustani,' volunteered the ancient, graciously, 'do they understand that?'

'Certainly,' broke in Percy. 'In the part of India from which we come, we speak Tamil and Kanarese generally; and of course, English. But we all understand Hindustani.'

The old man smiled happily.

Then he queried, using Hindustani, 'Tell me about yourselves and how come you to be here? Obviously you are strangers to these parts. Are you servants of the "sarkar" (government)?'

Othi thereupon launched into a sketchy account, and explained the circumstances of their presence at the ferry.

As he finished his talk, Seshagiri spotted the ferry-boat returning and said in obvious relief, speaking in English, 'Thank goodness, the ferry is returning.'

Hearing him, Percy explained to the Sikh, 'My friend is most anxious to continue our journey. He has heard stories about a famous dacoit named Man Singh who inhabits these parts, and is much afraid of meeting him.'

Then he asked the old man, 'Are these stories true? Have you seen this Man Singh at any time?'

Into the Sikh's eyes sprang a merry twinkle. But he never answered the question. Instead, he asked another, addressing all three of them conjointly.

'Tell me, Sahibs, are stories of this rascally dacoit really reaching as far as southern India?'

'Oh yes,' Seshagiri answered that one, 'and to other parts of the world also. We often read accounts in the newspapers about his daring raids, and of how the police have been trying for years to catch him, but failed.'

'What do people think of him in your part of the country?' pursued the old Sikh. He appeared to be very interested.

'Well,' broke in Percy Rahu with a chuckle, 'that depends on the people. Fellows like my friend there,' he indicated Seshagiri with a nod of his head, 'consider him to be a bloodthirsty murderer who kills on sight, and are mortally afraid. Personally, I should very much like to meet and speak with him. I don't know what my other friend Othi here thinks, but you can ask him for yourself.'

'Splendid fellow,' put in Othi, jocularly, 'a man after my own heart. I wish I could join him. I really mean that, you know. I would like to rob a few people.'

'I wonder how sincere you are,' mused the old fellow softly, in an undertone. With all that the others heard him and speculated in silence as to the reason for that remark.

In the meantime the ferry-boat had arrived.

They noticed that its construction was simple, consisting of a platform made of bamboos about twenty-five feet long and half as wide, super-imposed upon two ordinary river-boats, held parallel to each other by the platform itself.

The ferry could not be brought close to the shore, but was halted about twenty feet out in the river. The crew consisted of four men and a leader. Two of these men stuck long bamboo poles into the mud of the river bottom. The edge of the raft was allowed to come to rest against the poles which prevented it from floating down the river with the force of the current.

The leader jumped into the water and waded ashore. Then he walked towards the bus.

Othi and Ranjit Singh had stepped outside again. Othi addressed the leader of the raft's crew, in Punjabi.

'Friend, we are in a hurry and want to get to the other side as soon as possible. What is the charge for taking this bus across?'

'Ten rupees,' replied the leader, briefly.

'Okay,' agreed Othi, 'now, what is to be done?'

The man gazed at the bus with a professional look, as if to gauge its bulk and weight. Then he said, 'The ferry cannot be brought closer to shore. The water is too shallow and the boats will ground in the sand. You will have to drive your bus out into the river to where the ferry is. Don't be afraid; the water is barely two feet deep.'

Meanwhile all the inmates of the bus had alighted and were standing by the riverside, assessing the situation.

'How will the wheels climb on to the platform on the ferry?' asked Othi.

'We have taken many buses and lorries across before,' said the leader, condescendingly. 'I have two planks on board. We will wedge one end of each of them in the sand at the river bottom, and place the other end upon the raft. But do be careful to see all four of your wheels keep on the planks and don't go off.'

So saying, he shouted to the other two raftsmen who had been squatting idly on board.

'Oh fellers! bring the planks.'

Each of the men addressed stepped into one of the boats on which the raft's platform was fixed and drew out a plank of wood. From where they were standing, they could see that each plank was about eight feet long, but less than eighteen inches wide.

The leader of the raftsmen paced off with his feet, toe to heel, the distance between the centres of the tyres on the front wheels of the bus. Then he waded across the water, stepped on to the platform on the raft, and carefully measured out the same distance again, heel to tow, marking the spot from where he had begun, and where he ended.

His assistants lifted the planks and shoved the ends into the water, taking care that the middle of the eighteen or so inches, representing the width of each plank, coincided with the places marked. That done, they stood on the planks in turn, to ensure the ends sank into the sand at the bottom of the river securely.

'We are now ready', announced the leader blandly, 'the rest is your responsibility.'

'For heaven's sake, Othi, let the regular driver do the driving,' counselled Percy Rahu, wisely. Then if he throws the blamed thing into the river, we won't be responsible. If one of us handles it and anything misfires the driver is sure to say in headquarters, just as soon as he returns, that we didn't let him do the driving. Then a hundred-and-one questions will be asked.'

Othi agreed, and called to the driver, 'Sattar, you are the regular driver. So take charge of the vehicle and do your stuff.'

Sattar, the driver, looked at the bus and looked at the two narrow planks. Then he scratched his chin, dubiously.

'Come along, man,' said Othi, 'let's get a move on. Don't be scared. It's really quite simple. I could do it myself, in a jiffy.'

'Then why don't you, Sahib?' asked the driver, pointedly.

'Because you are the assigned driver, Sattar. Why should I take the responsibility,' answered Othi, with a touch of annoyance in his voice.

Once again the driver studied the distance between the wheels of the bus and the narrow planks of wood facing him, leading on to the platform of the ferry.

Then he climbed into the driver's seat.

He pressed the self-starter, allowed the engine to idle for a few moments, and then raced it. Letting it run slowly again, he depressed the clutch, engaged first gear, and revving the engine slightly, removed his foot gently from the clutch pedal.

Slowly the bus moved into the river and finally the front wheels reached the two planks. The spectators noticed the water was abreast of the footboards on both sides.

Then the front wheels began to climb the gradient of the two planks.

But the driver had given insufficient acceleration to the engine, which spluttered and came to a stop beneath the load. He declutched, and the front wheels rolled slowly backwards down the planks and into the water.

'Accelerate more next time, Sattar,' shouted Othi, 'now try it again.'

Once more the driver started the engine and engaged first gear. Once again the front wheels climbed the plank. Then the engine cut out. The driver pressed the foot brake and held the bus in position.

'Go on, race the engine. Don't be afraid,' advised Othi.

For the third time Sattar tried. But he was nervous and once again bungled it. On this occasion, in removing his foot from the brake pedal to the accelerator he wasted time. As he pressed the self-starter the front wheels rolled backwards into the water. The engine started, and stalled.

'Damn it, man; what's wrong with you?' spluttered Othi. 'Here, let me show you.'

Regardless of his shoes and socks he waded through the water, motioned to Sattar to move over, and climbed into the driver's seat in his place.

Othi then started the engine, depressed the clutch, engaged first gear, raced the engine wickedly and let go the clutch.

The bus bounded forward with a jerk. The front wheels climbed the planks and came on to the floor of the raft. The rear wheels started to follow.

But in the various attempts that had been made, and with the front wheels moving back and forth, the plank to the right had gone askew. The right-hand rear wheel rolled off it and fell, with a mighty splash, into the water, dragging the left rear-wheel with it, which followed with a second splash.

The two front wheels of the bus now rested on the raft, while the two rear wheels were in the water. The uneven weight caused the nearer end of the raft to slightly submerge, while the further end was lifted clear above the surface.

'Now you've done it,' said Percy, unnecessarily.

Othi tried to start the engine which had once again cut out. But the end of the exhaust pipe was below the surface of the water, and the back-pressure so caused prevented it from starting.

He got out of the driver's seat, scrambled over the front mudguard, and jumped on to the raft, from where he reviewed the situation.

After a minute he said, 'Let's replace the planks, boys, and try to push the damned bus up.' They did that and pushed with might and main. But the weight of the bus was too great, combined with the gradient. They could not budge it an inch.

The time was exactly 5.30 p.m.

Othi spoke to the leader of the crew controlling the raft. 'Is there no village nearby? Cannot you get some more people to help? I will pay you an extra ten rupees.'

That worthy smiled derisively. 'The nearest village is seven miles away, Sahib. Besides it is too late now, and we must be getting home ourselves for nobody will stay out after dark in these parts. It is a dangerous area. Man Singh stays near here.'

And he laughed mirthlessly.

Percy thought he caught him exchanging glances with the old Sikh.

Then he went on to add, 'Sahib, we will be back tomorrow morning and will bring some men with us. But it will cost you one hundred rupees to get your bus out of the river and not just ten rupees. And you must do it soon. Otherwise, it will cost you more; for you have immobilised our raft and we shall be losing business. Keep your one hundred rupees ready—that is, if you are all still here and alive in the morning and the money is still with you.'

At these words he, and his four companions, laughed meaningly.

Then they commenced wading through the water to the shore.

'Come back you blackguards,' called Othi after them, 'let us try once again to push the bus on to the raft.'

'There are not enough of us and it will require another dozen people to do that,' returned the leader, 'besides, as I have just told you, it will be dark soon and we dare not be abroad at that time. Keep a careful watch during the night, Sahibs,' he added, addressirig all of them, 'and take my advice—stay awake! That is most essential.'

Once again the whole company of them tittered and then commenced walking away. Only old Ranjit Singh, the Sikh, remained.

The six men who had come in the bus looked at each other blankly.

'I do not advise you to remain in the bus at night, Sahibs.'

It was the voice of the old Sikh speaking.

'There are many dangers. For one thing, the river may rise suddenly and you will be drowned. Apart from that, there are other dangers, too.' His voice trailed to an end.

'What dangers?' queried Othi, deliberately.

Ranjit Singh just smiled an enigmatic smile, but did not answer.

'Are you referring to Man Singh and his bandits?' asked Seshagiri, nervously.

'Maybe to his bandits,' answered the old man, vaguely. Then he chuckled aloud.

What the devil is he driving at, mused Seshagiri, in an abstracted fashion.

'If you will be gracious enough to accept the shelter of my poor hut for this one night, Sahibs, and such food as my miserable hospitality is able to bestow, you will at least be safe. Tomorrow will see you on your way. It is but one mile from here,' he added apologetically.

'Percy! Othi!' interrupted the frightened Seshagiri, in English, 'for God's sake let us accept. It is far too dangerous to spend the night in the open in this awful place.'

So they wrapped up their bedrolls, and each of the six of them, carrying his own suitcase, bedding and such other things as were left in the bus, started following the old man, who led the way walking downstream along the bank.

At least he was fairly correct as far as his estimate of distance was concerned, for they had gone just a mile when they saw a neem tree growing about two hundred yards from the water's edge. Under the tree was a grass hut.

As they came closer, a man came out of the hut, which proved to be larger than they had first thought by looking at it from a distance. This individual was much younger, had piercing black eyes, rather a long, oval face and a medium-sized beard. He was tall and strappingly built, wore a turban like the Sikh and a similar type of trousers; but no coat. A long shirt hung outside his pants, reaching almost to his knees.

'That is my servant,' said Ranjit Singh by way of explanation. Then, addressing the man, he said, 'Ganga, prepare some cha for the sahib and their attendants.'

'It is already prepared, huzoor,' answered the servant, promptly.

The hut was a rectangular affair, the roof of grass supported by a long bamboo held at either end by forked sticks, some ten feet high, planted in the ground. The roof itself sloped downwards on both sides. It appeared to be empty, except for a small steel trunk and some clothes bundled on top of the trunk, the lot being stored in a corner at the further end.

The newcomers also noticed that a smaller hut stood at the back. This had not been visible behind the larger construction up to now. From this second hut came the delicious smell of food being cooked.

'Keep your samans (belongings) in that further corner, inside,' invited the ancient. 'Then you may go down to the river and wash; or bathe if you like. It is quite safe; there are no 'mugger' (crocodile) in this part of the river. After that, khanna (food) will be served. It is but poor fare, Sahibs,' he apologised, 'but such food as I have you are most welcome to share.'

'Thank you very much, Singh-ji,' returned Othi, 'it is most kind of you. I really fear that we are putting you to a great deal of inconvenience, besides eating up your reserve store of food. Pray don't bother. We have some tinned provisions with us that will serve the occasion and which we beg you to share.'

Percy and Sesh joined in with their thanks.

'It is very good of you, Sahibs,' said their new friend, 'but as long as you are the guests of Ranjit Singh, you must not refuse his hospitality.'

They could see that, if they persisted, it would cause the old man hurt, if not open offence. So they accepted with renewed thanks.

Just then the servant, Ganga, appeared from the hut at the rear, bearing a large kettle of tea and seven enamel mugs. He served his master first; then Othi, Seshagiri and Rahu; and lastly the bus driver and the two mechanics.

Greatly refreshed by the tea, the six of them took soap and towels and walked down to the river for a bath. Within half an hour they were back, and now another pleasant surprise awaited them.

A clean mat had been spread in front of the main hut. As it was rapidly growing dark, a lantern had been lighted and stood in the centre of this mat. Upon a large aluminium platter, to one side, had been heaped a pile of freshly-made chappatties—there must have been at last fifty of them; and beside the platter stood a large degchie (a deep aluminium utensil), containing something else. For a moment they did not know what it was, as the degchie was covered.

'Please be seated, Sahibs,' Ranjit Singh invited; and then, to his servant, 'Ganga, spread another mat over there for the gentlemen's attendants.'

The old man uncovered the degchie to reveal its contents—delicious looking, and delicious smelling, cauliflower and home-made cheese, made into a curry.

'Here are plates,' he offered, 'but I am afraid you will have to eat with your hands. I have no spoons except the one large ladle for dishing out the curry. And, please take as many chappatties as you want, sahibs. There are plenty more in the kitchen, at the back.'

The curry was delicious and the chappatties soft and fried to perfection. Nobody spoke for the next ten minutes, as they were too busy with the food spread before them. In spite of Seshagiri's oft-repeated assertions that he would not eat anything that had not been prepared by a Brahmin like himself, he was so hungry that he ate heartily with the rest of his companions.

Meanwhile the servant, Ganga, served the driver and the two mechanics who had seated themselves upon the second mat he had spread for them.

Now and again the Sikh looked up and smiled a half-smile of contentment as he regarded with satisfaction the obvious relish with which his guests were consuming the curry and chappatties.

Fifteen minutes or so, later, they slowed down their eating. Almost all the curry was gone; and the chappatties, too. They had more than done justice to the meal.

Finally, with a bucket of water held in his hand a few feet away, Ganga beckoned to them. One by one they washed their hands as he sloshed the water over them.

Now that his stomach was full, Percy had been thinking, and the course of his thoughts apparently worned him a bit. Once or twice he made as if to speak to Ranjit Singh, but hesitated at the last moment. At last he came out with what was on his mind.

'Tell me, Singh-ji,' he asked innocently, speaking in Hindustani and addressing the old man, 'how comes it that you appear to have so much food—and cha, too—ready on hand to serve, when there is just yourself and your servant here? Do you often have guests or people like us dropping in?'

Just for a fleeting instant his habitual half-smile died from the old Sikh's face. But only for an instant. Then it was back again, as benign and as pleasant, as before.

'No, Sahib; very rarely guests like yourselves. But frequently many buses and convoys of lorries pass this way and are held up because of the ferry. The drivers are hungry and come here to eat my food. Of course, I make a business of it then, by selling.'

Percy remembered that at the crossing-point the number of vehicle tracks showing in the soft sand had been comparatively few. Also the ferry crew had clearly said that remaining out after dark in this region was considered a highly dangerous undertaking and never done. Was their host deliberately lying? The traffic at the ferry-point was scarce; they had not seen a vehicle of any kind for the last hour.

'I see, Ranjit-ji,' broke in Othi, 'then you must really permit us to pay you for the excellent fare you put before us and that we have enjoyed so heartily.'

The old man held up his hand in protest. 'No, Sahib. This time you are my guests,' he explained, 'but perhaps if you pass this way again I might charge you with a little interest thrown in,' and he laughed softly at what he considered a good joke.

After they had washed their hands, they sat down for some more tea.

Then from the steel trunk inside the hut the old man took a straight and much-blackened clay pipe, together with a small cloth bag filled with powdered tobacco. He loaded his pipe, lit it, and drew on it contentedly, exhaling a stream of blue smoke from his nostrils and lips.

He said to them, 'Tell me some more about yourselves, Sahibs. Do you not work for the Government? Are you not the servants of the sarkar?'

Othi began speaking in Punjabi and told the old man all over again that they were employees of a private industrial organisation in the south of India, and had been entrusted to drive the bus to the new branch opened by the company at Srinagar.

Ranjit Singh seemed very interested in all Othi told him, and asked a great many questions as to what sort of work the company to which they belonged was doing in the south, what work they were doing, what was their pay and positions, and so forth. Othi answered his questions fully and was pleased that the Sikh was such an attentive listener.

Then the old man said, 'A little while ago, while seated, in the bus by the riverside, you mentioned that this sahib,' here indicating Seshagiri with the stem of his clay pipe, 'was very afraid of the bandit, Man Singh. Why is that so? What rumours are circulating about him in southern India?'

Was it their imagination, or did his voice hold an aggrieved tone?

Percy heard the question and again began to ponder.

Othi answered with a laugh, slapping Sesh good-humouredly on his knee. 'You see, Singh-ji, this friend of mine has never left his part of the country before. He is a voracious reader of the newspapers, which make out that this Man Singh is a cruel and bloodthirsty outlaw who murders everyone he sees for money. Naturally, when our bus fell in the river, he was afraid that this brigand might come at night and slit all our throats,' and he chuckled.

But Ranjit Singh seemed far from amused. His smile faded and his face grew serious. There was a noticeably peculiar expression on it now. It was a look of resentment, mixed with sorrow; an aspect of apology, as of one striving greatly to be understood; a manifestation of hurt, struggling to give vent to its own excuses and wanting to offer its own explanations.

Seeing these changing expositions in the ancient's eyes and face, Percy commenced to ponder more deeply than ever before.

Whatever thoughts came to his mind did not appear to be very satisfactory or comforting, though. For Percy glanced around him, and noticed the utter blackness of the night that had set in by now and began just outside the narrow circle of light cast by the feeble and flickering glow of the lantern on the mat.

Some minutes later, Seshagiri said, 'It's half-past nine and I am feeling sleepy. Do you mind if I turn in? But you chaps can continue talking. It won't disturb me.'

Although he had so far given no indication of being able to understand or speak English, Ranjit Singh evidently guessed what had just been said. For he broke in, 'If this gentleman, or all of you are tired, let us go to bed then.'

'I think it is an excellent idea,' said Othi, climbing to his feet.

They all got up. In the meantime, having finished their dinner, the bus driver and the two mechanics had curled themselves up on the other mat and were already fast asleep.

'Sahibs, you must all sleep inside the hut. Yes, and your servants, too. I will sleep across the entrance and keep the lantern burning dimly outside.'

THE THREE TRAVELLERS

Othi hesitated for a second. Then he said, 'Singh-ji, I am afraid it will be frightfully hot inside at this time of the year. I think, if you don't mind, I should prefer to sleep out here on this very mat. It will be cooler.'

The Sikh turned on him, rather impatiently it seemed. 'Please do as I ask, Sahib; it is not safe for you to sleep outside. No, nor your servants either. They must also sleep inside the hut, along with the three of you. There is enough room.'

Momentarily, Othi felt like contesting the point. He did not want to be cooped up in the confines of a hut with five other human beings on a hot summer night like this one. But the old Sikh had already turned away apparently taking it for granted that he would be obeyed. He walked across to the three men sleeping on the other mat, and awoke each in turn by gently shaking his shoulder. As the three of them 'sat up drowsily, he pointed with his right hand towards the large grass hut and said in Hindustani, 'Un-dher chalo' (get inside).

Obediently the three of them got up and came to the grass hut.

In the meanwhile Percy closed his hand over Othi's left elbow and whispered into his ear, in English, 'We have got to listen to him and sleep inside. I think I can guess the reason, but there is no time to tell you now. God knows if the old devil understands English or not.'

By this time Ranjit Singh was walking back. He laid down the mat on which they had just dined to one side of the rectangular hut, and indicated that the three of them should sleep upon it, their heads to the centre and feet towards the outside.

Then he told the bus driver to fetch the other mat on which they had just been sleeping. The driver obeyed him. Ranjit Singh said that it should be spread along the opposite side of the rectangular hut and instructed the three of them to sleep upon it, their head also towards the centre and feet to the outside.

In a very few minutes the six men had laid out their respective bedrolls on the two mats. They then lay down upon them in the positions the old man had pointed out. Percy was nearest the entrance to the hut, Seshagiri next to him, and Othi furthest away.

Meanwhile Ranjit Singh had spread his own simple bed across the entrance. Before lying down himself he lowered the wick of the lantern to a dim glow and placed it just outside the hut within his reach. As he settled down for the night he told them to sleep soundly without fear.

Percy was dog-tired and wanted, badly, to sleep. But he struggled against the feeling and strove to keep himself awake. Within a few minutes Othi, on the distant side, began to snore—a loud, gurgling sound with the exhalation of each breath; followed by a deep, rasping intake.

Sesh was breathing evenly, indicating that he, too, had fallen asleep.

One of the mechanics began to mutter in his slumber. No sound came from the other two men, or from Ranjit Singh at the doorway.

Percy began to think that he was grateful to Othi for the loud noise he was making. It would help to keep him awake. Because, at all costs, he at least should remain so. It would give rum a chance to warn the other two when danger eventually threatened.

For he was convinced above everything else that the six of them were in very real danger.

But tired Nature invariably asserts herself. At least she did so that night. After a vain struggle lasting for perhaps half an hour, Percy himself fell fast asleep.

He had no means of telling how long after that he suddenly woke up, or why. But he did; abruptly and very completely.

The lantern, which had been burning dimly at the entrance, had gone out and they were in Stygian darkness. Percy sensed there was somebody standing in the hut.

Then came a faint scratching sound and a match was struck. He closed his eyes and pretended to be asleep, but contrived to keep the eyelids of his left eye ever so slightly apart to see what was going on.

And he saw the face of Ranjit Singh, with match held aloft above his head, peering at each of them in turn. Then the match went out.

This time, Percy made a better job of it at keeping awake, and remained so. There was no other sound from the Sikh. But he momentarily expected to feel the sharp blade of a knife stick into his chest, or perhaps its edge run across his throat. Involuntarily, he drew his chin inwards.

Quite some time after that, he did not know how long, Percy heard the deep, booming 'Who—o—o' of a horned owl calling some distance away. It hooted thrice and was silent.

Immediately it was answered by another owl. But this bird must have been very very close to the hut, mused young Rahu. Perhaps it was even seated on the top. Twice it hooted weirdly, dismally in reply, like a lost soul answering its mate. Then it was silent.

The minutes dragged by and Percy grew more and more nervous. A sixth sense kept pounding into his brain the message that they were in very great danger. He thought of awakening Seshagiri first, and then Othi; but considered that the noise they might make in getting up would surely give them all away.

Then he heard the faint whisper of voices speaking in a hushed undertone. It appeared to come from just outside the hut.

Percy turned his head ever so slowly, opened his eyes and strained to see out into the darkness. But he could make out nothing more than the faint outline of the entrance.

Two or three men were talking in whispers. He could hear their words. They were speaking in some language that he did not know. Punjabi perhaps; or maybe some other dialect. Of the six of them, Othi would be the only one who might understand what was being said.

But he was sleeping on the other side of Seshagiri, and he was snoring again.

Percy wondered what he should do. Then an idea came to him. Sitting up, on hands and knees he gently crossed over the slumbering Sesh and crouched down beside Othi.

Now came the problem of awakening him without causing him to make any sound.

Leaning forward on his right elbow, Percy blew air through pursed lips, gently but persistently, into Othi's face.

The rhythm of Othi's steady snore was broken. He gurgled and groaned. Then he turned on his right side, away from that annoying draught, and continued snoring.

Percy propped himself up on his knees, lent over the stout figure, and continued to blow air gently, but steadily, on the sleeper's face. The snoring stopped; then started again. Othi gurgled and grumbled in his sleep.

Would this fat fool never wake up, Percy began to wonder, anxiously? Was he going to snore all night?

So he blew harder than ever before.

The snoring stopped abruptly.

Percy knew that Othi was awake at last.

Leaning over still further, Percy whispered very softly into his ear, 'Othi, Othi; wake up and listen. There are voices whispering outside. What are they saying?'

'Where? Who? Why is it so dark? Where are we?' Although Othi also spoke in a whisper, his voice seemed inordinately loud. Clearly he was confused; and also afraid.

Re-assuringly, Percy pressed his arm; then whispered again, 'Hush! Be very careful. Make no sound, whatever. Listen; what are they saying?'

Othi sat upright, so as to be able to hear better.

The voices were murmuring in Punjabi, and he could understand what was being said. He listened in silence for awhile.

Percy, who could not follow, was becoming increasingly anxious and impatient. At last he whispered, 'For God's sake; what are they saying?'

Othi whispered back, 'Two men are questioning a third. They say they saw our bus at the river and were about to set fire to it because it looked to be a Government vehicle. Then they decided to consult the old man and so came here.'

'Where is the old man?' inquired Percy.

'It is he who is talking to them. Keep quiet now, and let me listen.'

The whispering continued and Othi hearkened.

Then he breathed excitedly, 'Percy, they are dacoits.
I just heard them say so. Wake up Sesh and our men. We must escape from here while the going is good. Hurry.' Rahu turned and started blowing air against Seshagiri's face to awaken him, as he had done to Othi.

Sesh did not awaken immediately. Then, quite unexpectedly, he said irritably and aloud, in English, 'What the devil are you trying to do? Let me sleep.'

The whispering outside stopped immediately, and they heard approaching footsteps.

In a few seconds they made out the tall form of Ranjit Singh at the doorway. This time he shone the beam of an electric torch in their faces. He saw all three of them sitting up on the ground, and noticed Percy was now in another place.

'So you are awake, Sahibs?' he queried, an amused jilt in his voice, 'and you have been listening no doubt, eh?'

They did not answer.

'Sometimes it is very dangerous for one to hear things not intended for him to hear,' he continued, seriously; 'but it doesn't matter this time. We will excuse you.'

Turning his head, he called out, 'Oh, my brothers and children; our guests are wide awake. Would you like to speak to them?'

There was an unintelligible murmur from outside which they could not make out.

Ranjit Singh addressed them again, 'Alright, Sahibs; bring your mat with you and come outside. It is cooler here and we shall talk.'

Without thinking of disobeying they walked outside, Seshagiri carrying the mat they had all been lying on.

The reflection from the stars, scintillating in myriads in the clear sky above them, cast a diffused glow over the entire scene. In that dim light they saw many figures standing around them.

'Spread the mat and sit down, gentlemen,' invited Ranjit Singh.

They complied.

'Well sirs,' he went on, 'one of you, earlier this evening, expressed fear of meeting the dacoits of this region. Another one of you said he would very much like to meet them. In fact, two of you said that. Those men's wish has been granted. Around you,' and here his voice assumed a dramatic touch, tinged with pride, 'are all dacoits.'

'And who are you?' It was Sesh who blurted out the question.

'I? Well, I am Man Singh, of course.'

There was a gasp of incredulous surprise from both Othi and Sesh. But Percy murmured, 'I thought so. I might have known it all along.'

Man Singh addressed him seriously. 'Young man, I had strong doubts about you from the beginning. From your demeanour, I know you suspected something. Then, when I came into the hut after midnight and struck a match to see if you were all asleep, I found you pretending to be so while peeping at me with one eye half-opened. Death stood very close to you at that moment, Sahib. I began to think you might be a police spy. Don't do it again, young man. You might not be so lucky the next time. Remember, men do not sleep with one eye closed and one eye opened.

'However, I have decided to spare your lives and let you go free, as I think you are all harmless and innocent. Also, I want you to do me a favour. I want you to take a personal message from me, and when you go back I want you to tell as many people as you can what I am now about to say to you. Tell it to the Government; tell it to big people; tell it to the newspapers; tell it to the poor; tell it to the rich; tell it far and wide.

'In fact, give my message to the whole of India and to the whole world.'

Man Singh's voice rose in crescendo and vibrated with earnestness.

'Listen carefully, then. This is the message I am about to give you.

'Man Singh Rathore, the dacoit, sends his greetings and this message to the Government and the people of India and to the people of the world.

'He was an honest, upright man, coming from an honest family, till some wicked people besmirched his honour and disgraced his family. The law was powerless to punish the evil individual who had first accused this innocent man and dragged his family's name into the dust. So I, Man Singh, who was that innocent man, punished that wrongdoer for the evil he had performed.

'Because I destroyed him and his vagabond brood, the law calls me a murderer. Why did it not punish him for what he did? Then it would have been a just law. Now it is an unjust law; seeking only to protect the rich and powerful against the poor and weak.

'I, Man Singh, am here to oppose this unjust law. I seek to help the poor and weak against the rich and powerful.

'Was I such a bad man as people sometimes say, I could kill and rob all of you right now. I know you each have money with you. I could also burn your bus to ashes.

'But I will not do it as you have harmed no one and I have no quarrel with you.

'Tell the people of India when you go away from here, Sahibs, that Man Singh is a true son of India and brother of theirs. He loves the country and is proud of being an Indian; and he loves them, too. But he hates oppression and injustice in any form, whatever.

'Therefore, Man Singh will continue to fight such oppression and injustice to the very end till he conquers them; or, maybe, till they conquer him; who knows?

'That is my message, Sahibs; and I entrust the three of you, on your word of honour as gentlemen, to deliver it to India, and, through India, to the rest of the world.

'At dawn today, before the crew of the raft returns, my men will put your bus on board. Rajah Man Singh Rathore, has spoken.'

And so it came to pass that, when the leader and the four members of the crew of the raft, accompanied by many other men from the village, turned up at about seven o'clock that morning, expecting to make at least one hundred rupees from the stranded strangers by pushing their bus on to the raft, they were petrified with amazement to find the work already accomplished and the bus safe and sound on board the raft, with all six of the men who had travelled in it sitting unconcernedly inside, smoking cigarettes.

Now would any of the six tell them how that miracle had been accomplished.

And they only received ten rupees for themselves, which was the normal fee for ferrying any bus or lorry across the river.

∼

This incident, strange in itself, brought a still stranger sequel.

Othi and his two companions returned by air to their headquarters in the south after leaving the bus at Srinagar; the driver and the two mechanics travelling by the slower train route.

Once back, all six of them as might have been expected kept to their promise and gave wide propaganda to their adventure, and Man Singh's personal message was repeated far and wide.

Most people did not believe them and felt their story was but an ingenious improvement on the usual fisherman's yarn. Could it be possible that the notorious murderer Man Singh who had spent so many years of his lifetime slitting people's jugulars, had not only spared them but had refrained from robbing them and well, in addition to feeding them and putting their vehicle safely on the ferry-boat? It was far too much to believe and should be taken with more than the proverbial pinch of salt!

But here and there, few and far between, people did believe them and the reputation for nobleness of Rajah Man Singh became enhanced.

And thus it came to pass that an American journalist, touring India in his private capacity, came to hear the story.

He did not know whether to credit it or not. So like most Yanks, he decided to do the common sense, plain thinking thing.

He made up his mind to first meet the men who had brought the story, and judge for himself whether they appeared to be reliable types of people or just obvious liars.

And he decided that, if he felt they were telling the truth, he would visit Man Singh if possible himself, and get the message at first hand from his lips to convey it himself to the people of the United States of America.

Thus he made it his business to trace the story to its origin and met Othi, Rahu and Seshagiri. All three of them assured him they had been speaking the plain truth, and produced the bus driver, Sattar, and the two mechanics who had been with them, as further evidence.

The journalist was satisfied. He waited just long enough to find out where all this had happened and what would be the shortest route to the ferry-crossing where the bus had been held up.

Then he got there.

Let us hand it to this Yank for being a brave man. Bear in mind he was a total stranger to India and could not speak a single word of any dialect. Yet he proposed to call upon Man Singh at his own headquarters in the midst of the Chambal ravines.

Now Johnny Carter, which was the American's name, had plenty of common sense and grit to make up for the handicaps of not knowing the people, country or language. Also, like all Yanks, he appeared to have a fair amount of money.

He hired three interpreters who could speak English, and through them came to learn all the current stories and rumours about Man Singh that were afloat, in order to find out all he could about the outlaw chief.

Thus it came to pass that, amongst other things, he found out that the bandit leader was easily accessible through his hundreds of spies, informers and secret agents, to all who sought him for good and sufficient reasons.

Next, he told his three assistants to go into the marketplaces of the towns in the area, and into the villages too, and spread his message to the dacoit leader among all the people.

'Tell Rajah Man Singh Rathore that an American journalist craves audience with him. This American has heard and received the message the Rajah gave to the six men who came by bus and were stranded at the ferry, to give to the people of India. The American Sahib would hear it himself from the Rajah's own lips so as to be able to deliver it with assurance to the millions of people in his own country of America far beyond the seas. For this purpose the American is prepared to entrust the Rajah with his life and to come alone and unarmed to whatever place the Rajah may bid him.'

Having sent out the message through his interpreters, John Carter camped in a certain Travellers' Bungalow to await results.

These came on the third day. One of his interpreters brought the news.

He was highly excited. 'Carter Sahib,' he said, 'last night there came a tapping at the window of the room in which I was sleeping. Wondering who it could be, I glanced at the clock. It showed one o'clock in the morning. I opened the window but saw nobody. Then from the darkness in front of me a voice said, 'Tell the American Sahib that the Rajah has received his message and will gladly give him audience. If he is speaking the truth, not a hair of his head shall be harmed. If this is a police trap or he is lying, he will not see another sunrise. Tell him to start walking on the main road which leads to the town of Bhind at midnight tomorrow night. He is to tell nobody—not a single soul. The Rajah will find his own means of contacting the American. And there is one other thing. Should any ambush or trap be laid due to this message, both the American and you will be killed. That is the message of Rajah Man Singh Rathore.'

'That is all, Carter Sahib. For God's sake be careful and tell nobody else what I have said. If you do, we shall surely both be killed.'

Johnny smiled very happily. He would tell nobody. And he would certainly keep the appointment.

At midnight the following day he left the gates of the friendly Travellers' Bungalow behind him. The road to Bhind passed directly in front of the building and led to the west.

So Johnny turned in that direction and walked onwards.

He walked for more than an hour and did not know how far he had come. As it was, the darkness was so intense that he had difficulty in keeping to the road itself. Had it not been for the trees growing on both sides he would have definitely strayed off it.

Suddenly things happened!

Without a sound or warning of any kind, John felt himself grabbed by two pairs of powerful arms, while a black cloth descended over his head.

This is it, he thought; and offered no resistance whatever.

More pairs of hands roped his arms behind him and his feet together. Then he was bodily lifted up and carried some distance.

Through the cloth over his head he thought he heard the neigh of a horse. He was right, for shortly afterwards the men who were carrying him lowered him to the ground and his feet were untied.

Then again they lifted him, but only long enough to guide his foot over the saddle of a horse. He felt the presence of a rider behind him. Strong arms encircled him from the back and took the reins. The horse started trotting at a slow canter. He could hear the hooves of other horses accompanying them, one on either side.

They rode for hours on end. Then the three horses were brought to a halt. John Carter was let down and led over the threshold of a building. Once inside, his arms were untied and the thin black bag removed from over his head.

He blinked his eyes and was surprised to find it was daylight. Two men, armed with double-barrelled shotguns stood at the door through which he had just entered.

Food was offered to him, and hot tea. Then a mat was brought, and he was motioned to lie down upon it and rest.

Despite the discomfort he had suffered for so long with the bag over his head and the ropes that had hurt his arms, John was well satisfied. His hopes were materializing. He fell asleep with that thought.

When night fell again the journey was continued. But by this time his captors had evidently come to believe that there was no trick in it, and that their prisoner was alone and unfollowed. They did not put the black bag over his head, but just blindfolded him with a towel. Nor did they tie his hands behind him.

Once again, with a man mounted behind him on the horse, John rode forward into the unknown.

Later in the night the horses were halted and he was taken down from the saddle. With hands holding his arms on either side to guide him, John was led forward.

They seemed to walk for hours and hours. The going was very rough and he tripped many times due to the cloth over his eyes, and would have fallen had not the arms on either side supported him. The terrain led continuously up and down. Carter began feeling exhausted.

Suddenly, out of the stillness, rang a challenging voice. The men around him answered something which of course Johnny could not understand. Then he was led forward again. He felt the chill of dawn and shivered a little.

At last that interminable walk came to an end. He heard the sound of voices and the hands holding his arms released him. He felt them fiddling at the knot of the cloth that had been used to blindfold him. Finally it was whisked away.

Before him stood a tall old man with abnormally high forehead, crowned with a tall turban. He had a flowing white beard, whiskers and a huge moustache. He was wearing a tight-fitting waistcoat of a maroon colour and white pants, made of silk, loose above the knee and very close-fitting below.

The old man bowed slightly, and salaamed in the fashion of the old days of regal India by raising his right hand and touching his forehead with his fingertips, palm turned inwards.

John Carter returned the greeting with a modern Indian 'namaste', by joining his two hands together before his face, palms and fingers touching each other, in the manner he had been taught to do.

'Welcome to the humble abode of Man Singh,' said the old man, in Hindustani.

But Johnny did not understand one word of what was being said. Instead, he looked interestedly at his surroundings.

Obviously they were in a cave of some sort, as the place was illumined by the light of four lanterns, suspended from the walls at different points. Besides Man Singh and the two men who had brought him, there were two others in the place. One of these latter carried a tommy gun in the crook of his arm. The other was a tall young man, unmistakably the old man's son, as he had the same high forehead and steely, boring eyes.

Man Singh noticed that the white man did not understand his welcome, and then remembered that he was an American and therefore unlikely to be conversant with any Indian language.

He turned to the young man beside him, and said, 'Tehsildar, my son, call Prithvi. He understands the white man's tongue and can speak to the American sahib.'

The young man so addressed went out of the cave. In about ten minutes he was back again, accompanied by a short, very dark wiry man of about 35 years of age, with a hooked nose and only one eye. The left eye. He was clean shaven.

Man Singh addressed the newcomer and spoke for awhile. Then Prithvi in turn addressed Johnny in quaintly-worded English.

'Maharaj Sahib, he say he very glad you come. You welcome. You eat something first; yes, no? Drink cha-tea? Then you tell Maharaj Sahib what you want, eh? Yes, no?'

John Carter was glad he could at last converse with the famous dacoit even if it was to be through an interpreter like the man who was now doing the talking. He said to Prithvi, 'Please tell the Rajah Sahib I am mighty grateful he granted me an audience, and I am glad to be here. Tell him that I heard the message he sent to the people of India and to the world through those folk he helped in the bus that got all bogged-up in the river. If he will be good enough to give me that message directly, I shall be real proud and happy to carry it to my own people in the U.S.A., thousands of miles from here.'

Prithvi took some time to translate this message to his leader, but at last finished talking.

The handsome old brigand was obviously greatly flattered and pleased. And proud, too. 'Tell the sahib,' be said, 'that today he shall be my guest. Let him rest first and feast with me. I shall show him my armoury and my treasure chest. Then tonight I shall deliver my message and send him safely back to the outer world. Also convey my apologies for the discomforts of the journey, but he will realise that I was compelled to take precautions.'

Prithvi interpreted all this to John in his quaint way. The American was touched. Spontaneously he held out his right hand to the dacoit leader. The old man took it between both of his and shook it warmly.

Then John was led through a passage in the wall of the cave which he had to negotiate bent almost double to an adjoining cave. Here food and water were served and he rested awhile on a carpet and silken pillows that had been provided for him.

At midday, more food was served. Prithvi appeared with it and said, 'You come after eating to Rajah Sahib? He show you pretty jewels; plenty, plenty. Also 'bundooks' (firearms); he got plenty more.' Then he ended with his characteristic, 'Yes, no?'

John ate heartily of the dry fried meat that was served, along with many thin, freshly-cooked delicious chappatties, dripping in ghee. He was given a large tumbler ot goat's milk after that, followed by a juicy watermelon. When he had finished eating and washed his hands, he stood up and announced he was eager to meet the dacoit-king again.

Prithvi led him along the same passage he had come by earlier and into the same cave where he had first met Man Singh.

The old bandit was there, but Carter noticed the man with the tommy gun had been changed. Also the son, Tehsildar, whom he had met the last time, was not present. In his place was a taller man, slightly older and having a pair of twinkling, jet-black eyes. He wore a black beard and a high, saffron-yellow turban.

Man Singh stretched out both his hands to shake John Carter's right hand again. Then he introduced his companion, through Prithvi. 'This is my beloved second son, Subedar Singh,' adding in an undertone, 'my eldest son, Jaswant Singh, was killed by the police years ago.'

Subedar greeted John pleasantly, with a welcoming, sincere handshake.

'I will show the American sahib my armoury first,' announced Man Singh.

At a signal from him, his bodyguard stooped down and opened a trap door that was concealed under a sheepskin laid on the floor of the cave. Man Singh led the way; the bodyguard followed. Then Subedar Singh invited John to go next. He came immediately behind, with Prithvi bringing up the rear.

They descended six or seven steps cut in the earth, into a low, dark room lit by two lanterns, both suspended from the ceiling. John noticed that there were weapons all around him. Along the further side of the room were lines of wooden rifle-racks. Neatly arranged in them were rows of .393 army service rifles. Along the next wall was another rack. This held a miscellaneous collection of firearms of all description and vintage. There were some modern big-game double-barrelled rifles among them, including a Jeffries .470 cordite rifle and a .500 blackpowder express; many .12 bore shotguns, a couple of them made by such famous makers as Holland & Holland, and three by Greener. And there were some single-barrelled .12 bore and .16 shotguns, too. Along the third wall were arranged the muzzle-loaders; some fairly modern and others very ancient, flintlock weapons. In between these were revolvers and pistols of all makes, shapes and sizes. The last wall of the armoury boasted the cream of the collection. They were British Army-issue Sten guns and tommy guns, mixed with Japanese and Italian automatic weapons, obviously all relics of World War II.

'Still further underground,' indicated Man Singh through the interpreter, 'are our hand-grenades, some bombs, and stores of gunpowder. But it is unsafe to go there just now with lighted lanterns.'

They reascended the earthern staircase to the cave above. Here Man Singh led John to a medium-sized iron safe standing by itself in a corner. He opened the door.

Against the back of the safe, bundled, tied and stacked closely together, were piles of one-hundred-rupee notes. How many such bundles there were he did not count.

In front of the stacks of notes stood a tin box.

Man Singh opened the box for John to gaze at its contents. There he saw gold watch-chains, diamond rings, and necklaces of gold set with emeralds, rubies and other, precious stones; women's golden nose rings and earrings; and trinkets of all descriptions, large and small. Among the collection was a very valuable gold watch of obviously old European make. Man Singh took it out and held it up for John to see. Then he wound it and listened gleefully as it chimed prettily, and struck the hour.

When Man Singh had closed the safe, he turned to the American and said, through Prithvi, 'Go back and rest now, sahib. Tonight you shall have dinner with me and a few guests. After that I will give you my message for your people and send you back, safely.'

That dinner was a memorable event. Man Singh sat John next to him on his left on the floor of the cave while his armed bodyguard stood behind. To the right of the chieftain sat Subedar Singh. To John's left was Tehsildar Singh. There were also five others present whom Man Singh variously introduced as Nawab Singh his elder brother; and four of his lieutenants, Charna, Roopa, Lakhan Singh and Devi Singh. The last invitee to the banquet was the interpreter, Prithvi.

The meal consisted of several courses of well-cooked food, all entirely strange to the American journalist. To end the feast, a bottle of Exshaw Brandy was opened; and finished by them. Only Man Singh himself never touched a drop.

Finally came the closing enactment in the whole unusual drama. Man Singh delivered his message for John Carter to convey to the American people, to England and the world, and Prithvi interpreted it in his comical way.

But it is far too great and wonderful a message to be spoilt by repeating it in the way in which Prithvi said it, although he did his best as interpreter with the poor knowledge of English at his command.

So, rather let us render it as Man Singh originally gave it in his own mother tongue, the dialect of Rajasthan.

'To the President and the people of the United States of America; to the Sovereign and the People of England and the British Empire; and to the People of all the World; I, Rajah Man Singh Rathore, send by you, John Carter, my warmest greetings.

'I am no thief or brigand by choice or by nature. Evil men made me so.

'As the people of all your countries fought, and still fight, for that which is right, so do I fight now. I love my country, India; and I am proud of being one of her sons. I would not exchange this heritage for any other.

'But I grieve over the evil that still happens here, just as it still happens in your lands. Tell all your people to join me in fighting against oppression of the poor in all its forms in all our lands, wherever such wicked practices may exist.

'Only then will my country and your countries become great—and remain great—for all time!

'Many of us will fall in this fight and lose our freedom and even our lives, for the forces of evil are widespread and powerful. But those who die for this cause shall live forever in the histories and memories of the peoples of their lands. Is not that worthwhile? Is it not the greatest reward a man could seek?

'Speak this message aloud, John Carter. Write it in a book and send it to all the countries of the world. For then you will be serving a good cause, and a noble one. And may God be with you always.

'I, Rajah Man Singh Rathore, have spoken.'

From the third finger of his right hand, Man Singh removed a gold ring, set with a single blood-red ruby. He handed it to John Carter directly, saying to Prithvi,

'Tell the American Sahib to please accept it as a personal gift from me; to keep it and wear it, in remembrance of me. Tell him it is my own ring; not stolen from anyone.'

And the illustrious old man shook with laughter at his own joke.

John Carter began the journey back later that night. He was not bound this time, nor was the black bag put over his head. He was merely blindfolded. And it was done with his consent and in his own interest. For then he could truthfully answer the authorities that he did not know the way to Man Singh's secret cave.

What happened thereafter is not known in India. But we sincerely hope John delivered the great message entrusted to him that day.

Perhaps, as he gazes at that gold ring and that blood-red ruby, his memory conjures up a picture of that grand old bewhiskered warrior, imbued with the solemn and noble principles of the cause for which he was prepared to lay down his life and become a martyr—Man Singh, the gentleman dacoit.

Chapter Seven

The History of Man Singh

Rajasahib Man Singh Rathore, king of the Dacoits of India, did not earn his distinction easily or lightly. It was not just a name, given to an ordinary man. He earned every letter that went to make up that proud and extraordinary title. His is a history beyond imagination that beggars description and is fascinating, transcending words.

Just think of it. One single man, who was pursued by 1,700 policemen of four states for 15 years in an area of approximately 8000 square miles. He was the victor of over 80 encounters with the police. And the cost of the operations, that eventually led to his death, was one and a half crores of rupees. In figures, this reads as Rs. 1,50,00,000. Or, if you should prefer to write it in another way, Rs. Fifteen millions of rupees! About one and one-eighth millions of pounds sterling spent on the elimination of just one man!

For his arrest, or his dead body, many rewards were offered, the highest being Rs. 15,000—well over pounds 1000 sterling!

Records and paperwork, dealing with his adventures his depredations, and his pursuit, were estimated to weigh over a tonne. He was directly responsible for more than 200 murders and a thousand acts of dacoity, pillage, ransom and raid.

But all the loot he was accused of having taken, both proved and unproved, did not amount to anywhere near half the sum of money the Government spent in trying to catch him.

And bear in mind always dear readers, this is not mere romancing. These are plain, hard, true facts.

There was nothing petty, mean, ignoble or churlish about this man. Everything was noble, brave, sporting and on a grand scale. Justice was something he not only preached, but lived and followed himself.

Read what the Bhind Morena Crime Inquiry Committee, appointed by the Government of the State of Madhya Bharat in 1953, has to say about this most unique personality:

'The case of Man Singh is representative of the peculiar problems of this area. He is reported to be a man with no private vices. Stories are told of him in hushed voices of admiration, of how he helps good causes, kills informers and policemen only when pursued, just lifts a few men who have money to spare, respects Brahmins who give him blessings, and occasionally coerces Zamindars to contribute to desirable objects like school buildings.

'His admirers often remark that he represents the high watermark of dacoity, nobly practised. Officers of revenue, customs and education departments could run into him without fear. He could join marriage celebrations attended by thousands of people. Now, however, he is on the run. His case represents how the natural repulsion against heinous offences can be mellowed by adopting ingenious methods. In the opinion of the Committee, the public attitude towards crime is as serious a matter, if not more serious, than the prevalence of crime itself.'

Remember, those words do not represent the ideas of any one person or of the writer. Verbatim, they are the findings of a Committee appointed by Government to inquire into the causes and nature of such crimes.

Man Singh was reported to be a strict teetotaller and vegetarian, living a life of abject simplicity, close to nature. His morals were unimpeachable. He robbed the rich, to help the poor.

He was deeply religious, and bathed in the river at break of dawn, singing sacred songs in the water where he would offer ablutions to the fiery ball of the rising sun as it peeped above the line of distant hills. Fresh from his bath, he would walk straight to the temple of the Goddess Kali and worship her devoutly. The string of large, amber beads he wore around his neck served the purpose of a rosary. He would count them while enchanting his prayers, and they never left his person night or day.

As part of his religious life, he built several temples, the money for which came from the loot he obtained when robbing the rich. Many a temple, to this day, boasts a big brass bell, donated by the intrepid Rajah. You will find his name inscribed on them. It was his sincere belief that every time the bell was rung it would sound a prayer for him, if he was alive; or for his soul, if he was dead.

He donated schools, too, for the primary education of boys and girls; and 'chatrams' (or free shelters) for the aged, the poor and homeless, and the down-and-out.

There was one religious festival he would never omit to attend. It was held once a year, on a feast day, at the Bateshwar Nath Temple, and Man Singh never failed to be present on that day. Eventually, the police came to hear of it, and on that occasion they would surround the temple with a ring of uniformed men, and closely interrogate the thousands of pilgrims that would attend.

They knew that one among those thousands was the man for whom they were looking.

They would talk to the pilgrims and cross-examine them. Year after year, one of the men they might speak to, and question, would be the man they were so desperately in search of, the bandit leader, Rajah Man Singh. They knew it, but they did not know which was the man. How could they? He was too well disguised. And so, year by year and each year, he would literally slip from their fingers, only to be back again the following year, but with the same results.

Many an evening would he spend at a village, sitting in the open of the 'maidan' (grassy space), or on the doorstep of a house, smoking a clay pipe, the end of which he would hold to his lips with cupped hands, and talk to the villagers, discuss their problems, and help them with advice and money, when required.

The police knew this too, from information conveyed by their agents. But by the time they reached the spot, Man Singh would no longer be there. Evidently his spies—or more likely, his well-wishers—were as efficient as those on the police side. Perhaps more so. But he always just managed to elude their grasp.

A very human story is prevalent about him among the villagers of Bhind.

One evening, as the smoke of the village fires curled heavenward while cooking the evening meal of chappatties, Man Singh sat on the step of the Patel's (headman's) house, talking to the headman and several other villagers.

The Government, through the police, had engaged spies and informers on monthly salaries and had liberally distributed these persons in all the villages, far and wide over the area. One of these individuals came to know of the dacoit's presence and hastened to inform the police. They surrounded the village and converged on the Patel's house. But, as was to be expected, Man Singh had vanished into thin air.

To say the least of it, the Inspector in charge of the police party was peeved. With scowling mien he confronted the Patel.

'Fool, and son of five generations of idiots, why did you not detain him, until we came?'

'Because, your honour, the man who could detain Rajah Man Singh has not yet been born.' The Patel spoke quietly, but there was an air of finality in his tone.

'Don't talk rubbish,' almost screamed the police officer, sweat running down his face from the heat, his exertions, and the rage he was in. He began to speak in short gasps. 'I can lock you up for harbouring this murderer,' he shouted, 'don't you know it is against the law, to aid and abet criminals?'

'I know that quite well, sir,' flatly returned the Patel, 'but I was neither aiding him, nor abetting him. It was just that Man Singh turned up at my house quite unexpectedly and spoke to me. What could I possibly do, sir? Arrest him?'

Then the Patel continued in a quizzical tone. 'You say that I can be locked up, by law, for talking to the Rajah. Tell me, your honour, suppose I had tried to detain Man Singh and had lost my life in doing so. Would the law give me another life?'

The Inspector nearly exploded. Then, just in time, he remembered he was nearing the age of retirement from service. The police doctor had advised him to 'take it easy' for the few months remaining before he would be relieved from duty. He was suffering from high blood pressure as it was, and carried far more weight than was good for him.

There was something, after all, in what the Patel had said, he mused. Neither the Government, nor the law would provide him with a second life. On the other hand, the former would swallow up his pension if he were to kill himself before his time through giving away to undue temper.

With all that, he could not refrain from calling Man Singh a very bad name.

Now, while all this was going on, the usual gaping crowd of villagers had assembled to see and hear all they could. Among them was a young widow whose name was Jaya. Very recently, Man Singh had sent her some money through one of his lieutenants to pay her eldest son's examination fees, to enable him to appear for the school final examination.

She heard the bad word, and she resented it. Hot-headedly, and from the midst of the crowd, she spoke up, addressing the Inspector.

'You do not know him, sir, and hence you have no business to call him that name. Why, he is a benefactor of the poor. Although I had never seen him at any time, he generously sent me money to pay my son's examination fees when I did not have an anna in the house. May God bless him; and protect him from the likes of you.'

Jaya said the words in a rush and then remained quiet, as she realised the magnitude of her offence to this high-ranking police officer. There was utter silence as the crowd waited to see what would happen next.

The Inspector pushed the peak of his service cap upwards, tilting the hat to the back of his head. He looked at the widow closely.

She was middle-aged and rather tall, and still had a comely face. The determined set of her jaw well became her finely-chiselled countenance, and she stood erect, displaying a figure that indicated that, in her youth she must indeed have been a very attractive-looking girl.

'It is because of people like you,' he stormed, 'that we cannot apprehend this scoundrel. Instead of informing us where to find him, you assist him to escape from the clutches of the law?'

'Police Officer,' she said slowly and clearly, 'to you he may be a scoundrel; but to me he is a brother; a very, very dear brother.'

The Inspector wondered what he should do next. All around him were grinning faces. They were laughing at his discomfiture. It was quite evident to him that the whole population of this village, from the Patel downwards, stood behind the bandit-leader and would shelter and support him. They were openly exuberant at the disconcertion of the police posse. He would dearly enjoy beating every man jack of them. But, as that could not very well be done, the next best thing seemed to be to withdraw as gracefully as possible from the scene.

'Squad, fall in!' he ordered. The men fell in, in three ranks. 'Left turn; by the left, quick march.' And the police went away.

A certain old man with a white beard, moustache and whiskers, lying in a hayrick less than a hundred yards away, pulled the wisps of straw from his beard and face, as he watched the departing policemen benignly.

The widow lived in a hut not far away. It was the third turning to the left, as you went along the main street of the village; and her's was the sixth hut, again to the left.

The following day was the celebration of the Diwali festival. That night, there came a soft knocking on her door. Wondering who the caller might be at such a late hour, she timidly opened up, to see a tall and stately figure standing on her threshold, his noble countenance partly hidden in a white beard, whiskers and huge moustache.

'I am Man Singh,' he announced without hesitation. 'Yesterday, I heard you refer to me as your brother to that stout policeman. I have come to thank you for what you said to him, and to tell you that, indeed, I now look upon you as my sister. Please accept this little gift as a token of my esteem and affection. Henceforth, till the day of my death, no matter how far away I may be at the time, I will visit you on Diwali night, my sister.'

With the words he thrust some folded paper into her hands.

Jaya looked down to unfold the paper and see what it was.

Man Singh had given her five one hundred rupee notes.

She looked up to thank him with tears brimming in her eyes.

But he had gone.

Thereafter, every Diwali night, till the year of his death, Man Singh kept his promised tryst with Jaya the widow, who had called him her brother. And each time he gave her five hundred rupees.

The villagers say, in hushed whispers, that after his death Man Singh still visits Jaya on Diwali night. He comes as a spirit, but the money he leaves is real.

Man Singh organised and ruled his gangs of followers well, generously and justly. And there was always discipline amongst them.

The men knew their leader's noble disposition. They were afraid to commit any act that would reflect against the Rajah's, and thereby the gang's, own reputation.

Accounts were kept strictly, and all loot shared equitably.

In one skirmish with the police at a much later date, Tehsildar Singh, the dacoit leader's third son, was captured. On his person was found a diary, which revealed that he served as the steward of the gang, inasmuch as all the day-to-day expenses incurred by them were noted in it. Reading through the items, the police were amazed to find that the dacoits paid for all the food they ate, and did not rob it. Each merchant had been reimbursed in cash for what had been purchased by the band.

Is it any wonder then, that wherever this amazing character went, he was greeted with the deepest respect and profound salaams? Everyone helped him, and no villager would betray or give information about his whereabouts or movements.

Some of the stories told about him may have been exaggerated. Rumours are always that way. But never was he accused, even by the police themselves, of a single act of rudeness to any poor man. Veritably and truly, he was the friend and succourer of the down-trodden.

Just like Robin Hood of Sherwood Forest fame in England, Man Singh was of aristocratic birth. He was a Rajput (which people are a martial clan of Hindus), and his birthplace was the village of Rathore Khera not far from Agra. The year he was born, 1890.

From young, Man Singh loved Nature and everything connected therewith. He revelled in the hard work of ploughing and sowing his fields, and the harvest was a delight and a period of thanksgiving to God, as he gathered in the golden grains of wheat. It was the reward of his labour. He loved each inch of the soil. No work was too hard for his rippling young muscles as he laboured bare-bodied beneath the tropical sun. Every night he would lay himself down to rest, sometimes still soiled with the grime of the day to fall asleep at once; exhausted, but very very happy.

In his spare moments, which were few and far between, he would stroll into the forest that skirted his fields. There he would sit in solitude under a spreading fig tree and hearken with harmony in his soul to the music of the birds of the wild; the plaintive call of peafowl, the harrying and worrying notes of the 'brain-fever' bird, the cheery crow of the jungle-cock both morning and evening, the peculiar sound made by nightjars at dusk and the mysterious and frightening hoot of the great horned owls at night. He asked nothing more from life than these things. He was simple; he was contented; and he was happy.

Bihari Singh, his father, was the village headman or patel. He was rich and lived comfortably with his two sons, Nawab Singh, the elder, and Man Singh, the hard-working, peaceful farmer youth.

As with most other Indian boys romance and marriage were brought early into Man Singh's simple life in the form of a beautiful Rajput lass to whom he was married by his father while still very young. Through her, he had four sons—Jaswant Singh, Subedar Singh,

Tehsildar Singh and Dhuman Singh; and one pretty daughter, whom he named Rani.

When he was only 24 years of age, he was elected as the Mukhiya of his village and made a member of the Agra District Board. The British Government at that time benefitted by his valuable help as a good and honourable citizen during the dark days of World War I. He was always an honest man.

But nothing gave him greater joy than the cultivation of his wide lands, and the income he derived from them more than rewarded him for his hard work.

His outstandingly tall figure, his affable personality, and the beard that he wore from young made him well-known and respected everywhere; both as Mukhiya when he arbitrated over village disputes, and as an active member of the District Board. He had an outstandingly lofty forehead, and on his head he would wear a large and high turban. These increased his physical height and imbued him with a dignified bearing.

Then Fate decided, by one of her quirks that things were going too well with this happy and contented family and started a chain of circumstances that eventually made this upright son of India into one of her most feared and dreaded brigands. Fate went even further than that. It made this man write his history in a queer mixture of chivalry and blood as the greatest dacoit of all time that the country had ever known and at the same time most benevolent.

Bihari Singh his father became engaged in litigation over some land with a man named Talfi Ram, a cunning and plotting Brahmin who was jealous of Bihari Singh's wealth and of Man Singh's increasing popularity and position.

The elder brother, Nawab Singh, had already left the family and was leading a peacefully nomad life in the jungles at this time.

Suddenly a dacoity occurred in the village. The word 'dacoity' signifies a raid accompanied by robbery and violence. In this case a baniya's (moneylender's) house was attacked at night, the baniya stabbed but not killed, and some money taken.

The malicious Talfi Ram falsely informed the police that the nomad elder brother, Nawab Singb, had perpetrated the act, aided and sheltered by the father, Bihari Singh, who did not like the baniya because he was a friend of Talfi Ram. He also stated that Nawab Singh's brother, Man Singh, knew an about the raid and had assisted actively in it.

The police, as police all over the world will do, called both Bihari Singh and Man Singh to the station, closely interrogated them about the missing Nawab Singh, and warned them to be of good behaviour. Nothing more than that was done, because nothing could be proved. There was absolutely no evidence.

But old Bihari Singh, because he was innocent of the charge, took the incident greatly to heart as an irreparable insult to his family's honour and dignity. Young Man Singh supported his father wholeheartedly. His hot Rajput blood was up, and he determined to be avenged on the rascally Brahmin Talfi Ram and his whole family.

It was the fateful year 1928 when matters came to a head and the underlying feud burst into open conflict.

Man Singh went into the forest with his four sons, a relative named Roopa, and a large number of friends and well-wishers. There he joined his brother, Nawab Singh, who had been accused by Talfi Ram of perpetrating the original dacoity.

One night the combined party raided Talfi Ram's house. The Brahmin had been anticipating the attack and had hired some men, as mercenaries, to defend him. A bloody fight took place, in which Man Singh and his party eventually emerged victorious. Several of their opponents were killed and many wounded.

This single incident wiped out, for all time, Man Singh's name from its place of honour as a respectable, useful and law-abiding citizen. Instead, it was now inscribed in letters of blood and murder, as Man Singh the Dacoit, who was later to be hailed as the king of all dacoits.

The police acted quickly and creditably after that, and Man Singh and his whole party were arrested; only his brother, Nawab Singh, his eldest son, Jaswant Singh, and a nephew, Darshan Singh, escaping.

Man Singh was imprisoned for the first and last time in his existence. He was brought on trial and convicted to transportation for life.

As time passed and the tension died down, the three fugitives, Nawab Singh, Jaswant Singh and Darshan Singh, occasionally and secretly visited old Bihari Singh in his house. Talfi Ram came to hear of these clandestine visits. He had sworn to be revenged after his recent defeat and had unobstrusively regathered his forces and friends to attain this purpose.

One day, while the three men were gathered in the house with the old father, Talfi Ram and his band counter-attacked, and a gun battle ensued. At the same time, very cleverly Talfi Ram sent word to the police for help, saying that the three fugitives were in town and trouble was afoot.

The police heard the shooting and concluding that the three wanted men were the aggressors, arrived at the spot as an armed posse. Meanwhile Talfi Ram and his followers had craftily faded from the scene, leaving the three fugitives inside the house and the police on the outside.

Foolishly, Nawab Singh and the other two men opened fire on the armed police. But they were outnumbered and out-gunned. Jaswant Singh, the eldest son, and Darshan Singh, the nephew, were shot dead. Nawab Singh was arrested, brought to trial, and also sentenced as a murderer to transportation for life.

Talfi Ram gloated over his revenge, which had been swift and highly successful.

There had been a Judas among Man Singh's relatives. A distant cousin, named Khem Singh, had deserted and gone over to join the Brahmin who had paid him for his betrayal. In fact, it was this man who had told Talfi Ram that the three fugitives were in the house with Bihari Singh, and had caused the counter-attack. He had also been the one to summon the police.

Man Singh nursed his revenge in his heart for ten long years. His home had been wrecked, the good name of his father, Bihari Singh, and that of the whole family irretrievably besmirched. No longer were they a household that was looked up to and respected. They were but a family of brigands and murderers. Worst of all, the old man, his father, was heartbroken.

The wily Brahmin, Talfi Ram, was responsible for it all. For the death of his son, Jaswant, and his nephew, Darshan Singh. And for sending him, and his brother, Nawab Singh, to jail for years upon end.

Yes; Talfi Ram was the cause of it all. Talfi Ram, and that other traitorous dog, Khem Singh, doubly a traitor because he belonged to old Bihari Singh's family.

Man Singh made up his mind what he would do when he was released.

At last came the year 1938. Ten long years had passed while he had been in jail. During those ten years, Man Singh had been an exemplary convict, and one of the best behaved. He lived for revenge, and revenge only.

Because of his excellent conduct, he was released that year.

No sooner was he out of prison than he got entangled in disputes and open quarrels with the families of Talfi Ram and Khem Singh. Once more the police intervened. They warned him that he would be thrown into jail again. He was bound over to be of good behaviour for two years—up to May 1940. But Khem Singh was excused and went scot-free.

This added insult to injury, and yet more did Man Singh fret and fume. But he had now been taught the need for caution, and bided his time, behaving as a reformed citizen, till May 1940, which marked the expiry of the period for which he had been bound over to be of good behaviour.

At last the sun set on that glad day of May 31st, 1940. Man Singh was now a free person once more.

He waited just one short month to take his revenge.

On the night of 4th July, 1940, assisted by his remaining three sons, the faithful Roopa, and other relatives and friends, Man Singh launched a sudden attack on the houses of his two enemies.

Except for two women, Talfi Ram and his family, or such of them as were at home, were butchered; while Man Singh's youngest son, Dhuman Singh, personally cut off the heads of two of Khem Singh's close relations.

The die had been cast forever. There was now a barrier of blood and guilt between Man Singh and his followers, on the one hand, and law and society on the other—a barrier that could not be forgotten, surmounted, or circumvented. Henceforth, they were outlaws for ever and ever—and the feud that had started against mankind could only be expiated by the death of everyone of the outlaw band.

A person of lesser character would have quailed in the face of this inexorable fate. Everybody's hand was against him, thirsting for his blood. He was feared by all and hated by all. The police of four states were searching for him. He was a lost soul in a lost body. Where should he go, where should he hide? How was he to eat and live? Nowhere could he seek employment; nowhere earn an honest living. His beloved fields, and his beloved home, father and wife were lost to him, forever. He was an outcast; thief, robber, murderer, dacoit!

Truly, most men would have succumbed through sheer fear, desperation and helplessness, to a fate such as lay ahead of him.

But Man Singh never flinched for one moment. He was made of sterner stuff than that. Indeed, he had guts and was veritably a man.

He merely accepted the situation for what it was worth and made the best out of it.

And that best was a very, very great deal, indeed.

From an insignificant outcast, he became, in 15 years, the greatest dacoit India has ever known. To emphasise that achievement, he came to be called throughout the peninsular as the King of Indian Dacaits. He started his career as an ordinary outlaw; hated, feared, and despised by everybody. He ended it by being respected, loved and even revered by millions throughout the length and breadth of the land. He ran away, penniless; but lived to donate money and temple bells, and to build schools and temples themselves. He fled from the scene of his acts of futile vengeance; but lived to save and help many others who, themselves had become the victims of revenge. He had done and still did, much harm; but he also lived to do very much good.

It is not for mortal and sinful men to judge Man Singh and his misdeeds. That supreme judgement is given only to the all-wise Creator who made Man Singh and knew why He had made him and allowed him to sin. But the whole of India acclaims and proclaims that Man Singh was, in veritable truth, a 'man' in every sense of the word—a man with unbounded courage and indomitable spirit.

Perhaps those who read his adventures may come to hold the same opinion.

⁓

At the time, Man Singh embarked upon his career as a dacoit, four states of India converged on an area watered by three rivers. The states were Madhya Bharat, Vindhya Pradesh, Rajasthan and Uttar Pradesh; and the rivers were the Chambal, the Kunwari and the Jamuna.

The country was extremely broken and the land eroded. In between the ravines so formed flowed the three rivers named above, and their tributaries; mostly dry nullahs in the summer, but raging, impassable torrents of water when the rains came. It was wild country; wooded with scrub and interlaced by watercourses, furroughed ravines, and caves, covering an area of well over 8000 square miles.

For purposes of cultivation, the land and the soil were worthless. For purposes of sheltering a band of outlaws, who could hide in the caves, creep along the ravines, strike at their victims, and then vanish into thin air, the terrain was ideal.

Man Singh was a born general. He at once knew that among that maze of ravines, caves, dried waterways and thorny scrub, he and his followers would be safe from surprise attack. Paths were few, and they were tortuous. High grass grew everywhere. Few people, if any, came near the area. It seemed a land of the dead, fit for nothing but ghosts and ghouls and the huge horned owls that sailed soundlessly along the nullahs, seeking a rodent or a rabbit at night for prey.

But Man Singh made it his kingdom; a wide kingdom, forbidding and austere. Here he established his stronghold and headquarters, from where he launched his bands of dacoits upon raid after raid and in which it was very difficult for the police to ever dream of catching up with him.

As his fame and authority spread, more and more outlaws and vagrants were attracted to his banner. Dacoits who had hitherto carried on operations on their own initiative, now decided to throw in their lot with him. Some of them had already earned reputations that caused people to tremble at the very mention of their names. All of them were experienced. One by one, and in groups, they rallied to the standard of this new leader; whom they recognized as a man who possessed both the required strong personality and the organisational capacity to hold such a motley band of hard, cruel desperadoes, together.

Outstanding among his followers, we find the following names. Subedar Singh, Tehsildar Singh, who later became known as 'the Terrible', and Dhuman Singh, his remaining three sons; Charna, 'the Ferocious', who was to grow into his most able general, and Shyama, both dacoits who had hitherto been operating in the United Provinces; Prithvi, Shankar and Dhawan, brigands from Rajasthan; Sultan, Lakhan Singh, 'the Lion', and Amrit Lal, from Madhya Bharat; Pratap and Devi Singh, from Vindhya Pradesh; and his old friend, distant relative and trusted follower, Roopa, 'the Faithful', who outlived him and still operates as a dacoit today.

Just as Robin Hood of England gathered his merry men around him in the fastnesses of Sherwood Forest, from where they would launch their raids and then vanish back into the little-known labyrinths; Man Singh of India gathered his band of outlaws, making the Chambal ravines as they were known, as famous as Sherwood Forest, because they came to shelter a man every bit as brave, and chivalrous, as Robin Hood of undying fame.

His initial attacks were still in pursuit of the old vendetta that had made him into a dacoit, and were directed against the residual members of the families of Talfi Ram and Khem Singh, which he started to systematically exterminate in cold blood. We are told that Khem Singh's relatives were finally completely wiped out with the murder of the last remaining grandson. There is no record as to whether the same fate befell the Brahmin's kinsmen, but the fact that they were never heard of again appears to indicate that it was so. Or perhaps the few that were left fled the area forever.

While this was happening, Man Singh's band of followers and desperadoes increased by leaps and bounds. And men cannot live on revenge. They require food. And food costs money. So Man Singh was forced to extend his raids merely to procure that commodity, money, which meant food and hence life, for all of them.

His initial plans were simple but intelligent. And back of them was the full force of his brain—a brain that had once been clever and devoted to constructive progress—now warped beyond repair, to revel in lawless adventure, and daring, atrocious brigandage.

From the very beginning, Man Singh revealed himself as an organiser of immense capacity and forethought, a strategist of outstanding merit and ability.

He split his gang into groups. One lot were just spies and informers. They would wander into villages and towns, noting who were rich and well-to-do persons. Later, they would kidnap them, or perhaps one of their sons or other beloved relative, and hold him to ransom in the fastnesses of the ravine kingdom.

The kidnapped person, be the zamindar, businessman or landlord, or the heir of such a person, would be compelled to write a letter home to his relations, plainly stating he had been kidnapped and that the gang demanded ransom money. In addition he would have to say that, if the money was not paid within a stipulated period, he would most certainly be done to death.

Invariably the ransom was paid. People did not dare to report the matter to the police, because in any case the police were helpless, and could do nothing about it; while, if Man Singh came to know the police had been told, there was the great danger that the person held to ransom would be put to death at once.

Another group was formed to function as a striking force. The leader of this advance corps was the brigand named Charna. He earned the epithet of 'the Ferocious', and indeed he was the most merciless of all Man Singh's lieutenants. A fearless man, and an inherent tactician, he selected as the men who were to serve under him the most bloodthirsty and toughest members, whom he trained in jungle warfare and the use of tommy guns and modern equipment. He had been a soldier in his time and was given the choice of the best equipment in the possession of the band, which included hand-grenades, Sten guns, tommy guns, and .303 service rifles, all procured illegally along with vast stores of ammunition.

The 'spies' would inform the 'advance corps' who very often did the actual kidnapping.

Not only that, but Charna's men served as a commando unit in more senses than one. It was their duty to look out for police movements, and to counter-attack, ambush and harass them, and keep them engaged till the main body of dacoits could escape, or wolf around to surround the police and tackle them from the rear.

Tehsildar Singh, the third son, was the marksman of the band. He was an excellent sniper. Even in pitch darkness, he had taught himself to fire at the author of the slightest sound. Invariably that individual never made another sound in this life again.

Or Tehsildar would throw a stone near some police picket on a pitch-black night. The sentry would challenge, or open fire. Tehsildar would locate the spot where the challenge came from, or watch the flash from the policeman's rifle. The next second the sentry would be dead.

Lakhan Singh, called 'the Lion', and Devi Singh were two others among Man Singh's lieutenants who earned for themselves the reputation of being most ruthless, and daring beyond compare.

The great leader never went alone. Invariably he would be accompanied by a bodyguard with a tommy gun, sworn to protect and defend him at the cost of his own life.

There was always a spirit of good comradery among the members of the band; a spirit of honesty; faithfulness and loyalty; a spirit of genuine love and sacrifice for their popular chieftain, to safeguard whom, or at whose command, any member of the band would willingly and gladly lay down his own life at a moment's notice. In fact implicit obedience was one of the main factors that led to the gang being able to operate so successfully over such a great length of time.

To replenish their stock of firearms and ammunition, frequent raids were made by the band on police chowkies and outposts, whose inmates were exterminated and their equipment stolen. Other agents were employed solely to rob such weapons and ammunition, wherever and whenever they could, from army and police supplies and sources, or get them from deserters.

A trick often used, solely for the purpose of procuring firearms, would be for Charna and his band to force an encounter with a police patrol, when Charna would employ one or two dacoits only to engage the enemy. Fire would be exchanged, and then one of the dacoits would pretend to fall dead. The other, if there had been a companion, would act as if he was running away. The police patrol would advance upon the 'dead' man with the object of seeing if they could find any incriminating evidence in the way of documents or other information about the gang. upon his person. When they were well in the open, the rest of Charna's advance corps would enfilade them from all points and wipe them out. Then, of course, the rifles and other firearms they had been carrying, together with all their ammunition and equipment, would be robbed.

Man Singh and his men lived this self-chosen life of violence, pillage and murder, in the ravines of the river Chambal and its vicinity, camping in the open or hiding in caves, for years. But never once in all this time did he harm a villager, a poor man, or the petty merchants that kept him supplied with food. His prey were the zamindars, the rich landlords, and the haughty, arrogant moneylenders of the area. His avowed enemies were the police, and all their agents and secret informers.

During the whole period of his regime, he and his followers always behaved fairly and even generously with the working-class folk and the humble, downtrodden farmers. Having been once a farmer himself, he was particularly partial to the poor agriculturists he encountered.

Thus it came to pass that he was looked upon as their best friend and saviour. They loved, respected and obeyed him. They would give no information that might betray his whereabouts. And many a time, when the police made a surprise attack, they would hide him and his followers in their own huts, inside their own granaries, even down their own wells. It was almost a case of the law and the police, on one side, versus the dacoits and the villagers on the other. The murders he committed were translated and glorified by the people into acts of commendable courage; and his robberies, as a means of justice, to wrest money from the rich and undeserving, with the purpose of feeding the poor and helpless.

When India gained independence in 1947, many criminals and convicts were released by the Government as an amnesty to celebrate the occasion. One of these was Nawab Singh, Man Singh's elder brother. The first thing this man did, upon coming out of jail, was to go to his old village, borrow a gun, kill the only two remaining relations of Talfi Ram and then join his redoubtable younger brother.

Not one soul now remained alive of the once large families of the Brahmin, Talfi Ram, or of Man Singh's own distant relative, Khem Singh, who had once betrayed him.

Man Singh and the members of his family that were with him had indeed taken an awful revenge.

Not content with wiping out both families, they then proceeded to mercilessly slaughter all who had been their adherents, their witnesses, their informers, and even their sympathisers.

The lust for revenge seemed to imbue Man Singh for some time after this. Not satisfied with having annihilated his personal enemies and their followers, he even went on to embark upon a campaign of retaliation on all who had stood witness against any of his dacoit band at any one time or another. These included the police, their secret agents, spies and informers, and the relatives of these people. They were also killed.

Even the magistrates in the land received warnings that they would be eliminated if they dared to institute any active measures against the band or any members who had been arrested and brought to trial.

The Military Take a Hand

Matters had now gone from bad to worse. With the latest policy of indiscriminate revenge that had been adopted by Man Singh and his men through systematically wiping out each and every police spy or informer, their relatives, and even sometimes innocent people suspected of having helped the police in some way or the other, directly or indirectly, action by the civil authorities became puerile and abortive. The regularly paid police agents either resigned, reported sick or absconded from their posts. Their terror became contagious and spread to the uniformed constables stationed at distant and isolated police chowkies, who felt they were beyond the pale of help from the authorities, who had evidenced complete inability to support or protect them, anyhow.

So they, in turn, deserted.

Conditions were growing chaotic.

Civil law and order had been brought to a standstill and became a laughing stock.

At this stage, Government decided to call upon the military for assistance, and small units of the regular army were stationed at strategic points.

It did not take very long for the dacoits, who had become increasingly self-confident, to clash with the military, and a number of gun battles and skirmishes ensued, with the result of many fatal casualties on both sides.

With all this, the power of Man Singh grew and grew, and the villagers loved him more and more. They refused point-blank to assist the military or the police in any way. The authorities found themselves in greater difficulties than ever before.

Man Singh had attained such heights of fame that, apart from the depredations committed directly by him and his henchmen, numerous lesser bands of maurauders, raiders and dacoits operating for hundreds of miles around became subservient to him. In return for the protection afforded by his name and often by members of his gang in person, they proudly proclaimed him their suzerain and punctiliously paid him from 10% to 25% of the loot and money they took in their raids. This payment was known as a 'nazrana' (tribute money), and not only enormously increased Man Singh's exchequer, but his reputation soared to be regarded as almost that of an emperor among thieves. It extended over thousands upon thousands of square miles, in all the affected areas of the four states converging in that region.

This last state of affairs stung the authorities to desperation, and the four governments concerned decided to pool their resources. They raised an army of policemen between them numbering 1,700 selected men, and committed them as a full-time job to wipe out the dreadful menace that had arisen. An experienced Deputy Inspector-General of Police was placed in charge of the whole operation, and hundreds of men from the C.I.D. branches of the police forces of all the states throughout India were distributed over the area, in villages big and small, to glean information about the bandits and their movements; particuiarly regarding their leader and his ravine stronghold.

This concerted effort did not take very long to gain its first result.

A police spy came to know that Charna, the Ferocious, intended to visit his wife in a certain village, upon a certain day.

The police laid a trap.

Unsuspectingly, Charna and some of his men entered the village. The police did nothing till they had gone right inside the house. Then about 60 of them surrounded it and tried to break the door in.

Charna found he was trapped and determined to sell his life dearly. From windows on the top storey of the building, the dacoits opened fire and the police returned it. For 24 hours a vigorous gun battle raged, but the 60 policemen were unable to advance a step further.

Desperately they called for help.

More police answered the call, and 400 especially trained policemen were sent to help the 60 policemen already there.

Inside the house were only 14 dacoits, and their chieftain, Charna.

Surrender was out of the question. The attackers fired volley after volley and even used tear-gas shells.

But the bandits returned their fire and held their own.

So the 460 policemen, after besieging the 15 dacoits for 3 whole days and nights, sent for military help.

An Army unit from the Dogra Regiment was sent to the spot, and an artillery detachment.

Two cannon shots were fired at the house at point-blank range, and the building collapsed. With a yell, the combined force of soldiers and policemen charged into the debris.

There they found 14 dacoits, all dead. But not Charna.

Somehow, miraculously he had fled, while his loyal followers had laid down their lives to a man to cover his escape.

Little wonder then, that when so few men could fight over 33 times their number of better-equipped and trained regular policemen for 3 days, and only stopped fighting when they were killed by cannon fire, entirely in devotion to a petty chieftain; what must have been the loyalty, the respect, and the utter, selfless love which the main band of dacoits had for their leader, the matchless Rajah Man Singh Rathore, as he was now called.

This happened in 1951.

In 1953, Charna, once again at the head of the advance guard, ambushed and wiped out a police patrol. Unfortunately for him, that patrol had a portable wireless transmitter, and when the attack was launched had sent out a desperate S.O.S. for help. Police reinforcements from all directions, who had picked up the message, rushed to the assistance of the beleagured party, although they failed to arrive in time to save it.

But Charna did not know about the transmitter.

When the first of the reinforcements came on the scene, they were in time to see the dacoits relieving the dead bodies of the police patrol of their arms, ammunition and equipment. They opened fire, and the dacoits retaliated briskly.

More and more policemen arrived, and this time there was no friendly building to shelter the dacoits as they fought. They had ambushed the original police squad in the open; and now in turn they found themselves in the open, but surrounded.

Once again a grim gun battle was fought, and this time lasted for 10 hours. But the outlaws were at a disadvantage as they had but little cover, while the many police units that had arrived upon the scene poured in volley after volley upon the little band.

Ten hours later the sounds of gun and rifle fire subsided, and the smoke of battle gradually drifted from the scene.

It revealed Charna and nine of his outlaw band stretched dead upon the sward. Not one had escaped, this time.

The Fall of Man Singh

The death of Charna appeared to be a bad omen for Man Singh and his followers, and the forerunner of many evils to come, culminating with his own doom. Not only had the dacoit leader lost a very staunch and brave supporter, but the advance guard was now bereft of a chieftain who had been a strategist by natural gift and knew exactly when, and where to attack, and when not to. His successor had not these qualities and the advance unit soon began to run into serious trouble itself. Rather than continue to remain the most efficient striking force it had hitherto been under the leadership of the late Charna, it became an additional liability for Man Singh to look after.

In a skirmish shortly later several dacoits were seriously wounded, and one of the C.I.D. agents brought in word that these wounded men were to be moved at night from the caves where they had been kept in hiding, across the river Chambal, to a place called Etawah to be attended to by a doctor; and that Man Singh himself was in hiding in a ravine beside the Bhua Kher.

Large numbers of police surrounded the area in a huge circle and then slowly closed in upon the ravine where Man Singh was said to be. By midday they received notice of the presence of the dacoits when a solitary rifle shot broke the silence and a sergeant fell dead. Then a voice shouted, 'Come any closer, and your agent, Kama, who is a prisoner with us, will be shot.'

In reply to this the police began to crawl forward cautiously. Another single rifle shot broke the silence.

After that a sharp battle ensued. The outlaws employed hand-grenades, Sten guns, tommy guns and rifles, and the police used the same.

By weight of numbers the forces of law began to advance, and the outlaws broke and ran for safety. Man Singh and Roopa, firing tommy guns escaped down a connecting ravine. Others scrambled over the sides and rocks for safety. Tehsildar Singh, the bandit leader's third son—he who bore the title of 'the Terrible'—made a dash for liberty on horseback, but he and his mount were wounded. Later he was caught, and in his possession was a big-game rifle—a .500 bore double-barrelled black powder Express.

When the police searched the camp, they found their agent, Kama. The outlaws had carried out their threat. 'He had been shot through the head. That was the second shot they had heard after being warned not to advance closer.

A domestic tragedy overtook the dacoit leader about this time. Lakhan Singh, who was called 'the Lion', had married Man Singh's daughter, Rani. But this girl proved unfaithful to her husband, and took unto herself a lover from among the dacoit band. This news infuriated Man Singh. It outraged his high ideals and his strict sense of justice. In the very presence of Rani, his daughter, he shot her paramour dead.

The old man had performed his duty as a father-in-law in keeping with the strictest principles of justice. But the shame of his daughter's conduct lived with him to his last day. And that same shame drove Lakhan Singh, her husband, who was also one of Man Singh's ablest lieutenants, to leave the band and go far away to operate and die on his own.

With the loss of these three very competent supporters, Man Singh suddenly grew tired and remorseful at the life he had been leading—a life of bloodshed, a life where he had no home to call his own, where he could never settle down and was always on the run; the restless life he had loved so dearly for so long but was now tired of following.

He wanted rest; he wanted peace; he wanted a home.

So he did a remarkable thing.

He offered the Government an amnesty.

He wrote a letter to the Government of India—unique in the annals of this country and, for the matter of that, of any country in the world. He began his letter by saying he was not a thief or murderer by choice, but fate and circumstances had forced him to be one. When he had not committed dacoity and was innocent, he had been called a dacoit and accused of a crime he had never done. He said the police had shamed and warned him without cause. So he had been compelled to punish the liar Talfi Ram, who had so blamed him. Now, however, he was willing to come back home and live a respectable life once again. He also went on to make what he termed a sporting offer to the Government. As a measure of his earnest desire to become a good and useful citizen of India, he stated that he and his band of dacoits would proceed to Goa, and free that foreign pocket by throwing the Portuguese out, and if necessary into the sea.

The Government of India did not reply. It could not negotiate peace terms with a multi-murderer.

This disheartened Man Singh and demoralised his followers. Unrelentingly the police pursued them from hideout to hideout. One by one the outlaws were arrested, wounded or killed. Now many started deserting, the zeal and fight knocked out of them.

Finally, only 18 remained. Among them were Nawab Singh, his aged brother; Subedar Singh, his second son; and Roopa, the Faithful.

By this time Nawab Singh had become an old man, and his failing sight and physique often made him a burden to his companions. He begged his brother to abandon him. But the Rajah was not the sort of man to desert a friend, far less his own elder brother. He kept Nawab Singh with him to the very end.

Although depleted in numbers, Man Singh resolved that the reputation of his followers should never be sullied. He committed dacoity after dacoity upon the rich, while his fame for generosity and kindness towards the poor increased yet more.

The authorities were almost berserk. The 1,700 uniformed policemen searching for him, and the horde of plain-clothed C.I.D. detectives were stirred to greater efforts.

But Man Singh and his remaining 18 outlaws continued their depredations.

On a day in November, 1954, the Home Minister of Madhya Bharat, Mr. Dixit, undertook to resign from the State Cabinet if Man Singh was not brought to book within a year from that day. To accomplish this, he called upon those most famous fighting men of India, the Gurkhas, to help him. He raised a special company, comprised entirely of these hardy hill soldiers, to eliminate Man Singh, who had become a curse to the four states in which he had eluded all efforts to catch him.

Things became more and more hot for the quarry now, so that Man Singh adopted a ruse. A cremation was held in an obscure village with a corpse dressed up to resemble him and the rumour was circulated that the old brigand had died of a sudden illness and had been cremated, according to custom.

The authorities and the police were jubilant. The rich zamindars and landlords and oppressors of the poor slept soundly in relief. The humble and harassed wept bitter tears at the loss. There was a lull in the pursuit.

After some time, Man Singh struck again. Indeed, he was alive in right earnest and had fooled the authorities thoroughly.

Many who believed he had really died were now convinced he had come to life again. This bestowed upon the Rajah a reputation of being immortal.

The police took up the pursuit once more and the crack Gurkha company went into action.

Man Singh was traced to a hideout in the Morena district which the police besieged at dawn. Heavy firing continued all day till nightfall, when the outlaws retreated, leaving a good quantity of arms and ammunition, including Sten guns behind them. Man Singh was supposed to have been wounded in this battle, but he made good his escape.

The forces of authority followed harder than ever on his trail. For seven months after that, from February to August, 1955, they relentlessly hounded him from pillar to post. By the middle of August they had him literally sealed up in the ravines of the Chambal River. All outlets were guarded.

The Last Glorious Fight

Somehow this amazing man and his 18 followers got clean through the police net. He escaped to the district of Bhind and tried to cross the Kunwari River.

Here Fate played him a cruel trick. The Kunwari was in full flood and totally unfordable. Man Singh and his band fled back to the village of Bijapur, and the crack company of Gurkhas, under the command of an officer named Chaihale, pursued him.

Man Singh fired the first shot; and the last battle of his brilliant, but criminal career, was fought.

A platoon of the warlike Gurkhas, led by one of their own countrymen, Jamadar Bhanwar Singh, attacked; and the fight was fast and furious. Guns rifles, tommy guns, Sten guns and grenades were freely used. Man Singh himself a crack shot, accounted for many of his foes, and thousands of rounds were fired.

But his time had come and the Great Reaper, whom he had eluded so often, claimed him at last. The most illustrious dacoit of all time fell to earth, his body riddled with bullets.

With a hurrah of victory, the sturdy little Gurkhas rushed forward to take his corpse.

But there was yet an epic to be enacted in this great battle before it was finally over.

The dacoits counter-attacked vigorously to prevent the earthly remains of their beloved leader from falling into the hands of the foe. The fight waged more furious than ever.

Then from the ranks of the outlaws rushed forth a stalwart figure, red with his own lifeblood that streamed from many wounds, while tears flowed unrestrainedly down his leathery dark cheeks and on to his beard.

It was Subedar Singh, valiant second son of the stricken leader. He rushed to cover his father's body with his own so that it should not receive any more bullets.

And he succeeded in his purpose.

Riddled himself with rifle, tommy gun and Sten gun bullets, he fell dead over the corpse of his beloved father, to protect it in death.

The battle was over. Roopa, the Faithful, badly wounded, was able to get the aged Nawab Singh away, together with a handful of those remaining alive.

But most lay dead on the field of that last and most glorious fight.

Even the little Gurkhas, men of war and blood that they were, stood mutely in respect before those huddled corpses. Then, one by one, they saluted the dead with honour; the esteem of gallant men for one another!

The police were again jubilant. The public throughout India rejoiced. The newspapers announced the victory, in leading headlines.

Mr. Dixit, the Home Minister, had kept his pledge; and so he did not have to resign. Prime Minister Jawaharlal Nehru; Home Minister, Pant, of the Central Government; and the Congress President, Mr. Dhebar, were informed by telegram, and were relieved.

While the poor throughout the land, whom Man Singh had loved and defended, and who loved him in return, wept bitterly.

Dr. Sampurnanand, Chief Minister of the United Provinces, issued this announcement:

'It is not a very happy thing to express joy over the death of a person. Man Singh is dead, and the people who were awestricken on account of the depredations of Man Singh and his gang, have heaved a sigh of relief.'

But the sighs and the tears of widows and children, and the incense and the prayers of the temple priests, and the chimes of the bells that Man Singh had donated, went up to God for his soul, throughout the land.

The Last Rites

The police brought the bullet-riddled bodies of the great leader and his staunch son, under heavy armed guard, to the town of Bhind. Their bodies were tied to charpoys (cots made of a wooden frame, interlaced with rope), and exposed in a standing position for the public to gaze upon. It is estimated that over 40,000 people filed past the dead men. Some of these did so out of a morbid curiosity; some out of joy and relief. But thousands who paid their last homage cried openly and bitterly, like children.

From there, the corpses were taken to Gwalior City for cremation. Man Singh's widow petitioned the Government by telegram that the bodies of her husband and son be given to her, as a matter of justice, so that she could perform the last rites. From jail, Tehsildar Singh, the third son, begged Government to allow him to light his father's funeral pyre and to put the ceremonial fire in his mouth. This ceremony is called the 'mukhagni', and is the final bounden duty enjoined upon a surviving son towards his father at the latter's death.

Both petitions were refused.

That last day another 60,000 people filed past the dead bodies at Gwalior City to pay their final respects. The hushed silence was broken by the hum and murmur of prayers for the departed spirits of the brave father and son, and throbbed to the sound of sobbing. Tears flowed freely, many of them to fall on the mute remains of the beloved brigand. People bent low to salaam him. Ex-soldiers and pensioners from all branches of the Services turned out in full uniform, wearing their war medals. The red coats, supplied by the British to their Indian soldiers before World War I were conspicuous on these veterans of long ago. Many of them were very old men, who had fought India's wars valiantly in the dim past. They knew what bravery and loyalty meant.

In the broiling sun, they joined the slowly-moving queue. When finally they stood before the dead body of the great leader, those frail and bent old backs were frail and bent no longer. They grew upright, as if once again on parade. The old, stooping shoulders squared. The medals, earned so long ago, flashed in the sunlight once again as the aged feet clicked together, at attention. The feeble right arms, trembling a little perhaps, went up to the salute and remained there for a full minute. Tears they could not restrain brought salt to their lips as they murmured, 'Farewell, Maharajah Sahib! May God rest your brave soul in peace.'

Then they shuffled on to the corpse of Subedar Singh. Once more the stiffening of the aged limbs; once again the click of heels and the salute; this time the words, 'Salaam, Subedar Sahib! Loyal and brave son of your father, we salute you!'

Under close armed police guard, both bodies were then cremated, the guard remaining while the flames licked hungrily at the piled wood surrounding the mortal remains of gallant father and son; while they hissed and crackled; and while the smoke went up in heavy yellow spirals; and even till such time as it died down again, leaving only the glowing embers and the ashes to mark the spot where two famous bodies, of two kindred souls, had stood.

People said it looked as if the police feared that the terrible father and his equally terrible son, might suddenly become alive again and escape once more from their very midst.

And that was how the greatest bandit leader India has ever known, came into being, and lived, and died.

He was a thief and murderer, no doubt; but also a gentleman to his fingertips. His prey; the rich. His enemies; the police and informers. He counted his friends by the thousands amongst the very very poor of the land. Never once did he harm a woman or child; never once did he owe any man an anna without repaying the debt; never once did he rob a person who could not afford it. And at the very end he, and his beloved son, Subedar, remained united in gallantry; and died as they had lived, as heroes.

We do not condone the murders and brigandage he committed. We condemn those actions. It was not for him to have taken the law into his own hands. His revenge against, and murder of the enemies of his family, was wrong. For his misdeeds he was rightly punished by the loss of his life.

But as a living legend of India for all time; a very Robin Hood of the East; for his chivalry, his generosity, the magnitude of his nature, and his big-heartedness and bravery and sheer grit, in the face of insuperable difficulties, hazards and dangers, and his tenacity and determination, let us always respect him and never forget him. Let us keep a corner also in our memories for that loyal son who sought to shield the dead body of his father with his own live body, and succeeded at the cost of his life.

Let us join with those little Gurkhas on the field of battle that day; and with those ex-soldiers and pensioners who filed past in Gwalior City; by saying, 'Salaam, Rajah Sahib and Subedar Sahib! Illustrious father and loyal son. We salute you both and shall remember you.'

Epilogue

Even as the writing of these tales comes to a close, news is to hand that Roopa, the Faithful, staunch follower and a relative of the Rajah, is still at liberty and operating his trade as a dacoit.

In the next paragraph is the copy of a Press Report, dated 1st January, 1959.

DACOIT ROOPA KILLS 4

'GWALIOR, Jan. 1, 1959. Roopa, notorious dacoit and chief lieutenant of dacoit Man Singh, last night shot dead three persons and fatally injured another in a village in Morena District, according to a report reaching here this morning. The fourth succumbed to his injuries after he had been removed to hospital.'

www.ingramcontent.com/pod-product-compliance
Lightning Source LLC
Chambersburg PA
CBHW022054160426
43198CB00008B/228